INDIAN DEFENCE INDUSTRY

An Agenda for Making in India

INDIAN DEFENCE INDUSTRY

An Agenda for Making in India

Laxman Kumar Behera

INSTITUTE FOR DEFENCE STUDIES & ANALYSES
NEW DELHI

Indian Defence Industry: An Agenda for Making in India

Laxman Kumar Behera

First Published in 2016

ISBN 978-81-8274-905-4

Published by

PENTAGON PRESS
206, Peacock Lane, Shahpur Jat,
New Delhi-110049
Phones: 011-64706243, 26491568
Telefax: 011-26490600
email: rajan@pentagonpress.in
website: www.pentagonpress.in

In association with
Institute for Defence Studies and Analyses
No. 1, Development Enclave,
New Delhi-110010
Phone: +91-11-26717983
Website: www.idsa.in

Printed at Aegean Offset Printers, Greater Noida, U.P.

Contents

Preface

India has one of the largest defence industrial complexes in the developing world. Currently, it consists of 39 ordnance factories, 9 defence public sector undertakings under the administrative control of the Ministry of Defence (MoD); and 150-odd companies in the private sector. In addition, there are 50-odd dedicated research laboratories and establishments under the umbrella of the Defence Research and Development Organisation (DRDO), the premier research and development (R&D) wing of MoD. Together, these entities, which employ over 200,000 people, produced arms and other stuff worth over Rs. 46,428 crore ($7.6 billion) in 2014-15. India is one of the few countries to have designed and produced a fourth-plus generation fighter aircraft, nuclear submarine, main battle tank, and intercontinental ballistic missile with a range of more than 5000 km.

Despite these feats, India continues to be overwhelmingly dependent on arms and equipment imports. The target of 70 per cent self-reliance in defence procurement set for 2005 is still to be achieved. Currently, India's self-reliance is hovering at around 35-40 per cent. According to the Stockholm International Peace Research Institute (SIPRI), India with a 15 per cent share in global arms import during 2010-14 was the single-largest arms importer; and China was the world's third-largest arms exporter ahead of countries like France, Germany and the UK.

To reverse the country's huge arms import dependency and put the country on a self-reliance path, the National Democratic Alliance (NDA) government led by Prime Minister Narendra Modi has launched the ambitious Make in India initiative. Although it covers 25 different sectors, defence manufacturing, as stated by the Prime Minister in his Aero India 2015 address, constitutes the 'heart' of the initiative. Under Make in India, many reform measures have been taken to revitalise the moribund defence industry, particularly in the private sector, whose contribution to India's defence procurement continues to be abysmal even though nearly 15 years have passed since it was allowed to undertake defence manufacturing. The reform measures taken so far include a hike in foreign direct investment (FDI) cap from the earlier 26 per cent to 49 per cent through the automatic route; simplification and streamlining of defence industrial licensing, permitting the industry to undertake arms manufacturing without getting into bureaucratic entanglement; articulation of a first ever defence exports strategy along with a set of guidelines for grant of defence export licences; rationalisation of taxes; and certain measures to insulate the industry from currency fluctuations. In addition, MoD is working on a host of other reform measures, including the ones suggested by the 10-member Experts Committee set up by the current government with the specific task of suggesting measures to promote Make in India in defence manufacturing.

The key question that still remains, however, is whether Make in India will enable India to attain its long cherished goal of 70 per cent self-reliance in defence procurement. This book examines this question. In doing so, it examines not only Make in India as it evolves, but also the key constituents of defence industry and the policies surrounding Indian defence production, relying extensively on hard evidence.

Chapter 1 maps the various phases in Indian defence industrialisation. It observes that the latest phase is a continuum of the policy initiatives undertaken in the past several years, although it focuses more on the private sector, thus far the marginal players in India's defence production sector.

Chapters 2 and 3 examine the public sector defence production entities, namely the ordnance factories (OFs) and the defence public sector undertakings (DPSUs), the traditional pillars of India's defence industry. Their gross inefficiency has been the main reason why India has failed to become self-reliant in defence industrialisation. But given their size, experience, vast skilled human resources and huge public investment, much is expected of them in the foreseeable future, provided they manage to transform themselves. Radical steps such as shutting down non-performing factories, corporatisation of the Ordnance Factory Board (OFB) and the process of privatisation of DPSUs are among the steps that the government needs to take.

Chapter 4 deals with the private sector. Although the private sector has received a much-needed fresh lease of life under Make in India, many existing hurdles could prevent its performance. Lack of R&D and skilled human resources, uncertainty in procurement decision-making and the inherent bias of MoD in favour of the public sector entities are some of the hurdles that the government needs to address. The government should also bring in an enabling fiscal mechanism to make the defence sector attractive for a much larger private investment.

Chapter 5 deals with DRDO, the monopolistic defence R&D agency, which is often blamed for India's poor self-reliance in the defence sector. DRDO would have to perforce play a far more significant role to not only reduce India's arms import dependence but turn back India's traditional licence-based production approach to one based on own intellectual property, indigenous design and development.

Chapter 6 examines India's defence offsets policy, a key feature in India's defence capital procurement manual since 2005. The offsets have so far played a negligible role. Based on the experience of several countries including Canada, Israel, South Korea, UAE, Malaysia and Turkey, the chapter suggests a range of options to make the policy effective.

Chapter 7 discusses the policy recommendations made by the various committees set up after the Kargil conflict to look into various aspects of promoting indigenous defence production. Chapter 8 makes certain recommendations in the light of the preceding discussion.

Much of the work for this book was done well before the publication of the revised version of MoD's capital procurement manual, the Defence Procurement Procedure 2016 (DPP-2016) and the report of the Task Force on the Selection of Strategic Partners. Some of the issues highlighted in the book have some direct relevance with these two documents. For the benefit of the readers the major highlights of DPP-2016 and the main provisions of the Task Force Report are provided in an overview format in Annexures A and B.

Acknowledgements

This book would not have been possible without the support of the Institute for Defence Studies and Analyses (IDSA). For this, I am truly grateful to Shri Jayant Prasad, Director General, IDSA. It is his passion, support and encouragement which have immensely motivated me to undertake this comprehensive study.

I would like to thank Brig. Rumel Dahiya (Retd.), DDG, IDSA for his patience and support during the writing of this volume.

I am truly grateful to Shri VK Misra, former Secretary (Defence Finance), Ministry of Defence for his able guidance. His rich experience of dealing with myriad issues of Indian defence at the highest level, and his vast knowledge of the subject have greatly benefited my work.

My gratitude goes to Shri Amit Cowshish, Group Captain (Retd.) Vinay Kaushal and Col Kevin A Desouza of the Defence Economics and Industry Centre of IDSA for providing scholarly inputs and enriching my work.

I am particularly thankful to the two external anonymous referees for their valuable insights and comments.

Last, but not the least, I thank the members of IDSA fraternity, particularly Vivek, Suresh, Pitambar, Mukesh and Vikrant for their help in finishing this task.

Laxman Kumar Behera

List of Abbreviations

ALH	Advanced Light Helicopter
BDL	Bharat Dynamics Ltd
BEL	Bharat Electronics Ltd
BEML	Bharat Earth Movers Ltd
BRICS	Brazil, Russia, India, China, South Africa
CAG	Comptroller and Auditor General of India
CPSE	Central Public Sector Enterprise
CSIR	Council of Scientific and Industrial Research
DAC	Defence Acquisition Council
DAE	Department of Atomic Energy
DARPA	Defence Advanced Research Projects Agency
DDP	Department of Defence Production
DIB	Defence Industrial Base
DIPP	Department of Industrial Policy and Promotion
DPB	Defence Production Board
DPP	Defence Procurement Procedure
DPSU	Defence Public Sector Undertaking
DRDO	Defence Research and Development Organisation
DSIR	Department of Scientific and Industrial Research
ERV	Exchange Rate Variation
FDI	Foreign Direct Investment
FICCI	Federation of Indian Chambers of Commerce and Industry

GRSE	Garden Reach Shipbuilders and Engineers Ltd
GSL	Goa Shipyard Ltd
HAL	Hindustan Aeronautics Ltd
HSL	Hindustan Shipyard Ltd
IAF	Indian Air Force
IDSA	Institute for Defence Studies and Analyses
IL	Industrial Licence
IOP	Indian Offset Partner
IPR	Intellectual Property Right
ISRO	Indian Space Research Organisation
JV	Joint Venture
LC	Letter of Credit
LCA	Light Combat Aircraft
MBT	Main Battle Tank
MDL	Mazagon Dock Ltd
MIDHANI	Mishra Dhatu Nigam Ltd
MoD	Ministry of Defence
NDA	National Democratic Alliance
OFB	Ordnance Factories Board
OFs	Ordnance Factories
PAT	Profit After Tax
PIB	Press Information Bureau
PSU	Public Sector Undertaking
R&D	Research and Development
S&T	Science and Technology
SCAP	Services Capital Acquisition Plan
SIPRI	Stockholm International Peace Research Institute
VoP	Value of Production
VoS	Value of Sales
WIPO	World Intellectual Property Organisation
WTO	World Trade Organisation

List of Tables

Chapter 3

Chapter 4

Chapter 5

Chapter 6

Chapter 7

List of Figures

1

Indian Defence Industry
The Journey to Make in India

Like many other developing countries, India also follows a policy of autarky when it comes to arms production. Self-sufficiency/reliance has been the primary reason for developing a vast defence industrial base (DIB), which now comprises 52 defence laboratories and establishments under DRDO; and 9 defence public sector undertakings and 39 ordnance factories under the Department of Defence Production of MoD. Besides, there is a small but growing number of companies in the private sector. The DIB is responsible for design, development, production and upgradation of various types of arms primarily for the Indian armed forces. To the credit of this vast industrial base, India is among the few countries that has produced (or is at the advanced stage of production) a fourth-plus generation fighter aircraft, an aircraft carrier, a nuclear submarine, main battle tanks and intercontinental ballistic missile. However, India is probably the only country which despite having a vast DIB still imports majority of its armaments, including several low-tech items (including military transport vehicles). According to the Congressional Research Service, the policy research wing of the US Congress, India signed $46.6 billion worth of arms transfer agreements between 2004 and 2011.[1] According to the Stockholm International Peace Research Institute (SIPRI), India is the world's largest importer of major weapons, with a 15 per cent global share during 2010-2014.[2] During this period China, which was the largest importer of arms not so long ago, was the world's third-largest arms exporter behind the US and Russia.

India's heavy dependence on arms imports has been a cause for concern expressed by parliamentarians, oversight agencies, policymakers and defence analysts. In 2012, debating in the upper house of Parliament (Rajya Sabha) the state of defence preparedness, the legislators cutting across party lines voiced their concern over the county's inability to manufacture its own defence needs, and the strategic vulnerability in depending on others.[3] The Comptroller and Auditor General of India (CAG) in a 2011 report to Parliament had expressed its displeasure at the 90 per cent import dependency of the state-owned Hindustan Aeronautics Ltd (HAL) for 'raw materials and bought out items' for production of what is touted as indigenously designed and developed Advanced Light Helicopter (ALH) even though it was in production for a decade.[4] Commenting on the low indigenisation level of two of India's flagship indigenous programmes – MBT Arjun and Light Combat Aircraft (LCA) – the Parliamentary Standing Committee on Defence had earlier also expressed its concern.

In 1992, a Self-Reliance Review Committee (SRRV) under Dr A.P.J. Abdul Kalam, then Scientific Advisor to the Defence Minister, had formulated a 10-year self-reliance plan through interactions among the various stakeholders, including the Armed Forces and MoD. As per the plan, self-reliance index (SRI), measured as a percentage share of indigenous content in total procurement expenditure, was to progressively increase from the 1992-93 estimate of 30 per cent to 70 per cent by 2005.[5] The target is still to be achieved. A study by the Institute for Defence Studies and Analyses (IDSA), which was incidentally cited by the CAG in a report presented to Parliament in 2014 and also was a source of a Rajya Sabha question,[6] has estimated India's self-reliance index varying between 36 and 48 per cent during 2006-07 and 2010-11.[7]

It is in this context of high import dependency that the National Democratic Alliance (NDA) government of Prime Minister Narendra Modi has launched a spirited campaign under the Make in India initiative in 2014. This chapter looks at the concept of Make in India and at India's defence industrialisation process since 1947, in order to differentiate the new initiative from past initiatives.

Defence Industrialisation Phases

India's defence industrialisation can be divided into five different phases:[8] (1) from independence till the mid-1960s, when self-sufficiency was an overall economic principle behind India's industrial development; (2) from mid-1960 till the mid-1980s, when the term self-reliance replaced self-sufficiency in defence production; (3) from mid-1980s till the early 2000s, when the emphasis on self-reliance was through co-production; (4) from the mid-2000s to late 2014, when self-reliance was tried through greater participation of the Indian private sector. With the Modi government coming to power, Make in India has become the new model. The following paragraphs present a brief account of the different phases.

Phase 1. The Quest for Self-Sufficiency

India's defence industrialisation immediately after independence was influenced by the country's socialistic and centralised planning system reflected in the first Industrial Policy Resolution adopted in 1948. The resolution emphasised the importance to the economy of securing a continuous increase in production and its equitable distribution, and pointed out that the State must play an active role in the development of industries. The resolution, which was revised in 1956, reserved the key industries – including arms and ammunition, railways, air transport and atomic energy – in the domain of the public sector and the State assumed the exclusive right for their development.

All the 18 ordnance factories that India inherited from British India formed the core of the state-led defence industry. The OFs were supported by a rudimentary R&D setup (which in 1958 became a full-fledged organisation, DRDO) and an aircraft plant, Hindustan Aircraft Factory, which was set up in Bangalore in 1940 by the visionary industrialist Walchand Hirachand with the objective of promoting aviation industry in India.

The quest for self-sufficiency got a further push by the 1954 US-Pakistan strategic partnership and the border tension with China which became intense in the late 1950s. In 1954 Bharat Electronics Ltd (BEL) was set up with French assistance. The government also acquired two shipyards – Mazagon Dock Ltd and Garden Reach Shipyard – and placed them under the control of MoD with the intention of undertaking naval construction.

The self-sufficiency model was however limited in scope and was partly influenced by the 1948 report submitted by the British scientist P.M.S.

Blackett, who was invited by Prime Minister Nehru to advise the government about defence R&D requirements. Blackett's report, which was accepted by the government, articulated a plan of action envisaging indigenous manufacture, in large quantity, of what it termed non-competitive weapons, while setting out a long-term plan for producing high-performance and complex ('competitive') weapons. Non-competitive weapons meant technologically simpler weapons such as light anti-aircraft guns, 25-pounder field guns, light tanks, motor transport, naval escort aircraft, transport aircraft and trainers, whereas the latter category included jet fighters, bombers, airborne radars, high altitude anti-aircraft guns and heavy guns. Blackett believed that given India's weak economy and low industrial base – the latter's output being a fraction of the UK's (Table 1.1) – the country did not have the wherewithal to produce complex weapon systems. Bulk production of simpler weapons would largely compensate the need for competitive weapons and provide 'an extremely valuable stimulus to the economy and present a very considerable step forward in industrialisation'.[9]

Table 1.1: Industrial Production and Population in UK and India, 1945

	Industrial Production (£ million)	*Population (million)*	*Industrial Production Per Head (£ million)*
UK	7000	45	155
India	600	300	2

Source: P.M.S. Blackett, 'Scientific problem of defence in relation to the needs of the Indian Armed Forces', A Report to the Defence Minister, September 1948, p. 4.

Table 1.2: Approximate Cost of Armed Services as Percentage of National Income and Budget, UK and India (1948)

	National Income (£ Million)	*Central Budget (£ Million)*	*Cost of Services (£ Million)*	*Cost of Services as % of National Income*	*Cost of Services as % of Budget*
UK	9000	3000	800	9	27
India	500	250	100	2	40

Source: Same as of Table 1.1.

A vital component of Blackett's analysis pertains to resource availability to the cause of national defence. Blackett was realistic in his assumption that defence allocation, which was accounting for as much as 40 per cent of the central government budget (compared to 27 per cent in the UK) (Table 1.2), was unlikely to cross that level, without affecting the industrialisation process and economic growth. He therefore recommended that the defence budget should be below 2 per cent of GDP,[10] which was the norm throughout the 1950s, and in the early 1960s before India went to war with China in 1962 (Figure 1.1).

Figure 1.1: Share of Defence Expenditure in GDP, 1950-2016

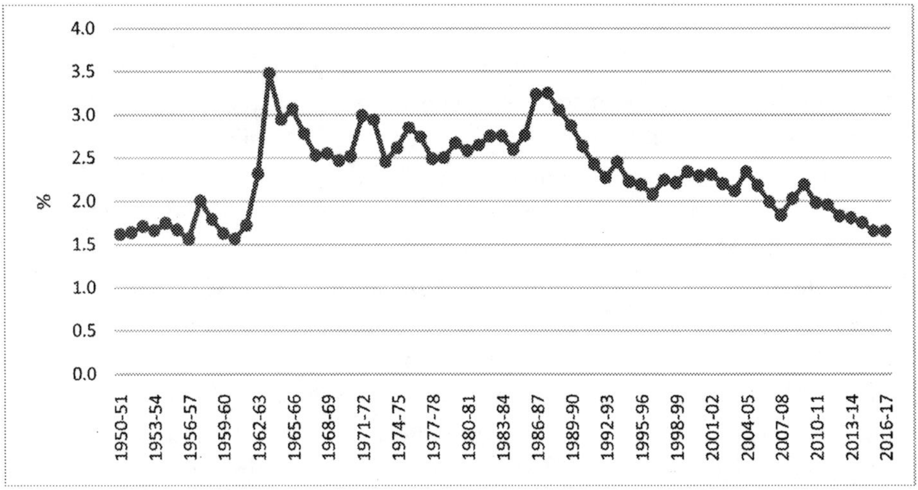

Note: GDP figures for up to 2010-11 are based on base year 2004-05 and between 2011-12 and 2016-17 on base Year 2011-12.

Source: Author's database.

With the self-sufficiency model designed around low-end technology and minimal dependency on state funding, defence production upto the mid-1960s was nonetheless quite remarkable, although certain weaknesses were prevalent. The production of ordnance factories in the 1950s had 'eased dependence on foreign (primarily British) sources, which accounted for no less than 90 per cent of India's military equipment and stores in 1950'. By 1953, 80 per cent of the Army's light equipment was produced indigenously and India was self-sufficient in non-lethal stores and equipment.[11] During this period, the government also undertook initiatives for the production of tanks, trucks, tractors and jeeps in the ordnance factories, for which technical assistance was sought from other countries.

In aeronautics, the self-sufficiency model was pursued at a more ambitious level at HAL, which was brought under the control of MoD in 1951. During the 1950s, HAL made a significant stride in aircraft assembling under licence including Prentice, Vampire, De Havilland and Pushpak trainers, the Douglas

C-47 transport and the Vampire fighter.[12] Along with assembling, HAL also undertook indigenous design and development of trainers and fighters, including the HT-2 primary trainer and HF-24 Marut fighter. The HT-2 project was first authorised by the government in September 1948 and the first prototype flew in less than three years in August 1951. A total of 161 aircraft were produced by 1962, when the production line was closed for lack of orders.[13]

HF-24 Marut was an ambitious project conceived by Prime Minister Nehru and his Defence Minister Krishna Menon, as a means of self-sufficiency in aeronautics.[14] The design and development of Marut started in 1956 under the guidance of the famous German designer Kurt Tank, who worked along with his German and Indian teams (the latter led by Dr V.M. Ghatage) in HAL. Initially, Marut was visualised on two versions: transonic Mark 1 version with Orpheus 703 turbojet engine and supersonic Mk 2 with single Orpheus 12 turbojet engine. Within four years of design and developmental efforts, HF-24 Marut took to the sky in June 1961, powered by two Orpheus 703 engines.[15] However, the engine was underpowered and efforts to integrate the fighter with a more powerful engine failed. This contributed to reduction in production from the projected 214 units to 164 units.[16]

Compared to indigenous production for the Army and the Air Force, Naval construction during the early phase of industrialisation was accorded a low priority, partly driven by the land- and air-centric threat perceptions from Pakistan and China, and also by the benign influence of British naval presence in the Indian Ocean. It was only in 1955 that a small order was placed on the domestic shipyard to construct a survey vessel.[17]

Despite the notable success achieved by the defence industry, the self-sufficiency model had certain weaknesses. Defence allocation was low, and the R&D and industrial base at that time was poor. Between 1950-51 and 1960-61, the share of defence expenditure in the central government expenditure was reduced by more than half from 33 per cent to less than 16 per cent.

The Blackett report had excluded the necessity for India to undertake R&D in advanced systems. Not surprisingly, R&D was accorded low priority, with DRDO accounting for about one per cent of the defence budget in the 1960s.[18] This coupled with lack of a civil industrial base had a major impact on indigenous content and the production schedule. The production programmes which were initiated with foreign assistance, such as Komatsu tractors, Shaktiman and Nissan trucks and Nissan patrol jeeps were 'considered behind schedule and heavily dependent upon foreign components.'[19] The situation in aircraft industry, which took some bold initiatives, was even worse. HAL, despite its success in designing aircraft, was not only dependent on foreign sources for special steel and aluminium but also for all instrumentation, undercarriage, braking systems, communication systems and electronic systems.[20]

Phase 2. Self-Sufficiency to Self-Reliance

The events of the 1960s, particularly the 1962 war with China and the India-Pakistan war of 1965 brought about a major change in India's defence policy. Not only India's defence budget as percentage of GDP increased in the subsequent years (Figure 1.1) but also the approach towards arms procurement policy and indigenous defence production changed. Post-1962, India sought and received military assistance from a host of counties including the US. However, the US embargo after the India-Pakistan war of 1965 became a major factor in India's forging close defence links with the Soviet Union. On its part, given the Cold War politics, the Soviet Union was willing to provide arms and assistance to India on terms which were considered favourable to New Delhi.[21] A major beginning of this close cooperation was made with the MiG-21 aircraft (signed in October 1962), which paved the way for the aircraft's licence manufacture by HAL.[22] By 1980, roughly 70 per cent of Indian military hardware was of Soviet origin.[23]

The war with China also led to a significant expansion of the defence industrial base. Between 1962 and the mid-1980s, 11 ordnance factories were established including the Ordnance Cable Factory in Chandigarh (1963) and the Vehicle Factory in Jabalpur (1969).[24] Two DPSUs were also created: Mishra Dhatu Nigan Ltd (MIDHNI) and BEML to produce special steel/alloys and military vehicles respectively. DRDO also got a major boost. Decisions were taken to expand DRDO laboratories to undertake research in aeronautics, electronics, naval technology, materials, life sciences and engineering equipment.[25]

In this phase of India's defence industrialisation, the focus was more on licence production rather than on indigenous production. Apart from MiG-21, a number of other programmes were taken up for licence production, including tanks, destroyers, etc.

While the first phase of defence industrialisation suffered from a poor R&D and industrial base, leading to import dependency, in the second phase, the dependency was formalised by way of forging a close relation with the Soviet Union for licence-manufacturing in India. The painstaking efforts made for indigenous production, particularly in aeronautics, paved the way for pure licence-based production, a feature of India's aeronautics industry that is continuing even now. The Soviet arms transfer and transfer of technologies for licence production no doubt helped India strengthen its military capability, but did little by way of strengthening its defence industrial and technological capability. As a former DRDO head notes: 'most defence production in India was under licence, which neither led to capacities to design nor develop advanced manufacturing techniques; licences for assembly of weapon systems simply followed one another in boring succession.'[26]

By the end of the Cold War, India was overwhelmingly dependent on the Soviet Union: 100 per cent for ground air defence, 75 per cent for fighter aircraft defence, 60 per cent for ground attack aircraft, 100 per cent for tracked armoured vehicles, 80 per cent for tanks, 100 per cent for guided missile destroyers, 95 per cent for conventional submarines and 70 per cent for frigates.[27]

Phase 3. Self-Reliance through Coproduction

Beginning with the mid-1980s, the government pumped up resources on R&D (Figure 1.2) to enable DRDO to undertake high-profile projects. A major beginning in this respect was made in 1983 when the government sanctioned the Integrated Guided Missile Development Programme (IGMDP) at the initial cost of Rs 388.83 crore to develop four missile systems – Prithvi (surface-to-surface), Akash (surface-to-air), Trishul (naval version of Prithvi) and Nag (anti-tank) – and a Technology Demonstrator, Agni.[28] In the same year, the government also sanctioned the Light Combat Aircraft (LCA) at a cost of Rs 560 crore to develop an indigenous fighter aircraft.[29]

The indigenous efforts were however not adequate to meet the growing requirements of the armed forces. This forced the government to look for alternatives from external sources. However, unlike in the past, the focus was shifted towards co-development and co-production with foreign companies. The beginning was made in 1998 when India and Russia signed an inter-governmental agreement to jointly produce a supersonic cruise missile, BrahMos. A joint venture (JV) was set up in India with an authorised capital of $250 million, shared 50.5 per cent by India and the balance by Russia

Figure 1.2: Share of R&D in Defence Expenditure (%)

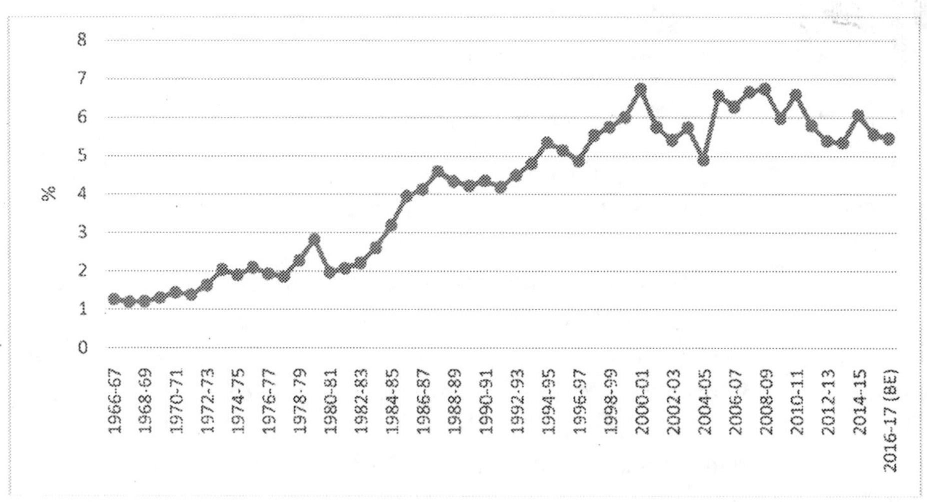

Note: Figures for 2015-16 and 2016-17 are Revised Estimates and Budget Estimates, respectively.
Source: MoD, *Defence Services Estimates* (various issues).

(the equity structure is designed to enable the JV to operate like a private entity for fast decision-making[30]). Since BrahMos, a number of collaborative programmes have been taken up by India, including for combat and transport aircraft and missile systems.

Taking the BrahMos model further, India and Russia signed in 2007 two inter-governmental agreements for co-development and co-production of a Multi Role Transport Aircraft (MTA) and a Fifth Generation Fighter Aircraft (FGFA). India's investment share in both projects would be 50 per cent.[31] Pursuant to the agreement, HAL, the designated Indian partner for these aircraft, has signed in 2010 Preliminary Design (PD) contracts with its Russian partners. The PD of FGFA, valued at $295 million, was planned to be completed in 18 months from February 2011, after which full-scale design work would be taken up. Initially, India planned to acquire as many as 250 FGFAs from 2018 onwards.[32] For the MTA, a JV was formed in 2010 with an initial outlay of $600.7 million (at 2006 prices), to be funded equally by both sides.[33]

Apart from Russia, India has also signed joint developmental programmes with Israel, which has become one of the top suppliers of arms to India. Cementing the growing defence trade between Tel Aviv and New Delhi, DRDO and Israel Aerospace Industries (IAI) are currently undertaking two missile systems: Long Range Surface to Air Missile (LRSAM) and Medium Range Surface to Air Missile (MRSAM).[34] The LRSAM was successfully test-fired by the Indian Navy on 30 December 2015.[35]

Phase 4. Self-Reliance through Private Sector Participation

While co-development/co-production remains a distinct feature of India's defence industrialisation process since the late 1990s, the approach towards self-reliance has taken a major turn since the early 2000s, when the government decided to allow 100 per cent participation of the private sector in defence production. However, the liberalisation process has been a long-drawn-out process, dating back to the constitution of six task forces in 1998 to explore the question.[36] Consequent to their recommendations, the government finally opened the defence industry in 2001 to the private sector, with the further provision of foreign direct investment (FDI) of up to 26 per cent. This did not however mean an easy access to defence contracts as MoD's Defence Procurement Procedure (DPP) – which stipulates detailed rules and procedures for capital procurement and the source of procurement– did not have enough provisions to facilitate private companies' participation in defence contracts. In order to create such provisions, successive DPPs have included a host of enabling provisions that include an offset clause, two new procurement categories – Make and Buy and Make (Indian) – and a host of other measures.

Under the offset clause, which was first announced in 2005, foreign companies winning MoD contracts worth Rs 300 crore or more are required to plough back 30 per cent of the foreign exchange component of the contractual value to the Indian defence enterprises. To facilitate the private sector to receive offsets, the government gave complete freedom to the foreign companies to choose their Indian partners. It was hoped that given the dynamism and flexibility the private sector would be the preferred partner for the foreign companies for the fulfilment of offset obligations and in the process to get to know the intricacies of defence production.

The Make category, announced in DPP-2006, is a somewhat revolutionary step, designed to provide the Indian industry, including the big private enterprises, an opportunity to indigenously design, develop and produce 'high technology complex systems'. The category was included in DPP-2006 following the acceptance of the 2005 report of the Kelkar Committee, which recommended a host of policy measures to enhance self-reliance in defence production. For the Make projects, the government makes a commitment to provide 80 per cent of the developmental cost to the industry. Consequent to the articulation of the Make category, two big Army projects – Tactical Communication System (TCS) and Future Infantry Combat System (FICV) – were initially identified with a further plan to award as many as 150-180 projects over a period of time.[37]

Complementing the Make category is the Buy and Make (Indian), under which MoD contracts will be given to Indian industry which is in turn required to form technology tie-ups with foreign companies. This is a marked departure from another existing Buy and Make category, which has been historically used by MoD to nominate its own enterprises to undertake licence production (based on technologies supplied by the foreign companies).

Apart from these initiatives, the government has also tweaked its DPP to create more opportunity for the private sector. As per DPP-2013, vendors participating in Buy (Global) contracts were given a degree of freedom to provide MToT (Maintenance Transfer of Technology) to an Indian private entity. Earlier, MoD had retained the power to nominate the Indian partner, which was invariably a public sector enterprise under its control. The biggest change in DPP-2013 however was the preferred order of categorisation in the order of: (1) Buy (Indian); (2) Buy & Make (Indian); (3) Make (Indian); (4) Buy & Make; and (5) Buy (Global). The significance of the order of categorisation is that while seeking in-principle approval from the government, the armed forces are required to use the higher categories or else give justification for not doing do. The intention was that by putting the onus on the armed forces to look for indigenous-centric categories as a default option, it would reduce large-scale import (through the Buy (Global) route which is now the least preferred option) and in turn promote self-reliance. From the private sector's perspective what is significant is the higher preference accorded to Buy and Make (Indian) over Buy and Make, which has traditionally been used by MoD to negotiate technology transfer agreement with foreign vendors and hand over the negotiated licences for production to public sector units on nomination. After this crucial change, there has been a favourable impact on the first two prioritised categories. In terms of the Acceptance of Necessities (AoNs) accorded by the Defence Acquisition Council (DAC), the highest decision-making body of MoD, during 2013-14 and 2014-15, the first two prioritised categories accounted for 93 per cent of the value of AoNs accorded. In the previous three years their combined share was 47 per cent (Table 1.3).

Table 1.3: AoNs Approved, 2010-15

	Buy (Indian) and Buy & Make (Indian)		*Buy (Global)*		*Other Categories (Rs crore)*	*Total (Rs crore)*
	Value (Rs crore)	*%*	*Value (Rs crore)*	*%*		
2010-11	77546	50.55	40547	26.43	35295	153388
2011-12	30593	54.16	20500	36.29	5387	56480
2012-13	19074	31.44	27114	44.7	14464	60652
2013-14	23736	85.96	371	1.34	3504	27611
2014-15	111070	94.26	6760	5.73	0	117830

Source: 'Make in India: the way ahead for indigenous defence production in India', 6th Y.B. Chavan Memorial Lecture delivered by A.K. Gupta, Secretary (Defence Production), MoD, at IDSA on 7 December 2015.

It is to be noted, however, that till the Modi government came to power, these measures did not have much impact on India's indigenous procurement, with the country remaining as import-dependent as ever. For the period between 2011-12 and 2013-14, India spent a whopping Rs 83,458.31 crore on defence imports.[38] This is apart from a huge amount of foreign exchange spent on what is considered India's indirect arms imports. These are undertaken by the public sector units in the form of parts, components and raw materials. The only thing that seems to have changed is India's number one supplier. If earlier USSR/Russia was the primary supplier, in recent times the US has taken the lead, at least for the period 2011-14 (Table 1.4). By the end of 2015, the US has sealed defence deals worth over $10 billion with India, of which agreements worth over $7 billion were signed between 2007 and 2014 (Table 1.5), indicating the increased bonhomie between the two countries after the nuclear deal was signed in July 2005. All these deals, however, came in the form of Foreign Military Sales (FMS) agreements.

Table 1.4: Top 5 Arms Suppliers to India

(*Rs crore*)

Country	*2011-12*	*2012-13*	*2013-14*	*Total*
US	7845.62	11327.57	13441.99	32615.18
Russia	5876.23	7947.12	11625.00	25448.35
France	4904.39	2566.99	4575.32	12046.70
Israel	1296.21	774.54	1234.65	3305.40
UK	378.84	966.93	312.36	1658.13

Source: Lok Sabha, 'Production of Defence Equipment', Starred Question No. 83, answered on 28 November 2014.

Table 1.5: FMS Agreements with India

US Financial Year	*Agreement ($ Million)*
1950-2006	354.5
2007	91.9
2008	1004.4
2009	10.4
2010	142.7
2011	4506.1
2012	167.9
2013	46.8
2014	1040.4
Total	7365.1

Source: Defence Security Cooperation Agency, US Department of Defence, http://www.dsca.mil/

What is of greater significance is that the private sector has not yet contributed significantly to the domestic arms production which continues to be dominated by the public sector units. The major reason for this is the MoD's failure to execute even a single major contract under two new procurement categories, Buy and Make (Indian) and Make which are key to big-ticket production by the private sector. At the same time, the private continued to face difficulties in its foray into defence business. The difficulties arise because of the host of unresolved issues pertaining to industrial license, financial terms of engagement and level playing field vis-à-vis government-owned entities. These are some of the hurdles that the Make in India initiative launched by the Modi government intends to remove.

Phase 5. Self-Reliance through Make in India Initiative

The Make in India initiative is not restricted to the defence industry; it covers 25 diverse sectors and constitutes a part of the Modi government's larger economic plan to propel the share of manufacturing in GDP to 25 per cent (from 16 per cent at present) and create 100 million additional jobs by 2022.[39] Also, the model is not very different from the previous model: both of them focus on achieving the same broad goal of self-reliance in defence manufacturing through greater participation of the private sector. But where Make in India differs from the previous model is the greater degree of political and bureaucratic will to achieve the objective. The new model reposes a great deal of trust with the private sector. More importantly, to facilitate private sector participation the government has brought in a host of 'ease of doing business' measures, besides bringing in an element of decisiveness in decision-making.

In less than two years of coming to power, the Modi government has already taken several broad reform measures pertaining to the defence industry. These pertain to industrial licensing, FDI cap, defence exports and level playing field between private and public sectors. The reform in licensing which came in the form of a series of government notifications issued between 26 June 2014 and 22 September 2015[40] is an attempt to codify and simplify the process of granting industrial licence (IL) and remove procedural hurdles and other complexities in the process. It may be noted that from the very beginning when the private sector's participation was allowed, there was no clarity, at least in the public domain, with regard to the items against which IL would be granted. Also, restrictive conditions were imposed while granting the IL and there was undue delay in the whole process. To streamline the process, the government has brought out a public version of a list of defence items. The list, while identifying the items which are subject to IL, has also made it clear that any item not included in the list is not subject to industrial licensing. It has also extended the validity of IL from the earlier three years to 18 years, removed the annual capacity norm as a condition for grant of IL and permitted sale of defence items to the government and public sector units and companies holding valid IL, without permission from MoD. The human interface involved in filling up the licence application has also been removed by putting it online. More significantly, the government has expedited the IL granting process. In the first year itself, it has granted some 73 ILs in comparison to 56 given in the previous three years.[41] (Some of the ILs granted by the new government were pending since 2009![42]) Post-rationalisation of IL, there is hardly any IL pending for approval. As Table 1.6 shows, only about 20 per cent of the ILs pending for approval were submitted before 2015.

Table 1.6: Year-wise ILs Pending for Approval

Year of Application	*No. of ILs Pending for Approval (As on 16 November 2015)*
2011	1
2012	3
2013	5
2014	4
2015	51

Note: For delay in obtaining IL in pre-Modi government period, see Table 4.6 in page 69.
Source: Department of Industrial Policy and Promotion, Ministry of Commerce, Government of India, http://dipp.nic.in/English/Default.aspx (Accessed on 16 November 2015).

The reform in FDI cap was first announced in the Modi government's first budget presented to Parliament on 10 July 2014. A detailed notification was issued on 26 August 2014, which has further been revised via Press Note 12 (2015 Series) issued on 24 November 2015. As per the November 2015 notification, the FDI cap stands increased from the earlier 26 per cent to a now composite cap of 49 per cent that includes, besides FDI, investments by foreign portfolio investors (FPI), foreign institutional investors (FII) and the like. Under the previous policy, investments from FPI/FII were either banned or capped at an arbitrary level. The new policy also allows all forms of foreign investment up to 49 per cent under the automatic route, requiring no prior government approval. For FDI beyond 49 per cent, the Foreign Investment Promotion Board (FIPB) is authorised to decide on each proposal 'whenever it is likely to result in access to modern and state-of-the-art technology'. The revised policy has also dropped an earlier onerous provision which required, for the purpose of control, the single-largest resident Indian shareholder of the JV to have at least 51 per cent equity share. As per the new policy, the control is now to be exercised by the resident Indian shareholder's power to influence the company's policy decisions and appoint a majority of the board of directors.[43]

Following the FDI cap increase, the government announced in early September 2014 a set of measures to promote defence exports. These include an export strategy and detailed standard operating procedures (SOPs) for grant of no objection certificate (NOC) to the industry. The export strategy outlines various steps such as formation of various promotional bodies and various diplomatic and financial support measures for the industry's export promotion. The SOP, which has further been revised in July 2015, gives clarity with respect to the processes and documentation required for export licence clearance. It may be noted that the private sector had long demanded an export policy that would take into account the country's security imperatives while promoting the commercial interests of the industry in a predictable and objective manner. The SOP is meant to meet that longstanding demand.

The private sector has also long demanded a level playing field with the public sector defence production units, which were long exempted from paying central excise and customs duties on goods supplied to the defence forces. In response, the government has withdrawn both exemptions on 30 April 2015.[44] These notifications have also encouraged foreign companies such as Boeing, Airbus, Lockheed Martin and BAE Systems to actively explore the scope of future investment in India.[45]

Make in India also emphasises putting the private sector at the heart of the procurement process. The Modi government's first year itself saw the clearance of 39 acquisition proposals, of which 32 proposals worth Rs 88,900 crore (or 96 per cent of total value) were under the Buy (Indian) and Buy & Make (Indian) categories.[46] Table 1.7 provides an overview of some of the big-ticket projects earmarked for the local industry. Of note is that in almost all the big proposals, there is a role for the private sector and in some cases (as in Avro Replacement Aircraft programme) the role is exclusive. For the P-75 (I) project for the procurement of six conventional submarines, the government has changed the previous government's decision (to import two submarines followed by licence-manufacturing of four by the public sector shipyards) and decided to construct all the submarines in the domestic shipyards in which the private sector will be given a chance to compete. In the Avro Replacement programme, the government has not only shown decisiveness in quickly overcoming certain reservations (about the exclusion of HAL from the programme) continuing from the previous government but also gone ahead in accepting the only single bid submitted jointly by Tata and Airbus – a rarity in India's decision-making scheme of things. In the LPD contract, the government has decided to exclude the public sector Cochin Shipyard Ltd and issue the tender to private shipyards only.[47] More significantly, it has taken some concrete steps for operationalising the Make procedure, which was in limbo since its articulation in 2006. In February 2015, the government awarded the first ever developmental contract to two shortlisted consortiums – one of which consists of two private companies, Tata and L&T – to develop the Battlefield Management System (BMS) prototype.[48]

Table 1.7: Select High-value Projects for Indian Defence Industry

Project	*No.*	*Value (Rs crore)*
P-75 (I) Conventional Submarines	5	50000
Battlefield Management System	–	50000
Light Utility Helicopters	384	40000
Landing Platform Dock	4	25000
Mounted Artillery Guns (155 mm/52 calibre)	814	15750
Avro Replacement Aircraft	56	11897
Fleet Support Vessels	5	9000
Survey Vessels	4	2324

Source: Author's database.

The trust factor with the private sector is perhaps best amplified in the government's recent decision to allow L&T to sign a Licensing Agreement for Transfer of Technology (LAToT) with DRDO for upgraded digital version of the Pilotless Target Aircraft (PTA), Lakshya.[49] This is the first time that technology of a high-value product developed by DRDO was given to the private sector for licence production. Earlier, the public sector units had the exclusive rights on DRDO-developed items. All these developments mean that the private sector will now play an equally major role in India's defence production sector.

The government is also considering additional steps to deepen the private sector's participation in defence production. The procurement manual is being given a Make in India outlook with particular focus on the private sector. In this regard, the government is examining the report of the Dhirendra Singh committee which was set up to suggest amendments to DPP-2013 and formulate a policy framework to facilitate Make in India. The report, submitted in July 2015, contains 43 recommendations. The major recommendations pertain to strategic partners (SPs) from among the private sector companies which would undertake manufacturing of big projects. The government has also set up a high-powered Task Force under the chairmanship of V.K. Aatre, former head of DRDO, to formulate guidelines to select SPs.[50] This along with the aforementioned measures suggests that the private sector, which was hitherto marginalised, will play an equally important role in India's defence production sector.

Can the Indian Defence Industry Make in India?

The Make in India initiative has no doubt created a buzz in India's private sector defence industry. However, the private sector currently constitutes the smallest segment of the Indian defence production and technology sector, which continues to be dominated by the public sector, including DRDO. As it would seem clear from the previous discussion, Make in India has so far not touched upon the state-owned entities, which for a variety of reasons have contributed much below their potential. But can the private sector-led Make in India really fill the void in India's self-reliance goals without the state-owned entities working to their true potential? This is a question that the succeeding chapters will try to probe in greater detail.

NOTES

1. Richard F. Grimmett, *Conventional Arms Transfers to Developing Nations, 2004-11*, Congressional Research Service, 24 August 2012, p. 47.

2. Pieter D. Wezeman and Siemon T. Wezeman, 'Trends in international arms transfers, 2014' *SIPRI Fact Sheet*, March 2015. SIPRI uses Trend Indicator Value (TIV) for measuring trends in arms transfers. The TIV does not however reflect the financial value of arms transferred, leading to its critique by analysts. For a critique of TIV, see G Balachandran, 'International arms transfers: a study', in Jasjit Singh (ed.), *Conventional Arms Transfers,* IDSA, 1995, pp. 48-59.
3. Rajya Sabha, 225th Session, Uncorrected debates, 8 May 2012.
4. CAG. Report No. 10 of 2010-11, http://www.cag.gov.in/content/report-no-10-2010-11-%E2%80%93-performance-audit-activities-public-sector-undertakings
5. Standing Committee on Defence (2006-07), 14th Lok Sabha, *Defence Research and Development Organisation (DRDO)*, 14th Report, Lok Sabha Secretariat, New Delhi, 2007, p. 3.
6. Rajya Sabha, 'Curbing indirect import reliance by DPSUs OFs', Unstarred Question No. 63, answered on 21 July 2015, http://164.100.47.5/qsearch/QResult.aspx (accessed on 3 November 2015).
7. Laxman Kumar Behera, *Indian Defence Industry: Issues of Self-Reliance*, IDSA Monograph Series, No. 21, July 2013, p. 52.
8. The phase-based analysis of India's defence industrialisation process is partly based on Manjeet S. Pardesi and Ron Matthews, 'India's tortuous road to defence industrial self-reliance', *Defense and Security Analysis*, Vol. 23, No 4, December 2007, pp. 419-438.
9. Blackett's report as quoted in Ramdas P. Shenoy, *Defence Research and Development Organisation 1958-1982,* DRDO, New Delhi, 2006, pp. 16-22.
10. Stephen P. Cohen and Sunil Dasgupta, *Arming without Aiming: India's Military Modernisation,* Penguin, New Delhi, 2010, p. 6.
11. Lorne J. Kavic, *India's Quest for Security: Defence Policies, 1947-1965,* University of California Press, Berkeley, 1967, p. 129.
12. Thomas W. Graham, 'India', in James Everett Katz, ed.,*Arms Production in Developing Countries: An Analysis of Decision Making,* D.C. Heath and Company, Lexington, 1987, p. 163.
13. Kavic, *India's Quest for Security* ..., n. 11, p. 132.
14. Chris Smith, *India's Ad Hoc Arsenal: Direction or Drift in Defence Policy?* Oxford University Press, Oxford, 1994, p. 160.
15. Kavic, *India's Quest for Security* ..., n. 11, p. 133.
16. Thomas W. Graham, 'India', in Katz, *Arms Production in Developing Countries...*,n. 12, p. 170.
17. Kavic, *India's Quest for Security* ..., n. 11, p. 135.
18. Standing Committee on Defence (1995-96), 10th Lok Sabha, *Defence Research and Development: Major Projects*, 5th Report, Lok Sabha Secretariat, New Delhi, 1995, p. 4.
19. Kavic, *India's Quest for Security* ..., n. 11, p. 136.
20. Ibid., p. 137.
21. Amit Gupta, 'The Indian arms industry: a lumbering giant?', *Asian Survey*, Vol. 30, No 9, September 1990, p. 855.
22. Ian Anthony, *The Arms Trade and Medium Powers: Case Studies of India and Pakistan 1947-90,* Harvester Wheatsheaf, New York, 1992, p. 58.
23. Raviderpal Singh, 'Indo-Soviet military cooperation: expectation, trends and opportunities', *Strategic Analysis*, December 1990, p. 1081.
24. See Ordnance Factory Board, *Annual Report 2006-07*, p. 12.

25. Amit Gupta, *Building an Arsenal: The Evolution of Regional Power Force Structures,* Praeger, Westport, 1997, p. 42.
26. Ravinder Pal Singh, 'India', in *Arms Procurement Decision Making: China, India, Israel, japan, South Korea and Thailand,* Oxford University Press and SIPRI, Oxford, 1998, p. 65.
27. Damon Bristow, *India's New Armament Strategy: A Return to Self-Sufficiency?,* Royal United Services Institute, Whitehall Paper 31, 1995, p. 30.
28. Standing Committee on Defence (2006-07), *Defence Research and Development Organisation (DRDO),* n. 5, p. 88.
29. Standing Committee on Defence (1995-96), *Defence Research and Development: Major Projects,* n. 18, p. 17.
30. Standing Committee on Defence (2006-07), *Defence Research and Development Organisation (DRDO),* n. 5, p. 63.
31. PIB, 'Joint manufacturing of aircraft', 15 March 2010.
32. PIB, 'Fifth Generation Fighter Aircraft', 07 May 2012; PIB, 'Joint development of Fifth Generation Fighter Aircrafts with Russia', 3 August 2011.
33. PIB, 'Agreement with Russia for Multirole Transport Aircraft', 10 November 2010.
34. Ministry of Defence, Government of India, *Annual Report 2010-11,* p. 97.
35. PIB, 'Successful conduct of LR SAM firing by Indian Navy', 30 December 2015.
36. The Boston Consulting Group and Confederation of Indian Industry, *Creating a Vibrant Defence Manufacturing Sector,* March 2012, p. 21.
37. Ajai Shukla, 'Defence Min signals growing acceptance of private sector', *Business Standard,* 30 March 2012.
38. Rajya Sabha, 'Defence Imports', Starred Question No. 496, answered on 12 August 2014.
39. Make in India website, http://www.makeinindia.com/policy/national-manufacturing/
40. The notifications are available at the website of the Department of Industrial Policy and Promotion, Ministry of Commerce and Industry.
41. PIB, 'Further boost to defence manufacturing, DIPP clears defence licences worth Rs 613 Crs', 3 July 2015.
42. Lok Sabha, 'Industrial licences to defence sector', Unstarred Question No 834, answered on 24 July 2015.
43. Department of Industrial Policy and Promotion, Ministry of Commerce and Industry, Press Note No. 7 (2014 Series)', 26 August 2014.
44. The notifications are available at the Central Board of Excise and Customs website, http://www.cbec.gov.in/cae1-english.htm
45. PIB, 'Big push to private participation in defence manufacturing: Government provides level playing field with Defence PSUs', 1 June 2015.
46. PIB, 'One year of NDA: Ministry of Defence', http://pib.nic.in/nda/Achievements.aspx
47. 'Rs 25,000 cr Navy tender only for private sector: Defence Ministry', *Financial Express,* 14 September 2014.
48. 'Tata-L&T consortium shortlisted for mega defence project', http://www.moneycontrol.com/news/business/tata-lt-consortium-shortlisted-for-mega-defence-project_1314651.html
49. Sushant Singh, 'In a first, DRDO transfers technology to private player', *Indian Express,* 19 July 2015; Lok Sabha, 'Pilotless Target Aircraft', Unstarred question No. 3198, answered on 7 August 2015.
50. 'Government plans strategic partnership with private firms, panel to give guidelines', *Economic Times,* 12 September 2015.

2

Ordnance Factories

There are 39 ordnance factories (OFs). OFs form the largest and oldest departmentally run industrial organisation in India. They have a vast infrastructure, skilled human resources and years of experience in defence production. They are responsible for the manufacture of arms, ammunition, armoured vehicles and ordnance stores required primarily by the defence forces. OFs as a whole have often come under attack for below par performance, as amply reflected in India's huge arms import dependency. The nature and degree of their relevance to the Make in India initiative would depend primarily on their performance in the near future. The question therefore arises: are OFs geared to face the emerging reality? This chapter tries to find out the answer by analysing OFs' performance with respect to a number of parameters including innovativeness, management dynamics, exports, pricing policy, productivity and contract execution performance. It also examines certain emerging issues arising out of Make in India.

Origin and Growth

OFs originated in the colonial period. To further Britain's economic interests and enhance the political holding in India, the colonial rulers considered some low-end defence production as a vital element. In 1775, the Board of Ordnance was established at Fort William, Calcutta (now Kolkata). The Gun Powder Factory was established in 1787 at Ishapore. The Gun Carriage Agency (now known as the Gun & Shell Factory), set up in 1801 at Cossipore, made the first production by an OF. The focus of expansion in independent India took place after the 1962 war. Sixteen factories were established between 1963 and 1995, compared to five factories that were set up during 1949-1962 (the British rulers had established 18 factories pre-1944). These 39 factories are in operation at 24 different locations. Two new OFs are being set up in Nalanda, Bihar (for the production of Bimodular charges) and at Korwa, Uttar Pradesh (for the production of new generation carbines).

Management

OFs are managed by a three-layered system. At the apex is the Department of Defence Production of the Ministry of Defence (MoD). The DDP takes the major decisions with regard to OFs' vendor development, product improvement/development and commercial interests.[1] At the mid-level is the Ordnance Factories Board (OFB), which was set up in 1979 in pursuance of the recommendations of the Rajadhyaksha Committee set up by MoD. OFB is headed by a Director General who is also its chairman. He is supported by nine members of additional director general rank. Of these, five head each operating division consisting of a group of factories. The remaining four are responsible for staff functions.

Operating Divisions

1. Ammunition and Explosives (A&E) – 10 factories
2. Weapons, Vehicles and Equipment (WV&E) – 10 factories
3. Materials and Components (M&C) – 9 factories
4. Armoured Vehicles (AV) – 5 factories
5. Ordnance Equipment – 5 factories

Staff Functions

1. Personnel
2. Finance
3. Planning and Material Management
4. Projects & Engineering and Technical Services

The OFB performs the executive functions, including laying down policies and procedures on the functioning of the factories, monitoring receipts of orders from buyers and determining the annual target for production. It also controls the overall budget of the organisation.[2] The factories are normally headed by a General Manger or Senior General Manager, who is responsible for the day-to-day functioning of their factories.

Employees, Production, Sales and Accounting

The OFs' product range consists of nearly 1,000 principal items, including tanks, infantry combat vehicles, artillery guns and rocket launchers (Table 2.1).

Table 2.1: Product Range of Ordnance Factories

1	Weapon Items	small arms (rifles, pistols, carbines, machine guns), tank guns, ant-tank guns, field howitzers, artillery guns, mortars, air defence guns and rocket launchers
2	Ammunition Items	ammunition for these weapon systems, rockets, missile warheads, mortar bombs, pyro-technique (smoke, illuminating, signal), grenades and bombs for the Air Force, naval ammunition, propellant and fuzes
3	Armoured and Transport Vehicles	Tank T-72 'Ajeya', Tank T-90 'Bhishma', infantry combat vehicles, armoured ambulances, bullet-proof and mine-proof vehicles, special transport vehicles and variants
4	Troop Comfort Items	parachutes for the Army and Air Force, high altitude and combat clothing, tents of various types, uniforms and clothing items, floats for light assault bridges
5	Opto Electronics	optical instruments and opto-electronic devices/fire control instruments for armoured vehicles, infantry and artillery systems
6	Others	special aluminium alloys for aviation and space industry, field cables, water bowser, etc.

Source: Standing Committee on Defence, 14th Lok Sabha, *Indigenisation of Defence Production: Public Private Partnership*, 33rd Report, Lok Sabha Secretariat, New Delhi, 2008, p. 7.

Table 2.2 provides the OFs' employee strength for the last five years. The number of employees has declined by 6.3 per cent during 2008-13, but OFs as a whole have a high ratio of officers to industrial employees (or direct labour). In 2013-14, the ratio was 1.97, meaning one supervisor for nearly every two direct labour!

Table 2.2: Employee Strength of OFs

Year	*Gazetted Officers*	*Non-Gazetted Officers*	*Industrial Employees*	*Total*
2008-09	3947	31105	67717	102769
2009-10	3481	30482	65411	99374
2010-11	8306	25302	65306	98914
2011-12	7917	25058	63572	96547
2012-13	8006	24409	63902	96317

Source: Author's database.

Table 2.5: Status of Indigenisation of Items under Technology Transfer

Contract Signed	*Item*	*Supplier*	*Cost (Rs crore)*	*Planned Period for Indigenisation*	*Status of Indigenisation (as in March 2013)*
June 2000	155mm screening smoke blue emission ammunition	Denel Swartklip, S. Africa	–	March 2003	25 per cent
February 2001	T-90 tanks	Rosoboronexport, Russia	2524	2006-07	59 of 78 codes (main assemblies)
October 2003	130mm cargo ammunition	IMI, Israel	40	2008-09	No progress due to ban on IMI
May 2004	AK-630 guns	Rosoboronexport, Russia	96	2007-08	48 per cent
February 2005	84mm rocket launcher Mark-III	FFV Ordnance, Sweden	460	2009-10	47 per cent

Source: CAG, Report No. 35 of 2014, p. 127.

reason behind the ineffectiveness of the vendor base lies in OFB's Procurement Manual which does not allow contracts with private industry for more than three years. Such a limited period has been a major hindrance for the local vendors to commit investment in new capability. It is therefore desirable that the manual be revised to allow a long-term partnership of minimum five years.

Table 2.6: OFB's Vendor Base

Year	*No. of Vendors*
2011-12	6231
2013-14	6910
2014-15	8124
2014-15 (up to December 2014)	8933

Source: OFB, *Annual Report 2014-15*, p. 7.

Table 2.7: OFB's Import Dependency

Year	*Import Content in Value of Issue (Rs crore)*
2009-10	2060
2010-11	2026
2011-12	1693
2012-13	1462
2013-14	1653

Source: OFB, *Annual Report 2012-13* and *2014-15*.

On the aspect of in-house R&D, it may be noted OFB has an elaborate infrastructure, consisting of a cell in each factory. Besides, there are 11 Ordnance Development Centres (ODC) with specific expertise in different generic areas. ODCs are the nodal agencies for planning, besides providing advice for R&D-related work. OFB is also vested with full powers to incur R&D expenditure. However, such powers do not seem to be exercised in right earnest. As may be seen from Table 2.8, OFB has a very modest level of spending on R&D, amounting to less than one per cent of its turnover. Except for some futuristic R&D projects (Table 2.9), OFB's current R&D efforts are largely confined to the modification of existing platforms and certain kinds of ammunition (Table 2.10). In this regard, it may be noted that about 90 per cent of OFB's current turnover comes from technology developed outside the organisation.[6]

Table 2.8: OFB's R&D Expenditure

Year	*R&D Expenditure (Rs crore)*	*Value of Sales (Rs crore)*	*R&D as % of Value of Sales*
2010-11	40	11215	0.4
2011-12	36	12391	0.3
2012-13	48	11975	0.4
2013-14	43	11123	0.4
2014-15	56	11344	0.5
2015-16*	89	13500	0.7

Note: *: Projected

Source: Standing Committee on Defence, *Demands for Grants: 2016-17*, 21st Report, Lok Sabha Secretariat, New Delhi, May 2016.

Table 2.9: OFB's Futuristic R&D Projects

Futuristic Infantry Combat Vehicle (FICV)	Electronic fuze for artillery 105/130/155 mm
Conversion of T-55 tank to Heavy APC	Development of assault gun
Commander TI sights for T-72 and T-90 tanks	5.56×30mm joint venture protective carbine
155mm/52 calibre SP tracked/wheeled gun system (ECWCS)	Development of extreme cold weather clothing
155mm future artillery gun	Development of NBC suit Mk-IV (small, medium, large and extra-large)
105mm LFG up-gradation with laser pointing and positioning system	Precision guided kit (PGT) for advanced artillery shell system.

Source: OFB, *Annual Report 2014-15*, p. 6.

Table 2.10: Products Developed though OFB's In-house R&D

Armoured Recovery Vehicle	LFG mounted on BMP
T-72 up-gradation	RGB mounted on BMP
Completer modernisation of BMP-II	Development of 155mm×45 calibre FH gun with Electronic Modules (Dhanush)
Modernisation/upgraded version of MPV for MHA	Development of indigenous propellant for 155mm BMCS of 155mm gun system

Source: OFB, *Annual Report 2014-15*, p. 5.

Execution of Orders

Timely execution of orders by OFB is a major source of disappointment. The OFs' production is often behind schedule, in spite of schedules reworked by mutual consultation between the parties concerned (see Table 2.11).

Table 2.11: Delay in Execution of Orders by OFB

Year	*No. of items for which demand existed*	*No. of items for which target fixed*	*No. of items manufactured as per target*	*% shortfall with regard to demand existed*	*% shortfall with regard to target fixed*
2007-08	628	507	360	43	29
2008-09	419	419	296	29	29
2009-10	605	434	300	50	31
2010-11	1016	639	414	59	35
2011-12	982	547	195	80	64

Source: CAG, Report No. 30 of 2013, p. 64.

What is perhaps a major concern is OFB's failure to meet the production target for ammunition. In view of the deficiency in the stock of various types of ammunition with the Army, MoD in January 2010 placed a consolidated roll-on indent for five years (2009-10 to 2013-14) on OFB for supply of ammunition in consultation with it. But OFB failed to meet the order. The shortfall varied between 54 and 73 per cent between 2009-10 and 2012-13. In value terms the shortfall ranged between 28 and 37 per cent. One of the reasons for OFB's inability to supply adequate ammunition was its overestimation of capacity.

The Indian Army's ammunition requirement is huge. In September 2013, the Army had projected ammunition requirement worth Rs 40,771 crore for the five-year period up to 2018-19. This translates to a supply worth Rs 8154.2 crore per year. To meet this requirement, OFB has to more than double its present production capacity. However, given the tardy progress in scaling up production by OFB earlier, there is a genuine concern about the fructification of the plan.

Army officials often complain that OFs have the tendency to inflate their capabilities in order to get increased number of orders. But there are several other factors which are beyond OFB's control, such as:

- Failure in purchase from trade sources due to ban on certain firms by the government, late receipt of material from vendors
- Delay in finalisation of procurement decisions in MoD
- Procurement delays due to exorbitant price hike and single-tender vendor situations
- Delay in product development by DRDO
- Delay in proof due to inadequate proof infrastructure
- Prolonged breakdown of plant and machinery

- Non-receipt of bulk production clearance from users
- Short supply from feeder factories

Pricing of OFB Products

OFs operate on a no-loss-no-profit basis. The products are supplied at a price that takes into account only the actual cost of production, which includes the cost of material and labour consumed and overhead charges. The overhead costs include those of the plants and machinery and are divided into fixed and variable overheads. However, this cost-plus mechanism of pricing is widely believed to be inefficient. The armed forces are vociferous in saying that OFB products are over-priced, affecting their budget and modernisation programmes. To keep the price under control, the Finance Division of MoD has since the last few years devised a system to determine and fix the price of major items supplied to the defence forces. The system is based on actual cost of production of the last two years, cost estimates for the year of pricing and the projected cost for the next year. The system also provides for interaction among the OFB, users and MoD's Finance Division. The advantage of the system lies in its in-built pressure on OFB to target for efficiencies. However, currently the rigour with which the mechanism works is far from satisfactory. OFB does not finalise its annual accounts in time, rendering the whole exercise a mere formality. The CAG has recently noted that OFB passed on a profit of Rs 97 crore earned though inputs sales of the sister factories to the factories assembling the final product. 'As a result, the cost of material at final product factories was inflated by Rs 97 crore since the cost at which these items were issued to the final product factories was taken as input cost by the final product factories and thereby jacking the input cost unnecessarily to the extent of profit element.' This, along with the absence of benchmarking against material procurement cost and the productivity gains over the years, renders the system of little use.

There are two other factors that contribute to the high price of OFB products. The first is related to efficiency in the usage of both labour and materials. Officials conversant with the functioning of OFs state that they have a very high input-usage rate, due to lack of process improvement and skill up-gradation of the labour force.

The second factor is related to 'surge capacity' that the factories are mandated to carry in order to meet the increased supply requirements during times of crisis. Surge capacity carries a minimum cost in terms of overhead charges. The only way the cost on this account can be reduced is through better utilisation of labour, plants, machinery and stores. In the last four years, however, there has been no visible improvement in overhead cost reduction (Table 2.12), with certain OFs having such cost in excess of 50 per cent (Table 2.13). Since large overhead costs are a sign of inefficiency and inflate the final cost of products, the users should look into this aspect more carefully.

Table 2.12: Overheads as Percentage of Cost of Production

Year	*Ammunition and Explosives*	*Weapon, Vehicles and Equipment*	*Armoured Vehicles*	*Materials and Components*	*Ordnance Equipment*	*Total*
2005-06	22.5	32.8	20.2	45.9	28.5	28.5
2010-11	23.0	33.8	19.8	39.3	32.7	27.5
2011-12	23.3	31.7	18.0	37.3	33.3	26.5
2012-13	23.4	33.6	20.8	35.7	30.8	27.5

Source: CAG, Report No. 35 of 2014, p. 122.

Table 2.13: Overhead Cost as Percentage of Cost of Production of Select OFs

Factory	*Main Product Line*	*2010-11*	*2011-12*	*2012-13*
Metal and Steel Factory, Ishapore	Barrel and casing forging, etc	65	61	53
OF Muradnagar	Castings for various ammunition	62	60	58
Rifle Factory Ishapore	5.56mm rifle, sporting rifle	58	59	59
OF Bhandara	Propellants and charges	77	73	54
OF Dehradun	Sighting instruments and equipment	64	62	61
Small Arms Factory Kanpur	Carbines, rifles and revolvers	54	56	54
Field Gun Factory Kanpur	Barrels, ordnance and revolvers	57	49	51
Ordnance Cable Factory Chandigarh	Cables and wires	63	65	52

Source: CAG, Report No 35 of 2014, p. 122.

Quality of Products

In reply to a question in the Look Sabha in 2007, the Minister of State for Defence Production reported a number of deficiencies in OFB products, including some batches of 5.56 mm INSAS rifle, 5.56 mm light machine gun, small arms ammunition, tank ammunition and delay igniter. The minister further reported that the affected items were segregated for investigation and corrective action.[7] Audit agencies have also reported deficiencies in OFB products. In 2005, the CAG observed that of the 47 items, test-audited by the agency, of weapons, ammunition and heavy vehicles produced in OFs, 18 had quality problems.[8] Recently, the CAG has noted that Rs 2432 crore worth of ammunition produced by OFs was rejected or was ineffective due to quality-related problems.[9] Between 1999 and 2004, the Army reported a total of 3210 defects in OFB-supplied products, of which more than 1500 were related to weapons, ammunition and armoured vehicles.[10] In some instances, the Army, frustrated with the consistent failures of some OFB products, has resorted to an 'expedient approach' by way of setting up its own in-house repair facility.

For quality control and assurance of OFB products, there is a twin-tiered system in place. Each factory has a quality control (QC) section which is entrusted with the task of inspecting and accepting the components on their receipt, checking at designated control points during the manufacturing process and finally conducting 100 per cent check of the final product. The Directorate General of Quality Assurance (DGQA) through its representative in each factory is mandated to provide quality assurance. This function is discharged by conducting a limited sample test and sentencing the product as either cleared for issue or rejected. This system does not, however, work efficiently. There are instances where quality assurance was given for products with 'defects that could have been detected in visual inspection'.[11]

Exports

Historically, exports by OFs had never been a primary focus. However, in a major policy change, the MoD, since 1989, has allowed OFB to venture into direct exports business. The intention of the policy decision was not solely revenue-driven. Rather it was intended that the international exposure would make the factories quality and price conscious. At the same time it was visualised that exports would allow the OFs to take advantage of the spare capacity, which in turn would drive down the per unit cost of production. To provide a competitive edge in the international market, OFB was also instructed to resort to 'strategic pricing', covering full material costs and a part of labour and overheads costs.[12] But over the years, exports have not gone up. Besides, not all the factories are in the export business (Table 2.14).

There are several factors behind OFB's poor export performance, some of which are not in its direct control. For instance, OFB's exports are limited to those countries which do not figure in the 'negativelist' maintained by the Ministry of External Affairs. Also, OFB cannot export some of its high-value systems such as tanks, some ammunition and infantry fighting vehicles because they are based on foreign technology, and require permission from the overseas collaborator for selling to third parties. The export potential is further constrained due to some of OFB products' non-compatibility with NATO specifications.

Table 2.14: Export Performance of OFs

Year	*No. of factories involved*	*Exports (Rs crore)*
1997-98	13	23.83
2000-01	15	11.79
2005-06	11	14.66
2006-07	13	15.12
2007-08	10	27.44
2008-09	11	41.07
2009-10	13	12.30
2010-11	8	35.70
2011-12	6	46.08
2012-13	—	15.0
2013-14	—	18.0
2014-15 (upto December 2014)	—	19.0

Source: Author's data base, based on various reports of CAG and OFB.

Measured in terms of the percentage of total sales, defence public sector undertakings such as HAL and BEL have higher exports, in the range of 4-5 per cent, compared to less than one per cent for OFB. Although OFB of late has taken a few measures, such as procedural simplification, hosting of an 'international generic' website (*www.ofbindia.com*) and product demonstration in major arms exhibitions – it has not resulted in any significant dividend. The customers' poor enthusiasm is primarily because of two factors. First, they are not yet convinced about the competitiveness of OFB products. Second, OFB has so far not taken a corporate approach in establishing a brand image for its products.

Capacity Utilisation and Impact of Modernisation

Efficient utilisation of key inputs, particularly plant and machinery (P&M) and labour goes a long way in controlling the cost of production. OFB has always maintained that its existing capacity with respect to P&M is optimally utilised. For instance, for the five-year period up to 2012-13, OFB's estimated utilisation of standard man hours was 127 per cent (Table 2.15). For standard machine hours, the utilisation was 74 per cent, which is not so bad considering that OFB has fixed the optimum utilisation rate at 80 per cent. These utilisation rates, though they sound incredible, belie certain basic international norms. It is widely known that government-owned companies including OFs are permitted to book exorbitantly high man/machine hours for any job they do. A clear example is HAL. For manufacturing indigenously developed Advanced Light Helicopter (series production), its average man-hours booked was nearly double the rates suggested by an international consultant.[13]

Table 2.15: OFB's Capacity Utilisation, Standard Man and Machine Hours (in million hours)

Year	*Standard Man Hours*			*Standard Machine Hours*		
	Available	*Utilised*	*Utilisation %*	*Available*	*Utilised*	*Utilisation %*
2008-09	116	162	140	170	129	76
2009-10	113	127	113	184	126	69
2010-11	108	135	125	183	131	72
2011-12	108	138	127	158	123	78
2012-13	103	132	129	160	121	76

Source: CAG, Report No. 35 of 2014, p. 120.

Related to optimum capacity utilisation is the induction of new plant and machinery. As per the instructions of OFB issued in 2004, each factory is required to assess the potential impact of induction of new machinery on 'cost reduction and quality improvement'. The CAG, which undertook a sample audit of 10 factories, has observed that 'factories did not conduct such a revision in 80 per cent of the machines commissioned during 2009-13', although OFB as a whole spent a huge sum of Rs 3109 crore during 2008-13 on new P&M.[14] Such high expenditure on P&M without any linkage with cost efficiency and quality improvement does not speak well for an industrial organisation. It is therefore imperative that a clear linkage is established in which new induction of P&M corresponds to a well-defined cost reduction and quality enhancement as well as improved timeframes for production.

Poor Inventory Management

OFB's total inventory was valued at Rs 10,490 crore as in March 2013, accounting for two-thirds of the cost of production. This has been identified as an 'area of concern' in the Review of Annual Accounts by the Principal Controller of Accounts, Factories (PC of A, Fys). CAG, which recently undertook a comprehensive review of inventory management of nine sampled factories, has observed that 90 per cent of their stores-in-hand (SIH)[15] exceeded the prescribed time limit as laid down in OFB's procurement manual. In the light of the above, it is desirable that procurement of stores should be closely linked to the production plan of the factories' supply, lead time and production cycle.

Outsourcing and Vendor Development

Currently, OFB's outsourcing is nearly 50 per cent of its total value of production (Table 2.16). These figures include purchases from both Indian and foreign vendors. Considering that OFB has a relatively low import dependency, the outsourcing to Indian vendors appears to be quite high.

Table 2.16: Outsourcing by OFB (Rs crore)

	Value of items Outsourced	*Value of Production (Excluding IFD)*	*Outsourcing as % of VoP*
2010-11	5725	11215	51
2011-12	6184	12391	50
2012-13	5740	11975	48
2013-14 (Provisional)	5231	11234	47

Source: *OFB Annual Report 2013-14*, p. 7.

It is, however, not clear to what extent OFB's outsourcing is part of a holistic strategy that takes into account optimum utilisation of existing resources while harnessing the potential of Indian industry for cost efficiency and for devoting greater focus on integration, product development and upgradation of existing products. As noted earlier, OFB's utilisation of existing resources, pricing of product and its focus on R&D and technology absorption are far from satisfactory. It is therefore imperative that outsourcing should be resorted to only when it is cost-effective and leads to overall efficiency in the organisation's performance parameters.

Corporatisation

Since MoD is responsible for OFB's major policy decisions, which are often tardy and sometimes also politically motivated, OFB's autonomy is curtailed, with no incentive to innovate. Compared to OFs, DPSUs are more autonomous, with powers to form joint ventures and strategic alliances, invest in modernisation projects, undertake R&D projects, and collaborate with foreign partners for technological know-how.

Similarly, unlike DPSUs whose board of directors is collectively responsible for their functioning, OFs are not board-managed. OFB's responsibility is restricted to giving policy directions to its factories which are more or less independent in their functioning.[16] This has led to poor monitoring of the individual factories.[17]

To address this deficiency in the management of OFs, various government-appointed committees and oversight agencies have suggested that the OFB should be corporatised. The rationale is to allow greater autonomy to the organisation to run its own affairs while at the same time being accountable for its performance. The Kelkar Committee had in particular recommended that 'all ordnance factories should be corporatised under a single corporation under the leadership of competitive management'. The committee also suggested the following:

- This corporation should be accorded the status of Nav Ratna
- The corporatisation could be on the lines of Bharat Sanchar Nigam Ltd. (BSNL)
- The existing dispensation by the Government to Ordnance Factories should continue for a period of three years to help them to steer the changed process internally
- Corporatisation does not necessarily mean privatisation.

CAG in its recommendations also says that 'the factories and the OF secretariat should be Board managed… similar to a Board of a company'. However, the government has not so far been able to implement this vital recommendation, apparently because of the strong opposition from the labour unions associated with the factories.

Challenges from the Private Sector

Under Make in India, the government has taken a host of measures for ease of doing business to promote the private sector in the defence industry. Two developments in this regard have a huge consequence for OFs. First, the withdrawal of the excise and customs duty exemptions granted earlier to public sector units has caused an estimated additional burden of Rs 1000 crore to OFs.[18] Second, post-launch of Make in India, the government has issued industrial licences pertaining particularly to ammunition, which was earlier the exclusive domain of OFs. Recently, L&T won a contract in a globally competitive bidding for the guns which were historically the production forte of OFs.[19] The private sector is also aggressively looking at other defence items such as Future Infantry Combat Vehicle (FICV).

Conclusion

Poor management and gross inefficiency have eroded OFs' relevance as a prime supplier so arms and ammunition, particularly to the Army. Given their record of poor focus on R&D and product development, high overhead cost, poor labour productivity, quality concerns and delay in execution of orders, it would be difficult for OFs to tread the business-as-usual path.

Currently, OFs have little autonomy. The government needs to introduce an effective management system by way of corporatising OFB and giving it autonomy. But corporatisation may not be the ultimate panacea. As discussed in the next chapter, DPSUs, which are corporate entities, also suffer from a host of inefficiencies. But being corporate entities they follow certain transparency norms that include disclosure of accounts. Corporatisation is also the first step for further reforms such as divestment of government equity and ultimately privatisation, if required.

OFs that have high overhead costs should be shut down. Alternatively, the government may like to put those factories on public-private partnership.

With 90 per cent of the turnover coming from technologies developed outside, the OFs' commitment to indigenisation and self-reliance calls for a major review. There is a need to substantially augment the in-house R&D capacity for both product improvement and the design and development of new products. A minimum 3 percent of turnover should be earmarked for R&D efforts.

OFs need to assume greater responsibility with regard to the price and quality of their products, Benchmarking with the best in the class must be undertaken to get rid of redundancies to stay relevant in the emerging competitive defence sector.

NOTES

1. Standing Committee on Defence (2005-06), 14th Lok Sabha, *Defence Ordnance Factories*, 7th Report, Lok Sabha Secretariat, New Delhi, 2005, p. 5.
2. CAG, 'Procurement of stores and machinery in ordnance factories', Union Government (Defence Services), Ordnance Factories, Report No. 15 of 2010-11, p. 2.

3. The demand placed by one factory on another sister factory for supply of components, castings, forgings, etc. is called IFD.
4. MoD *Annual Report 2014-15*, p. 58. CAG Report No. 35 of 2014, p. 126.
5. *SIPRI Arms Transfer Database*, available at http://www.sipri.org/ (accessed on 14 May August 2016). For a critique of SIPRI Arms Transfer Database, see note 2 of Chapter one.
6. *Ayudh*, House Journal of the Indian Ordnance Factories Organisation, December 2014, p. 6.
7. Lok Sabha, *Unstarred Question No. 2231*, answered on 3 December 2007, 'Rejection of Indigenous Weapons by Armed Forces'.
8. CAG, Report No. 18 of 2005, p.15.
9. Of the total, ammunition worth Rs 1618 crore, which was accepted by quality assurance (QA) was later found 'not up to the mark due to persistent quality problems'. The balance Rs 814 crore worth of ammunition was 'declared unserviceable within the shelf-life by the depots due to poor quality.' See CAG, Report No. PA 19 of 2015, p. vi.
10. CAG, Report No. 18 of 2005, p.18.
11. CAG, Report No. PA 19 of 2015, p. 31.
12. OFB, *Annual Report 2005-06*, p.21.
13. CAG, Report No. 10 of 2010-11, p. 32.
14. CAG, Report No. 35 of 2014, p. 120.
15. SIH is raw material held in the stores section of a factory.
16. The independent functioning of individual OFs is, however, limited to certain financial powers delegated to them.
17. CAG, Report No. 15 of 15 of 2010-11, note 2.
18. Shishir Arya, 'Central excise tax dropped like a bomb on ordnance factories', *Time of India*, 20 May 2015.
19. Vivek Raghuvanshi, 'Domestic firm shares $1B Indian gun tender with Korean partner', *Defense News*, 17 October 2015.

3

Defence Public Sector Undertakings

For the same reasons of huge capital investment and existing capabilities in terms of infrastructure, skilled human resources and years of manufacturing experience as in the case of ordnance factories (OFs), the defence public sector undertakings (DPSUs) will perforce play a key role in India's defence industrialisation process in the foreseeable future. However, given the changing focus of the country's defence industrialisation since 2001 and particularly the private sector-led Make in India initiative, the nature of DPSUs' involvement is likely to be determined solely by their performance, just like that of OFs. This chapter enquires whether DPSUs are geared to face the emerging reality, going by their performance parameters. In particular, it examines their innovativeness, labour productivity, R&D and technology absorption, and exports.

An Overview

India has nine DPSUs, as follows: Hindustan Aeronautics Ltd (HAL), Bharat Electronics Ltd (BEL), BEML (formerly Bharat Earth Movers Ltd), Bharat Dynamics Ltd (BDL), Mishra Dhatu Nigam Ltd (MIDHANI), Goa Shipyard Ltd (GSL), Garden Reach Shipbuilders and Engineers Ltd (GRSE), Mazagon Dock Ltd (MDL) and Hindustan Shipyard Ltd (HSL). Table 3.1 provides select statistics about them.

Table 3.1: DPSUs at a Glance, 2014-15 (Amounts in Rs crore)

DPSU	*Year of Incorporation*	*Government's Investment*	*No. of Regular Employees*	*VoP*	*VoS*	*PAT*	*Net Worth*
HAL	1964	486	31144	16289	15622	2388	16786
BEL	1954	80	9703	6659	6695	1167	7885
BDL	1970	115	3183	2770	2800	419	1533
BEML	1964	456	9599	2920	3130	7	2077
MIDHANI	1973	202	836	648	656	102	501
MDL	1934	279	9131	3593	2490	492	2443
GRSE	1960	145	2834	1613	2308	43	966
GSL	1967	53	1658	570	752	78	619
HSL	1952	674	1646	294	282	-203	-1023
All DPSUs	–	2490	69734	35356	34735	4493	31787

Note: Government's investment comprises paid-up capital and loans; VoP – Value of Production; VoS – Value of Sales; PAT – Profit after Tax.
Source: Author's database.

DPSUs are part of the larger setup of 290 Central Public Sector Enterprises (CPSEs) which operate under the administrative control of various ministries in different sectors of the economy. Unlike the OFB, which is a departmentally run organisation, DPSUs are corporate entities governed by their board of directors, subject to certain broad policy guidelines stipulated by the Department of Defence Production (the administrative department) and the Department of the Public Enterprises (DPE), Ministry of Heavy Industries and Public Enterprises. DDP monitors their performance while the DPE acts as the main interface between the administrative ministry and the CPSE and provides policy guidelines.

The board of directors comprises a chairman-cum-managing director (CMD), full-time executive directors, part-time government directors and independent directors. It enjoys autonomy in respect of 'recruitment, promotion and other service conditions of below board level employees'.[1] It also enjoys certain enhanced powers granted to profit-making CPSEs under the schemes of *Maharatna*, *Navratna* and *Miniratna*.[2] *Maharatna* status is given to *Navratna* companies that are listed on stock exchanges, had an average annual turnover of Rs 25,000 crore in the previous three years, and an average annual net profit of more than Rs 5000 crore in the last three years. No DPSU has that status. HAL and BEL have *Navratna* status, while BDL, BEML,

GRSE, GSL, MDL, MIDHANI have *Miniratna* status. HSL does not have a *ratna* status.

HAL is the largest DPSU, accounting for nearly half of all DPSUs' production. Formed in 1964 by the merger of Hindustan Aircraft Limited and Aeronautics India Limited, it is organised along four complexes – Bangalore Complex, MiG Complex, Accessories Complex and Design Complex. These complexes house 20 production centres and 10 R&D centres, employing over 31,000 regular employees. The company's primary area of activity is to design, manufacture and overhaul fighters, trainers, helicopters, transport aircraft, engines, avionics, and system equipment. It has so far produced 15 types of aircraft from its own R&D efforts and 14 types under licence. At present it is involved in nine major projects related to design, development and manufacturing. The design projects include Intermediate Jet Trainer, Light Combat Aircraft (LCA), Advanced Light Helicopter (ALH) Weapon System Integration, Light Combat Helicopter (LCH) and Aircraft Upgrades (Jaguar, Sea Harrier). Manufacturing projects include SU-30 MKI aircraft, Jaguar single seater, ALH and Dornier 228.[3] In the last 10 years (2005-06 to 2014-15), HAL's value of production has increased from Rs 5,917 crore to Rs 16,289 crore, while sales have increased from Rs 5,342 crore to Rs 15,622 crore. The company earned *Navratna* status in June 2007.

BEL, established at Bangalore in 1954 by MoD, is the country's premier defence electronics company, with nine production units and 31 manufacturing divisions across seven states. It is one of the two DPSUs (the other being BEML) which is listed on the stock exchange. From the initial production of transceivers for the Indian Army's radio communication equipment,[4] BEL has evolved to have around 350 products to its credit, including high-tech products such as radars, sonars, communication equipment, electronic warfare equipment, opto-electronics, tank electronics, and components. Some of the projects executed in recent years include Akash missile system, passive night vision devices, low-level light weight radar, Schilka air defence system, and software-defined radio. In 2014-15, BEL generated 13 per cent of its business revenues from the civilian sector, down from 17 per cent in the previous year.[5] BEL's R&D expenditure in 2014-15 amounted to 8.2 per cent of its turnover, the highest among all the DPSUs. The company claims that nearly 80 per cent of its turnover (in 2014-15) came from indigenous technology, with the balance coming from products manufactured through technology transfer from foreign companies.[6] BEL is currently setting up a 900-acre Missile Systems Integration Complex in Andhra Pradesh. The company jointly with Rolta India Ltd (a private company) has been selected as one of the consortiums to develop the prototype of Battlefield Management System (BMS) worth over Rs 50,000 crore.

BEML, which came into being in 1964, commenced its operation nearly one year later, with production of rail coaches and assembly of space parts at its Bangalore unit. The company with three product segments – Mining and Construction Equipment, Defence Equipment and Aggregates and Railway Rolling Stock, caters for the core needs of industry (mining, irrigation, steel, cement, power plants, infrastructure, etc.), defence services (trucks, diesel engines, and earth movers) and railways. The defence sector contributes much less to the company's revenue (only 6 per cent in 2014-15), compared to BEML's civilian business.[7]

BDL was carved out of DRDO in 1970.[8] It builds strategic and tactical missiles and allied equipment, either under licence or with technologies supplied by DRDO. Its licence-manufactured products include French Milan and Russian Konkurs anti-tank guided missiles (ATGM). The company attained prominence with the launch of India's Integrated Guided Missile Programme (IGMP) in the early 1980s.[9] BDL was its production agency. BDL has so far supplied to the Indian armed forces both the land and naval versions of Prithvi missiles (150 km and 250 km); and Agni I and II (700 km and more than 2000 km).[10] BDL is also involved in a number of other DRDO projects, such as K-15 (submarine-launched ballistic missile, SLBM) and ASTRA beyond-visual air-to-air missile.[11] At the end of 2014-15, BDL had a healthy order book of Rs 16,357 crore, largely due to the huge order placed on it by the Army and Air Force for AKASH surface-to-surface missile.[12]

Among the four shipbuilders under MoD, MDL is the largest, in terms of product range, value of production and number of employees. The company was mainly a ship repair yard when it was taken over by the Government of India from private owners in 1960.[13] Since then it has expanded its activities to shipbuilding, ship repair and construction of offshore platforms. Its present capacity is to build warships upto 6,500 tonne displacement and merchant ships upto 27,000 DWT. In the defence sector it specialises in design, construction and support of naval ships such as destroyers, frigates, missiles boats, offshore patrol vessels and submarines. It is the only shipyard in the country to build a submarine.[14] In the civilian sector it supplies cargo and passenger ships, supply vessels and various types of small craft. The company's order book includes three missile destroyers under project P-15A, four missile destroyers under P-15B and six Scorpene-class conventional submarines under

P-75. MDL has also signed a contract on February 2015 for construction of four stealth frigates under P-17A.[15]

GRSE was taken over by the Government of India in 1960[16] to develop a second line of shipbuilding facility. It is the only shipbuilder in India to have its own engineering and engine manufacturing division. Currently, it is executing four Anti-Submarine Warfare Corvettes under P-28, eight Landing Craft Utility (LCU), Offshore Patrol Vessels (OPV) and four Water Jet Fast Attack Craft.[17] The company achieved a rare feat in December 2014 when it made the first ever warship (an OPV) export from India. The vessel was sold to Mauritius and earned the company $58.5 million.[18]

GSL, established in 1957, is a leading shipyard on the west coast of India. By July 2014, it has built and delivered 201 ships to the Navy, Coast Guard, private sector and also foreign customers. Its product range includes 105 metre advanced offshore patrol vessels, 90metre offshore patrol vessels, 50metre fast patrol vessels, missile boats, etc. In February 2015, the Defence Acquisition Council (DAC), the highest decision-making body of MoD, nominated GSL to construct 12 Mine Counter Measure Vessels (MCMV) for the Indian navy. The project, by far the biggest for the shipyard, is estimated at Rs 32,000 crore.[19]

HSL was brought under the control of MoD in February 2010 to build 'strategic assets and warships'. The shipyard, the largest under MoD, has so far built 173 vessels besides repairing over 1900 vessels. When acquired by MoD, the shipyard's financial position was not healthy. The government had to pump in Rs 824.90 crore as a financial restructuring package.[20] The package has, however, not been enough to 'address the issue of negative net worth, working capital and order book improvement'.[21] Notwithstanding, the shipyard has recently teamed up with MIDHANI and BHEL, two other public sector units, with an eye to participate in the P-75 (I) project programmes under which the Indian Navy plans to procure six conventional submarines at an estimated cost of Rs 50,000 crore.[22]

MIDHANI was incorporated as a public sector undertaking in 1973 to achieve self-reliance in the areas of special steels, super-alloys and titanium alloys, which form the core needs not only of the defence but of space and atomic energy programmes. In the defence sector, MIDHANI is responsible for indigenisation of technologies and products to support programmes such as T-72 and MBT Arjun tanks, Kaveri engines (of LCA), Advanced Technology Vessels, and MiG fighter aircraft. Till 2014-15, the company has produced

105 grades of high-performance alloys for different applications in the defence, space and atomic energy sectors.[23]

From Nomination to Competition

For much of their existence, DPSUs, like the OFs, have been assured of steady orders through MoD's nomination approach, which essentially sidesteps the competitive bidding process and hands over contracts on a single tender basis. All the big-ticket items such SU-30 MKI fighter aircraft, HAWK advanced jet trainer, Scorpene-class submarine, Akash missile and a host of frigates, destroyers, corvettes, and mine counter measure vessels currently under production have been through this route.

With the entry of the private sector, MoD is however forced to taper down the nomination approach.[24] The decline is being institutionalised through the periodic changes in the Defence Procurement Procedures (DPP), giving primacy to competition. As a result, some of the DPSUs are loosing contracts to competition. For instance, BEL, which is exposed most to the competition, has lost 28 contracts, valued at Rs 1260 crore, in a matter of five years (Table 3.2).

Table 3.2: Tenders Lost by BEL to Competition, 2009-2013

Product	*Value (Rs crore)*
Radio Frequency (RF) Seeker	12
Wide Band Instrumentation Radar	13
Radar Air Warning L-band Mk III	45
Combat Management System (CMS)	239
Avian Radar	250
Digital Armoured Vehicle Intercom System (DAVIS)	280
Wide-band Code Division Multiple Access (WCDMA)	304
VLF with AMC	434
Small Projects (20 contracts)	47
Total	1624

Source: Author's database.

With Make in India, the nomination approach is being further eroded. Further, some contracts – such as the Rs 16,000 crore Avro replacement aircraft – have been exclusively reserved for the private sector. In this context, as explained subsequently in this chapter, DPSUs' performance, measured in terms of several parameters such as labour productivity, profit margin and value addition is anything but encouraging.

Defence Procurement: Share of DPSUs

DPSUs are by far the biggest players in the Indian defence production sector and have therefore a larger role in the country's self-reliance drive. But it is amply evident from Table 3.3 that there is a wide gap between the total procurement expenditure and the combined value of sales of all DPSUs. This gap is filled up primarily through imports.

Table 3.3: Defence Procurement: Share of DPSUs

Year	*Total Procurement (Revenue & Capital) Expenditure (Rs crore)*	*VoS (Rs crore)*	*VoS as % of Total Procurement Expenditure*
2006-07	39722	15849	40
2007-08	41799	16983	41
2008-09	44456	20007	45
2009-10	52498	25900	49
2010-11	62775	25980	41
2011-12	68963	28666	42
2012-13	71286	29456	41
2013-14	78887	28920	37
2014-15	81284 (RE)	34735	43
2015-16	92604 (BE)	–	–

Note: BE – Budget Estimate; RE – Revised Estimate; VoS – Value of Sales.
Source: Author's database.

Indirect Import

DPSUs themselves are significantly dependent on imported parts, components and raw materials. In the case HAL and MDL, for example, the average import dependency in the past five years has been 90 per cent and 67 per cent, respectively (Figure 3.1). This comes at a huge expenditure of foreign exchange. In the past five years, total utilisation of foreign exchange by all the DPSUs was Rs 78,740 crore (Table 3.4), which was 57 per cent of the total value of sales. HAL is the biggest spender of foreign exchange, accounting for about 62 per cent of total foreign exchange utilisation by DPSUs in the past five years.

Figure 3.1: Import Share of Parts, Components and Raw Materials Consumed in HAL and MDL

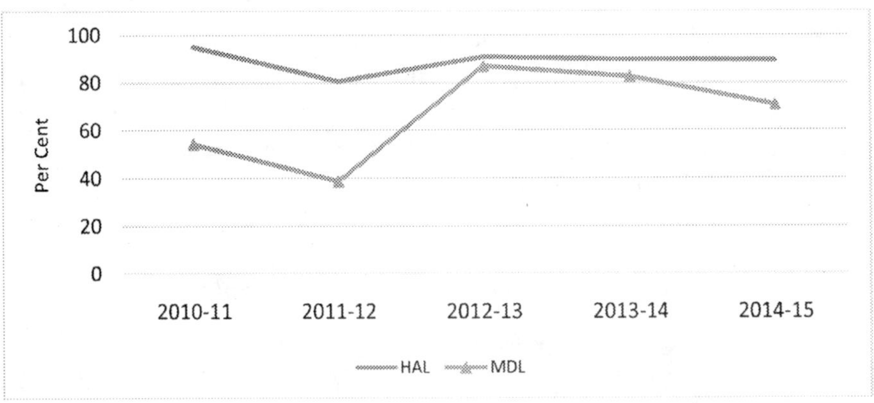

Source: Author's database.

Table 3.4: Foreign Exchange Utilisation by DPSUs (Rs crore)

DPSU	*2009-10*	*2010-11*	*2011-12*	*2012-13*	*2013-14*	*2014-15*
HAL	10520	11495	5803	8840	12401	10289
BEL	2146	1875	2217	2551	1671	1847
BEML	670	653	684	673	428	304
MDL	1766	1797	1751	2268	2610	1094
GRSE	294	277	249	285	341	271
GSL	105	217	95	141	150	235
HSL	423	305	195	104	129	82
BDL	262	263	419	546	411	534
MIDHANI	75	141	154	209	133	125
Total	16260 (63)	17023 (66)	11567 (40)	15616 (53)	18274 (57)	14781 (43)

Note: Figures in parentheses denote total foreign exchange utilisation as percentage of sales in respective years.

Source: Author's database.

Vendor Development and Outsourcing

DPSUs have traditionally been entrusted with the task of producing the final product along with associated major systems and sub-systems. Whatever was not economically feasible was mostly imported, with little going to the domestic industry by way of outsourcing. It is seen from Table 3.5 that combined outsourcing of all DPSUs hardly constitutes one-tenth of their combined value of production.

Compared to OFs, DPSUs' outsourcing is quite low. This could be because of the nature of items produced by these two different sets of players. Most of OFs' production falls in a relatively less complex area in which complementarity exists with the domestic civil sector. This is more so in areas of vehicles and troop comfort items. In comparison, DPSUs barring BEL and BEML have hardly any complementarity in the civilian sector. To make matters worse, until recently, there has not been an overarching policy either by DPSUs or MoD to develop a credible vendor base with a long-term vision for import substitution.

Table 3.5: Outsourcing of DPSUs (Rs crore)

	2010-11	*2011-12*	*2012-13*	*2013-14*	*2014-15*
HAL	261 (1.6)	280 (2.2)	366 (2.6)	380 (2.4)	491 (3.0)
BEL	1124 (20.4)	1314 (22.7)	1607 (25.5)	1945 (31.7)	1804 (27.1)
BEML	1083 (28.7)	1352 (33.2)	945 (28.1)	1063 (33.6)	937 (32.1)
MDL	87 (3.3)	89 (3.5)	70 (3.0)	74 (2.6)	101 (2.8)
GRSE	81 (7.7)	64 (5.0)	62 (4.0)	63 (3.9)	88 (5.4)
GSL	41 (4.1)	39 (5.8)	12 (2.4)	54 (10.7)	71 (12.4)
HSL	25 (4.2)	25 (4.4)	39 (8.1)	14 (3.2)	7 (2.4)
BDL	1 (0.1)	6 (0.6)	9 (0.7)	9 (0.5)	14 (0.5)
MIDHANI	38 (7.9)	51 (10.3)	50 (9.3)	41 (7.1)	87 (14.6)
All DPSUs	2742 (8.5)	3220 (11.1)	3159 (10.4)	3643 (11.0)	3601 (10.2)

Note: Figures in parentheses denote percentage share in Value of Production (VoP).
Source: Author's database.

Under the present government, MoD has formulated 'Outsourcing and Vendor Development Guidelines'. The policy, issued in May 2015, intends to enable DPSUs and OFB to focus on core activity while outsourcing the non-core activity with the objective of building a 'manufacturing eco-system in the country to attain self-reliance.' The policy also outlines a formula for measuring the outsourcing.[25] Consequently, some DPSUs have taken the plunge to indigenise many components through the participation of the local industry. Dedicated webpages have been created by several DPSUs for the purpose. The websites, besides putting out the list of items earmarked for indigenisation, also provide a list of testing facilities/infrastructure that can be used by the industry. BEL has, for instance, put up a list of nearly 550 items for indigenisation.[26] However, from the policy's perspective, there is no target nor accountability fixed.

R&D and Technology Assimilation

Like OFs, DPSUs also have a poor focus on R&D. This can be seen both in terms of inputs (expenditure on R&D) and output (patents, in-house design/development and technology assimilation and indigenisation). Going by the number of patents and copyright, which is by far the most common yet powerful indicator of R&D performance, DPSUs and OFs are way below their global peers (Tables 3.6 and 3.7). Of the nine DPSUs, four do not have even a single patent or copyright to their credit. In comparison, the US-based aerospace major, Boeing, claims over 1000 patents in a single programme, the 787 Dreamliner.[27]

Table 3.6: Number of Patents/Copyright held by DPSUs/OFs (as in March 2012)

DPSU / OFs	*No. of Patents or Copyright*
HAL	6
MIDHANI	5
BEML	3
BDL	2
BEL	6
OFs	1
Total	23

Source: Lok Sabha, 'Defence Research and Production', Unstarred Question No. 5056, answered on 7 May 2012.

Table 3.7: Patent Scorecard of Major Global Defence Companies

Company	*Patents Granted*	
	2010	*5-Year Average*
Boeing (US)	664	458
Lockheed Martin (US)	374	298
EADS (Europe)	328	169
Raytheon (US)	246	190
General Electric (US)	220	190
United Technologies (US)	220	132
Safran (France)	195	129
Honeywell (US)	143	99
Northrop Grumman (US)	130	163
Rockwell Collins (US)	123	72

Note: Patents include utility patents granted in the US.

Source: Lindsey Gilroy and Tammy D'Amato, 'The Patent Scorecard 2010: Aerospace and Defence', *Intellectual Property Today*, http://www.iptoday.com/issues/2010/11/the-patent-scorecard-2010-aerospace-&-defense.asp (accessed on 23 September 2013).

Barring HAL and BEL, which have dedicated R&D centres and spend 6-8 per cent of their turnover on R&D, other defence enterprises have what is termed by India's then defence minister a 'miserly attitude'[28] towards R&D spending (Table 3.8). Even the R&D of HAL and BEL is not necessarily comparable with their global peers. For instance, the French company Thales spends 20 per cent of its revenues on R&D,[29] compared to 8 per cent of BEL, arguably the most innovative defence enterprise in India. The lack of in-house R&D in most of the enterprises makes them perpetually dependent on others, either DRDO or foreign companies, for technology for production.

The separation of R&D from the defence industry has also created a unique problem for DPSUs and OFs. As observed by the then chief of DRDO, since most of Indian production agencies 'do not speak R&D language, it leads to difficulty in transforming research designs into manufacturing.'[30] The difficulty often results in delayed production. The delay in construction of Scorpene-class submarines by MDL with transfer of technology from France is one example of how the lack of R&D could lead to 'teething problems' in absorption of technology.[31] The undue delay in the production of MBT Arjun is partly due to the OF's problem in absorption of technology given by DRDO.

Table 3.8: R&D Expenditure by DPSUs, 2014-15

DPSU	*R&D expenditure*	
	Rs crore	*as % of sales*
HAL	1047	6.7
BEL	549	8.2
BEML	83	2.6
MDL	1.5	0.1
GRSE	3.5	0.2
GSL	6.5	0.9
HSL	...	...
BDL	23	0.8
MIDHANI	8.5	1.3
All DPSUs	1722	5.0

Source: Annual Report of the respective DPSUs.

HAL, India's biggest defence enterprise, is the classic example of the country's defence R&D backwardness. Notwithstanding its ambitious mission and vision statements of becoming a 'significant global player in the aerospace industry' and achieving 'self-reliance in design, development, manufacture and upgrade of aerospace equipment', HAL is at best a fringe player in the global aerospace sector. Its capability for designing aircraft seems to have drastically declined from that of fighter aircraft to trainers and helicopters. In the 1960s, HAL had shot into global prominence with the successful development of HF-24 Marut, which was then rated by experts as a good fighter.[32] Now the company plays second fiddle to others, such as DRDO or foreign companies. Even when HAL is a co-developmental partner, its role is limited. For instance, in the case of the Fifth Generation Fighter Aircraft (FGFA), HAL's contribution is believed to be around 15-25 per cent.[33]

Even though HAL's design capability has been reduced to helicopters and trainers, the company is still constrained in executing such capability in a reasonable timeframe, leading to imports. A case in point is the Indian Air Force's (IAF's) changing inventory of trainers. At one point of time, the IAF's entire trainer inventory consisted of HAL-designed planes such as HPT-32 (for basic training) and Kiran Mk-I and Mk-II (for stage-II and III training).[34] With ageing of these trainers and HAL making no credible replacement in time, the IAF looks set to make up its entire inventory with imported trainers. MoD has already signed contracts with UK-based BAE Systems for Advanced Jet Trainer (AJT) Hawk and Switzerland-based Pilatus for basic trainers. HAL's hope of complementing Pilatus with its HTT-40 seems to be running into a dead end. The IAF does not seem to be interested in HTT-40.[35] Initial reports suggest that MoD is not inclined towards HTT-40 on high cost ground, although recently HAL has made a fervent attempt to stay in the race.[36] Intermediate Jet Trainer (IJT), another plane being developed by HAL as replacement of Kiran, is also leading nowhere. The project, sanctioned in 1999, has not yet got initial operational clearance (as against the planned induction from 2005-06 onwards), causing frustration in the IAF, which has threatened to use Pilatus for the IJT's role.[37]

HAL's poor state of design capability is equally matched by its poor record in technology assimilation and indigenisation. The company is overwhelmingly dependent on foreign sources for production inputs (raw materials, parts and components). Between 2000-01 and 2011-12, the import dependency of inputs varied between 77 per cent and 95 per cent. The high import dependence is for both indigenously developed products and products manufactured under licence. For example, as reported in 2010-11 by CAG, the import content in HAL's indigenously developed ALH *Dhruv* (the design and development of which started in 1984, with the production beginning from 2000-01)[38] is 90 per cent as against 50 per cent envisaged originally.[39] The high import dependency in licence manufacturing is best amplified in SU-30 MKI, 222 units of which HAL is manufacturing in four phases since 2004-05.[40] Although HAL has commenced the last phase (supposed to be the highest form of indigenisation), the maximum indigenisation it has achieved so far is only 33 per cent.[41]

Value Addition

Value addition (VA) is the difference between the value of the product and cost of materials. It is a key performance parameter that measures the level of efforts and innovation put in by an enterprise to convert input materials into the final product. The higher the VA, the greater is the effort and innovation put in by the enterprise. Figure 3.2 maps the combined VA for all DPSUs (except HSL) along with the share of VA in total value of production in the past 10 years. It is seen that VA as a percentage share is in decline in most of the years.

Figure 3.2: Value Addition by DPSUs

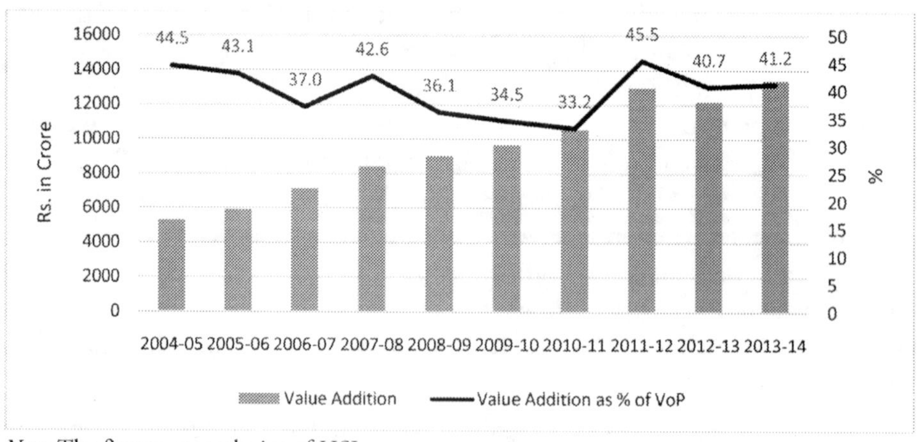

Note: The figures are exclusive of HSL.
Source: Data from individual Annual Reports of DPSUs.

Labour Productivity

As per official claims, the number of regular employees in DPSUs is regularly declining. Between 2008-09 and 2013-14, their number in all DPSUs (excluding HSL) has declined by nearly 10 per cent (Table 3.9). But between 2008 and 2014, the number of employees on contract has increased by

11 per cent, with the bulk of the increase coming from HAL and BEL (Tables 3.10 and 3.11). There is plenty of evidence that DPSUs are overstaffed. The top five arms producing companies in the world together have an average labour productivity of $370,000; whereas the eight DPSUs' combined productivity is around $67,000, or less than one-fifth of their global peers (Table 3.12 and Figure 3.3).

Table 3.9: Employees in DPSUs

	2008-09	*2009-10*	*2010-11*	*2011-12*	*2012-13*	*2013-14*
HAL	34822	33990	33681	32659	32644	32108
BEL	11961	11545	11180	10791	10305	9952
BEML	12600	12052	11798	11644	11005	10328
MDL	8018	8072	8090	8325	8670	8640
GRSE	4768	4345	4117	3792	3491	3133
GSL	1620	1701	1667	1604	1602	1545
BDL	2788	2894	2897	3142	3300	3266
MIDHANI	1229	1191	1121	1052	976	900
Total DPSUs	77806	75790	74551	73009	71993	69872

Source: Data from individual Annual Reports of DPSUs

Table 3.10: Break-up of Total Employees in DPSUs (As on 31 March 2008)

DPSU	*Managerial/ Executives*	*Supervisory*		*Non-Executives*		*Casual/ Daily Rated Workers*	*Contract Workers/ Employees*	*Total*
		Unionised	*Non-Unionised*	*Skilled*	*Unskilled*			
HAL	9379	0	0	24874	70	225	4206	38754
BEL	4340	335	447	7114	135	0	0	12371
BDL	618	0	0	1834	263	18	0	2733
BEML	2578	0	0	4958	4750	8	1686	13980
MIDHANI	249	0	153	790	72	240	21	1525
MDL	870	0	0	5793	1101	0	821	8585
GRSE	484	362	616	2517	992	129	191	5291
GSL	208	0	288	922	265	0	600	2283
HSL	503	947	0	1764	0	5	415	3634
All DPSUs	19229	1644	1504	50566	7648	625	7940	89156

Source: Author's database.

Table 3.11: Break-up of Total Employees in DPSUs (as on 31 March 2015)

DPSU	*Managerial/ Executives*	*Supervisory*		*Non-Executives*		*Casual/ Daily Rated Workers*	*Contract Workers/ Employees*	*Total*
		Unionised	*Non-Unionised*	*Skilled*	*Unskilled*			
HAL	9675	0	0	21409	60	396	11624	43164
BEL	5134	0	238	4052	279	2835	1573	14111
BDL	880	0	0	1975	328	0	102	3285
BEML	2482	3162	0	3722	233	0	4979	14578
MIDHANI	242	0	105	355	134	168	251	1255
MDL	1039	613	0	7264	9	0	2828	11753
GRSE	484	189	186	1500	475	0	0	2834
GSL	243	0	198	882	245	0	1492	3060
HSL	334	641	0	663	8	4	624	2274
All DPSUs	20513	4605	727	41822	1771	3406	23473	96314

Source: Author's database.

Table 3.12: Per Employee Sales of Select Global Defence Companies, 2013

Company	*Total Sales (US$ Million)*	*Total Employment*	*Per Employee Sales (US$ Thousand)*
Lockheed Martin	45500	115000	396
BAE Systems	28406	84600	336
Embraer	6325	19280	328
Raytheon	23706	63000	376
Northrop Grumman	24661	65300	378

Source: Adapted from Aude Fleurant and Sam Perlo-Freeman, 'The SIPRI top 100 Arms Producing and Military Services Companies, 2013', *SIPRI Fact Sheet*, December 2014.

Figure 3.3: Per Employee Sales of DPSUs, 2014-15

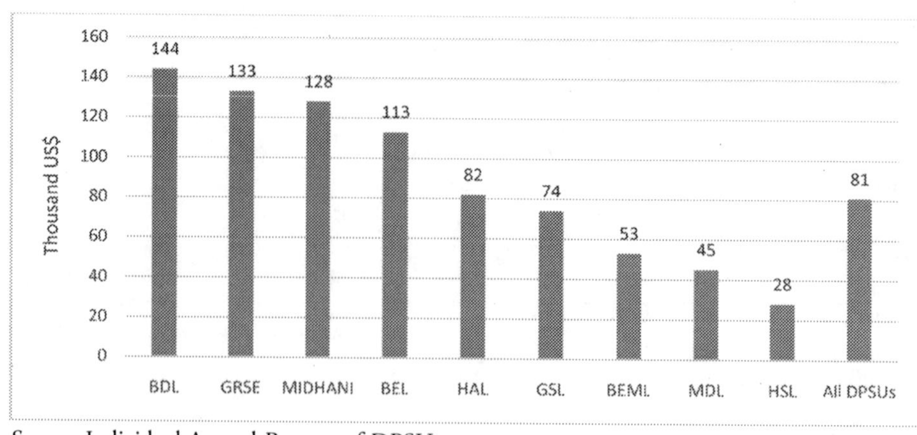

Source: Individual Annual Reports of DPSUs.

One reason for the high labour content in DPSUs is the absence of benchmarking with the global best. Like OFs, DPSUs are also allowed to fix labour norms for undertaking a particular job. HAL, for example, has registered a constant increase in capacity utilisation with respect to standard man hour (SMH) (Table 3.13). Although a part of the increase can be attributed to the decline in regular labour force and simultaneous increase in production, the high increase in capacity utilisation is also due to the way labour norms are fixed by the company. According to a former IAF official who functioned as Director (Cost Analysis), the standard norms followed by HAL were devised way back in the mid-1970s, although since then there has been a vast change in terms of improved operating environment, greater automation and better quality of labour force. There is no compulsion to revise the labour norms, mainly due to pressure from the labour unions. In the case of ALH, average labour hours booked for production are much higher than recommended by a hired consultant (Table 3.14). CAG, which undertook a study of the programme, has suggested that 'labour hour requirement needs to be reviewed de novo.'[42]

Table 3.13: Capacity Utilisation in HAL

Year	*Production (In Thousand Standard Man Hour)*	*Capacity Utilisation (%)*
2008-09	28722	104
2009-10	31032	106
2010-11	32328	112
2011-12	33310	118
2012-13	32870	116
2013-14	33731	122
2014-15	30523	110

Source: Author's database.

Table 3.14: HAL's Labour Hours for ALH

Labour Hours Prescribed by the Consultant	*Average Hours Booked by HAL*
38,500 hours for 1st ALH	88,768 hours for limited series production
30,000 hours from 50th ALH	58,367 hours for series production

Source: Adapted from CAG Report No. 10 of 2010-11, p. 32.

Analysis of Profit Margin

As Table 3.1 shows, except for HSL, other DPSUs have earned profit in 2014-15, with the PAT of six of them amounting to excess of 10 per cent of their sales. At first sight, this seems reasonable. However, much of the profit has little to do with their core activity. Table 3.15 analyses their profits in 2014-15. Nearly 11 per cent (or Rs 4262.7 crore) of the total income of Rs 34,796 crore comes from what constitutes 'Other Income (OI)', which primarily arises from the interest income that these entities earn by parking the huge advances received from the customers in the banks. If this segment is excluded, the profit margin reduces drastically to as low as 5.2 per cent, which is lower than the prevailing interest rates offered by commercial banks. If the tax component is factored in, the margin goes further down. This rate of margin is highly undesirable.

Table 3.15: Profit Analysis of DPSUs, 2014-15 (Rs crore)

	Revenue from Operations	*Other Income*	*Total Revenue*	*Profit Before Tax (PBT)*	*PBT Excluding Other Income*	*PBT as % of Total Revenue*	*PBT Excluding Other Income as % of Revenue from Operations*
Column	*1*	*2*	*3 (1+2)*	*4*	*5 (4–2)*	*6 (4/3*100)*	*8 (5/1*100)*
HAL	15629.9	2437.9	18067.7	3172.5	734.7	17.6	4.7
BEL	6842.7	478.0	7320.6	1466.7	988.7	20.0	14.4
BDL	2782.0	498.7	3280.7	614.2	115.5	18.7	4.2
BEML	2809.2	59.5	2868.7	6.9	–52.6	0.2	–1.9
MIDHANI	647.4	22.7	670.1	138.5	115.8	20.7	17.9
MDL	3618.9	562.6	4181.5	746.0	183.4	17.8	5.1
GRSE	1609.0	69.3	1678.2	76.0	6.7	4.5	0.4
GSL	575.5	105.3	680.8	53.2	–52.1	7.8	–9.1
HSL	281.5	28.9	310.4	–202.8	–231.7	–65.4	–82.3
All DPSUs	34796.0	4262.7	39058.7	6071.2	1808.5	15.5	5.2

Source: Author's database.

Exports

Only three DPSUs – HAL, BEL and BEML – have been relatively successful in exports (Table 3.16). In terms of physical exports, HAL accounts for nearly 27 per cent of total exports (on free on board basis) in 2014-15. In value terms, HAL's exports have grown from Rs 46.96 crore in 1999-2000 to Rs 414.08 crore in 2014-15.[43] During 2014-15, HAL booked export orders worth Rs 446 crore. The areas in which HAL has established its foothold in the international market include aero-structures – supplied to Boeing of USA and Aerospatiale, France – and 'spares and services for a variety of military and civil aircraft, engine, equipment, spares and devices.' In addition, HAL has been successful in terms of entering the export market in the area of Computer Aided Design (CAD) Modelling and Services. HAL's biggest achievement in exports came in 2008, when it bagged an order of seven ALHs worth $56.7 million from Ecuador. According to an MoD press release, HAL won the bid 'amidst strong competition' from other established international players and its bid was 'about 32 per cent lower than the second lowest bid'.[44]

Table 3.16: DPSUs' Exports on FoB Basis (Rs crore)

DPSU	*2009-10*	*2010-11*	*2011-12*	*2012-13*	*2013-14*	*2014-15*
HAL	204.7	221.7	326.0	365.1	408.5	414.8
BEL	99.4	161.7	187.9	166.1	246.2	358.5
BDL	0.0	1.4	0.0	0.3	1.2	0.0
BEML	132.0	179.4	116.1	179.2	73.3	258.5
MIDHANI	0.0	0.0	0.0	0.0	0.0	0.0
MDL	0.0	0.0	0.0	277.8	0.0	279.5
GRSE	0.1	0.0	0.0	0.0	0.0	0.0
GSL	0.0	0.0	0.0	0.0	0.0	206.5
HSL	0.0	0.0	0.0	0.0	0.0	0.0
All DPSUs	436.1	564.2	630.0	988.5	729.2	1517.8

Source: Author's database.

BEL's exports totalled Rs 358 crore ($57.8 million) in 2014-15, representing 5.3 per cent of its turnover – the highest among DPSUs.[45] It is the only DPSU which seems to have some sort of strategy to achieve 10 per cent sales from exports in the long run. Central to its strategy is the MoD defence offset policy, which it has been relatively successful in exploiting (Table 3.17). In 2014-15, BEL added $66.93 million worth of new orders, swelling its total export order book to $200 million. Some of the key items exported in recent years include Hull Mounted Sonar, Naval Surveillance Radar, Unit Level Switch Board, Electronic Voting Machine, Hand Held Radios, Radar Warning Receiver, CoMPASS, Radar Finger Printing System, Automatic Identification System, Radar Warning Systems, Casings, Stators, and Electro Mechanical parts.[46]

Table 3.17: Share of Offsets in BEL's Order Book ($ million)

Year	*Export Order Book*	*Offset Order*	*Share of Offsets in Export Order Book (%)*
2011-12	40.5	9.9	24.4
2012-13	94.1	13.0	13.8
2013-14	194.0	28.5	14.7
2014-15	200.0	45.0	22.5

Source: Author's database.

BEML has the unique distinction of exporting to more than 60 countries. In 2014-15, its total exports were worth Rs 484.33 crore, comprising of physical exports of Rs 106.78 crore and deemed exports of Rs 377.55 crore.

The overall performance of DPSUs on account of exports is, however, not satisfactory. The total foreign exchange earnings in 2014-15 – the major portion of which is through exports – of all DPSUs is just about 12 per cent of combined foreign exchange utilised by them. From a global perspective, DPSUs' exports as percentage of turnover also score poorly. Compared to 5 per cent for DPSUs as a whole, some global companies such as Israel Aerospace Industries (IAI) and Dassault Aviation of France generate more than three-fourths of their turnover from exports (Tables 3.18 and 3.19).

The biggest factor in the poor export base of DPSUs is the absence of a clear strategy on the part of both DPSUs and MoD. As mentioned in Chapter 1, MoD did not have a clear thinking on how to promote defence exports, which require active support from the government in terms of financial assistance and active diplomacy with friendly countries. In its absence, defence export was left to the DPSUs, which did not consider export as a major source of revenue.

Table 3.18: Foreign Exchange Earning by DPSUs, 2014-15

DPSU	*Foreign Exchange Earning*		
	Rs crore	*As % of Foreign Exchange Utilisation*	*As % of Turnover*
HAL	644.5	6.3	4.1
BEL	358.5	19.4	5.4
BDL	1.6	0.3	0.1
BEML	258.5	85.0	8.3
MIDHANI	0.0	0.0	0.0
MDL	279.5	25.5	11.2
GRSE	0.0	0.0	0.0
GSL	206.5	87.9	27.5
HSL	1.0	1.2	0.4
All DPSUs	1750.0	11.8	5.0

Note: Foreign exchange earning consists of exports of goods FoB basis; royalty; know-how; professional and consultancy fee; interest and dividend; and other income.

Source: Author's database.

Table 3.19: Share of Exports in Turnover of Select Global Defence Companies

Company	*Year of Reporting*	*Turnover*	*Exports as % of Turnover*
Dassault Aviation	H1 2015	€1675 million	79
IAI	2014	$3830 billion	78
BAE System	2014	£16637 million	35*
Raytheon	2014	$22826 million	29
Lockheed Martin	2014	$45600 million	20

Note: H1: First Half Year; * Export to non-UK/US customers
Source: Data obtained from corporate websites of respective companies.

An equally important factor for poor export base is the absence of own-designed quality product. Most of the big-ticket items produced by DPSUs are based on foreign technology, which prevents third-party transfer. The few items that are produced otherwise do not inspire much confidence because of the quality- and certification-related issues, which are critical especially in aviation assets. The biggest example of export efforts is HAL's efforts to market ALH in the international market. HAL has planned a major foray into the international market, especially in Latin America. However, the quality and certification problems have cut short its ambition to the domestic players.

Disinvestment and Listing on Stock Exchanges

Although the DPSUs are the corporate entities, they are not necessarily as dynamic as their private counterparts, which, driven by the profit motive, have the incentive to cut costs and constantly innovate to stay ahead of competition. The private sector is also far more inclined to introduce new technology and products; take quicker decision, better appreciate customer satisfaction, and more importantly give due diligence to labour management and leadership development. In regard to the leadership development, a critical aspect of corporate management, some of the private companies identify potential future leaders and nurture them for years before they are assigned the leadership roles. For instance, the Tata group has recently made public a plan to 'create a pipeline of future leaders who will be mentored by multiple chief executives for up to two decades.'[47] In comparison, many of the leadership posts in CPSEs lie vacant for a long time and often the appointments are made not on the grounds of competence but determined by various political considerations. Besides, the CPSE being the government-owned are constrained by many other problems resulting in an unhealthy situation that is perhaps best summarised by the Industrial Policy of 1991 unleashed by the Narasimha Rao government which initiated the beginning of the privatisation of the public sector entities through a process of disinvestment. The policy of 1991 has the following to say about the CPSEs:

> After the initial exuberance of the public sector entering new areas of industrial and technical competence, a number of problems have begun to manifest themselves in many of the public enterprises. Serious problems are observed in the insufficient growth in productivity, poor project management, over-manning, lack of continuous technological upgradation, and inadequate attention to R&D and human resource development. In addition, public enterprises have shown a very low rate of return on the capital investment. This has inhibited their ability to re-generate themselves in terms of new investments as well as in technology development. The result is that many of the public enterprises have become a burden rather than being an asset to the Government.[48]

Consequent to the Industrial Policy 1991, various governments have pursued a disinvestment policy, though the focus has changed over the years. What has not changed are the benefits of the disinvestment policy itself. Some of the benefits of disinvestment are listed below:

- Companies listed on the stock exchanges are mandated by various regulatory bodies to comply with higher level of disclosures, thereby bringing greater transparency in their functioning.
- Listed companies are required to have at least one-third of board members as independent directors (chosen from specialised fields) who are expected to bring in greater management efficiencies and enhance accountability.
- Shareholders' interest is likely to put constant pressure on the management to enhance productivity and unlock the true value of the company.
- Investor-centric research carried out by broking firm and other agencies provides a constant third-party assessment of the company, putting constant pressure on the management to benchmark its business model with the industry norms.
- Pubic listing allows a degree of level playing field in regard to accessing resources through the capital market.
- Listing enables ownership of development of people-ownership of CPSEs, thus encouraging participation and sharing in their prosperity.
- Disinvestment can raise substantial amount of resources to help bridge

fiscal deficit and meet various expenses of government. (In 2015-16, the government's target is to raise Rs 69,500 crore through this route.[49])

Immediately after the Industrial Policy of 1991, the government made a plan to disinvest 20 per cent equity in select CPSEs. The disinvestment cap has been reviewed several times since then. In an important review carried out in 1993 by an expert committee under C. Rangarajan, it was recommended that in sectors which are not exclusively reserved for CPSEs, the government's share could be either divested completely or brought down to 26 per cent. For sectors which are reserved for the public sector (such as defence industry), government's equity could be brought down to 51 per cent. The latter recommendation has, however, not been accepted by the government. Successive governments have pursued a policy which essentially means government retaining majority holding in all the key CPSEs, which include DPSUs.

When the Rangarajan Committee gave its recommendation in 1993, the defence industry was the exclusive purview of DPSUs and OFs. But in 2001 the sector was opened to 100 per cent participation of the private sector. By the logic of the Rangarajan committee, the equity shares of DPSUs could be divested by up to 74 per cent.

Conclusion

For Make in India to succeed, the government needs to transform DPSUs to perform optimally. Some of the measures that are needed in this direction are discussed here.

- List all DPSUs on stock exchanges. This will not only allow the government to raise resources but would also enhance DPSUs' level of accountability and transparency.
- At the same time, a roadmap may be prepared to completely privatise these entities in a time-bound manner.
- Lay down a clear roadmap for each DPSU to progressively reduce its dependency on imports. Make a holistic plan for development of domestic supply chain with a clear objective of import substitution.
- Encourage DPSUs to augment their in-house R&D efforts.
- Insist on their benchmarking their productivity with the global peers.
- Insist on their boosting their export potential, taking advantage of offsets, which has largely been a neglected focus of DPSUs.

NOTES

1. *DPE Annual Report 2013-14*, p. 8.
2. These schemes are designed to allow the CPSE concerned greater powers with respect to capital expenditure, investment in JVs/subsidiaries, mergers and acquisitions and human resources management, among others. The highest power is given to *Maharatna* companies, followed by *Navratna* and *Miniratna* companies. For the eligibility criteria and delegated powers to CPSE, see 'Delegation of enhanced financial powers to CPSEs', http://dpe.nic.in/sites/upload_files/dpe/files/pesurvey_13_14/val1/Chapter_7_ Delegation_ of_enhanced_financial_powers_to_CPSEs.pdf (accessed on 25 September 2015).
3. 17th Report of the Standing Committee on Defence (2006-07), 14th Lok Sabha, 'In-depth study and critical review of Hindustan Aeronautics Limited (HAL)', Lok Sabha Secretariat, New Delhi.
4. 9th Report of the Standing Committee on Defence (2005-06), 14th Lok Sabha, 'Defence Public Sector Undertakings', Lok Sabha Secretariat, New Delhi, p.17.
5. BEL, Annual Reports 2013-14 and 2014-15.
6. BEL *Annual Report 2014-15*, p. 1.
7. In 2005-06, 32 per cent of the turnover of Rs 2205.84 crore came from the defence sector. See BEML *Annual Report 2005-06*, p. 17.
8. Amiya Kumar Ghosh, *India's Defence Budget and Expenditure Management in a Wider Context*, Lancer Publishers, New Delhi, 1996, p.331.
9. IGMDP, sanctioned in 1983, encompasses five missile systems: Prithvi (150 and 250 km range surface-to-surface), Akash (25 km surface-to-air), Trishul (surface-to-air), Nag (fire &forget anti-tank). The latter is a technology demonstrator. For detailed description of the programme, see 14th Report of the Standing Committee on Defence (2006-07) of the 14th Lok Sabha, 'Defence Research and Development Organisation (DRDO)', Lok Sabha Secretariat, New Delhi, pp.58-65.
10. MoD, *Annual Report 2007-08*, pp.80-81.
11. Ibid., p.81.
12. BDL *Annual Report 2013-14*, p. 10; Lok Sabha, Unstarred Question No. 2062, 'Akash Missile System', 31 July 2015.
13. Ghosh, *India's Defence Budget...*, n. 8.
14. MoD, *Annual Report 2007-08*, p.62.
15. Standing Committee on Defence, Demands for Grants 2015-16, 6th Report, Lok Sabha Secretariat, New Delhi, p. 50.
16. MoD, *Annual Report 2007-08*, p.64.
17. Standing Committee on Defence, Demands for Grants 2015-16, 6th Report, p. 50.
18. 'India exports its first warship "CGS Barracuda" to Mauritius', *The Hindu*, 20 December 2014.
19. 'Defence ministry clears mine sweeping vessels, trainer aircraft', *Business Standard*, 28 February 2015.
20. HSL *Annual Report 2011-12*, p. 2.
21. HSL *Annual Report 2013-14*, p. 4.
22. 'BHEL, Midhani, HSL join hands for building submarines', *The Hindu*, 31 December 2014.
23. MoD *Annual Report 2014-15*, p. 63.
24. In one instance, A.K. Antony, then Defence Minister is on record, 'Antony hints at major

policy changes for defence industry', http://www.pib.nic.in/newsite/erelcontent.aspx?relid=66950

25. The value of sourcing is equal to value of producing excluding the value of direct import, raw materials procurement from the domestic market and in-house value addition.
26. BEL, http://www.bel-india.com/
27. 'Guarding the "Gold"', *Boeing Frontiers*, May 2010, http://www.boeing.com/news/frontiers/archive/2010/may/i_eot.pdf (accessed on 19 September 2013).
28. PIB, 'Antony asks industry to give up miserly attitude towards R&D', 31 January 2013.
29. Thales, 'Facts and Figures', http://www.thalesgroup.com/Group/About_us/Facts_and_Figures/ (accessed on 26 August 2013).
30. V.S. Arunachalam, 'In season of blame: a defence', *Deccan Chronicle*, 9 May 2013, http://www.deccanchronicle.com/130509/commentary-dc-comment/commentary/season-blame-defence
31. PIB, 'Scorpene Submarine', 14 March 2011.
32. MoD, *Annual Report 2010-11*, p. 60.
33. Ajai Shukla, 'India to develop 25% of Fifth Generation Fighter', *Business Standard*, 6 January 2010, http://www.business-standard.com/article/companies/india-to-develop-25-of-fifth-generation-fighter-110010600047_1.html; 'AK Antony to take up issues related to FGFA project with Russia', *Economic Times*, 17 October 2013.
34. Kiran Mk I, Mk II and HPT 32 were developed in 1968, 1976 and 1977, respectively. MoD, *Annual Report 2010-11*, p. 60.
35. Ajai Shukla, 'Indian Air Force at war with Hindustan Aeronautics; wants to import, not build, a trainer', *Business Standard*, 29 July 2013, http://www.business-standard.com/article/economy-policy/indian-air-force-at-war-with-hindustan-aeronautics-wants-to-import-not-build-a-trainer-113072800747_1.html
36. Ajai Shukla, 'MoD rejects HAL's proposal to build basic trainer', *Business Standard*, 19 December 2012; http://www.business-standard.com/article/economy-policy/mod-rejects-hal-s-proposal-to-build-basic-trainer-112121902013_1.html
37. Standing Committee on Defence, 14th Lok Sabha, *In-Depth Study and Critical Review of Hindustan Aeronautics Limited*, 17th Report, Lok Sabha Secretariat, New Delhi, 2007, pp. 39-41; Standing Committee on Defence, 13th Lok Sabha, *Demands for Grants 2003-04*, 19th Report, Lok Sabha Secretariat, New Delhi, 2003, p. 53; Ajai Shukla, 'IAF laments HAL delays in delivery of intermediate trainer', *Business Standard*, 5 February 2013; Biswarup Gooptu, 'HAL to work for quicker clearance of defence programmes', *Economic Times*, 7 February 2013.
38. CAG, *Performance Audit of Activities of Public Sector Undertakings*, Report No. 10 of 2010-11 for the period ended March 2009, p. 25.
39. Ibid., p. 23.
40. PIB, 'Indo-Russian defence deal', 18 March 2013; MoD *Annual Report 2004-05*, p. 78.
41. MoD, *Results Framework Documents 2012-13*, p. 4; MoD *Annual Report 2011-12*, pp. 64-65.
42. Report No. 10 of 2010-11.
43. HAL *Annual Report 2013-14*, pp. 10-11.
44. PIB, 'HAL bags order form Ecuador', 26 June 2008.
45. See 9th Report of Standing Committee on Defence (2005-06), p. 22; BEL *Annual Report 2007-08*, p. 20.
46. BEL Annual Reports 2013-14 and 2014-15.

47. Devina Sengupta and Baiju Kalesh, 'Cyrus Mistry's Vision 2025: Tata Group prepares to create potential future leaders', *Economic Times,* 21 September 2015.
48. Department of Industrial Policy and Promotion, http://dipp.nic.in/English/Policies/Industrial_policy_statement.pdf
49. Ministry of Finance, Government of India, *Receipt Budget, 2015-16*, http://indiabudget.nic.in/ub2015-16/rec/cr.pdf (accessed on 24 September 2015).

4

The Private Sector

For the first time since 2001, when the defence industry was freed from the clutches of the DPSUs and OFs, the private sector now sees an opportunity in the Make in India initiative to manufacture big-ticket items such as transport aircraft, submarines, Landing Platform Dock (LPD) and artillery guns. With Make in India focusing on ease of doing business and removing some of the hurdles, the private sector has a historical opportunity. However, will the opportunity materialise? This chapter argues that Make in India, despite its early encouraging reform measures, is yet to overcome certain concerns of the private sector.

Why Private Sector in Defence Production

Although India's defence production dates back to the early 19th century, the private sector's direct involvement began only in 2001 when the industry was liberalised. However, the question is why private participation was allowed in a sector which is still considered as a strategic one and its opening up is still viewed by some as a transgression of national security. There are primarily two factors behind this decision. The first is the inability of the state-owned industries to meet the diverse requirements of the armed forces. This has caused much embarrassment to the government, which has for long been advocating for enhancing India's self-reliance in defence production to 70 per cent. Expressing the government's frustration over high import dependency, A.K. Antony, the then defence minister, once termed this state of affairs as 'shameful and dangerous'.[1]

The second factor is driven by the success of the private sector after the economic liberalisation, which started in the early 1990s. In a quick span of time, the sector proved its credentials in the areas of management, high-end manufacturing and also its ability to raise capital from the market.

Defence Production: The Role and Scope of the Private Sector

Till 2001 the role of private companies in defence production was mainly restricted to supplying raw materials, semi-finished products, parts and components to the public sector units. After 2001, there has been a huge change in the private sector's involvement. This is clearly visible in the number of industrial licences (ILs) bagged by the private sector companies and their early success in winning contracts in direct competition not only with the established government-owned companies but also the foreign majors. As of October 2015, 182 companies have been issued 307 ILs for a wide spectrum of defence products (Table 4.1). Of these, 265 ILs, issued between 2002-03 and 2014-15, entail an investment commitment of Rs 13,370 crore. It is to be noted, however, that not all the ILs or investment proposals have yet materialised. Of the 182 companies, only 50 covering 79 ILs have intimated to have commenced production. This notwithstanding, some of the items produced by the private sector are even without formal tender issued to them, indicating its risk-taking capability.

Table 4.1: System/Sub-system/Component-wise List of Licences Issued to Indian Industry (As on 31 October 2015)

System/Sub-system/Components	*No. of ILs*
Armoured Vehicle/Arms Ammunition	34
Underwater Equipment/Underwater Ammunition	11
Ground Equipment/Ground Launch System	19
Night Vision/Sensor based Systems/Optical Goods/Display Systems	37
Radar/Electronics Systems/Radio/Avionics/Airborne Guidance & Control System/Simulators	88
Bulletproof Jackets/Ballistic Protection	14
Network-centric/Electronic Warfare System/Combat Management System	29
Rockets, Missiles, Torpedo Tubes/Air Defence Gun/UAVs System & Sub-systems	51
Warships/Submarines	9
Ship, Submarine, Maritime Equipment	11
Aircraft Engine/Airframe/Aircraft Systems & Sub-systems	38

Source: 'Make in India: the way ahead for indigenous defence production in India', 6th Y.B. Chavan Memorial Lecture delivered by A.K. Gupta, Secretary (Defence Production), MoD, at IDSA on 7 December 2015.

The risk-taking capability has started paying dividends. One area where the private sector seems to be dominating is Heavy Mobility Vehicles (HMV). In a series of wins within the span of a year, private companies have won contracts for the supply of 1694 HMVs worth Rs 1284 crore (Table 4.2), nearly eliminating the monopoly of BEML's controversial TATRA vehicles. In the non-vehicle segment, a major success for the private sector came in May 2011 when Pipavav Defence and Offshore Engineering Company (formerly Pipavav Shipyard) won a fiercely contested naval order valued at Rs 2,975 crore for building five naval offshore patrol vessels (NOPV) for the Indian Navy.[2] Pipavav was competing with GSL, which has expertise in building similar vessels.

Table 4.2: Heavy Mobility Vehicles (HMV) Contracts Won by the Indian Private Sector under Capital Acquisition

Type of Vehicle	*Quantity*	*Cost (Rs crore)*	*Date of Contract*	*Company*
6×6 HMV with Material Handling Cranes	1239	914.00	31 March 2015	Tata Motors
Vehicle Platform for GRAD BM 21 Multi Barrel Rocket Launcher	100	90.89	19 September 2014	L&T
6×6 Field Artillery Tractor for Medium Guns	100	63.96	23 July 2015	Ashok Leyland
8×8 HMV with Material Handling Cranes	255	215.04	31 August 2015	Ashok Leyland

Source: http://www.tata.com/media/releasesinside/Tata-Motors-awarded-contract-for-1239-vehicles-of-its-high-mobility-multi-axle-vehicles-by-the-Indian-Army; Lok Sabha, 'Defence Contracts', Unstarred Question No. 3232, answered on 18 December 2015.

Among the major domestic orders bagged by the private sector, three stand out: the IAF's Modernisation of Air Field Infrastructure (MAFI) project, the Indian Army's Self-Propelled Tracked Howitzers contract and its Integrated Electronic Warfare Systems for Mountainous Terrain (IEWS-MT) contract. In early 2011, the Tata Power SED won the MAFI project for the modernisation of 30 airbases. Valued at Rs 1094 crore, Tata won the contract against the Italian giant Selex Sistemi Integrati (a subsidiary of Finmeccanica).[3] Again in March 2013 Tata won the Rs 923 crore IEWS-MT contract by defeating Elta of Israel. (BEL, the established state-contracted player, even failed to clear the technical trials.[4]) In early 2015 L&T in partnership with South Korea's Samsung Techwinwon the Army's tender for supplying 100 units of 155mm, 52-calibre howitzer guns, the contract being worth nearly one billion dollars. The partnership was competing against Russia's Rosoboronexport.[5] The private sector has also been quite successful in exporting defence items. As may be seen from Table 4.3, the private sector now accounts for more than 63 per cent of arms exports for which the government has given no-objection certificate.

Table 4.3: Export of Defence Items Based on no Objection Certificate Issued by the Government (Rs crore)

Year	*Value of Export by DPSUs, OFs and Private Sector*	*Value of Export by Private Sector*	*% Share of Private Sector*
2011-12	512.5	137.5	26.8
2012-13	446.8	138.1	30.9
2013-14	686.3	286.0	41.7
2014-15	994.0	132.2	13.3
2015-16*	695.7	441.1	63.4

* Figures for 2015-16 are up to 30 September 2015.
Source: Author's database.

The private sector has also shown dynamism in acquiring foreign companies/production facilities and forming joint ventures with major global defence companies. The Mahindra Group acquired, in December 2009, majority stakes in two Australian defence companies, Aerostaff Australia and Gippsland Aeronautics, signalling its entry into the defence and aerospace business.[6] Bharat Forge of the Kalyani Group is believed to have acquired gun manufacturing facility from a Swiss firm, Ruag. In regard to the formation of JVs, the private sector is way ahead of its public sector counterparts. Out of the 34 JVs set up till date, 31 are led by the private sector companies (Annexure C). Leading in this endeavour are Tata, L&T, Bharat Forge and Mahindra.

There is a huge scope for the private sector, considering India's large and growing defence budget in general and the capital expenditure (most of which is spent on procurement of hardware) in particular. Figure 4.1 summarises projections over a 10-year period of India's capital expenditure till 2025-26. The projection is based on past trends. Assuming that nearly 80 per cent of the capital expenditure would be spent on capital procurement, the order of magnitude would be $300 billion. Much of India's defence procurement budget is spent on imports. If the private sector can capture a part of what is imported, there is still a huge opportunity to look for.

Figure 4.1: Defence Capital Expenditure: Projections up to 2025-26

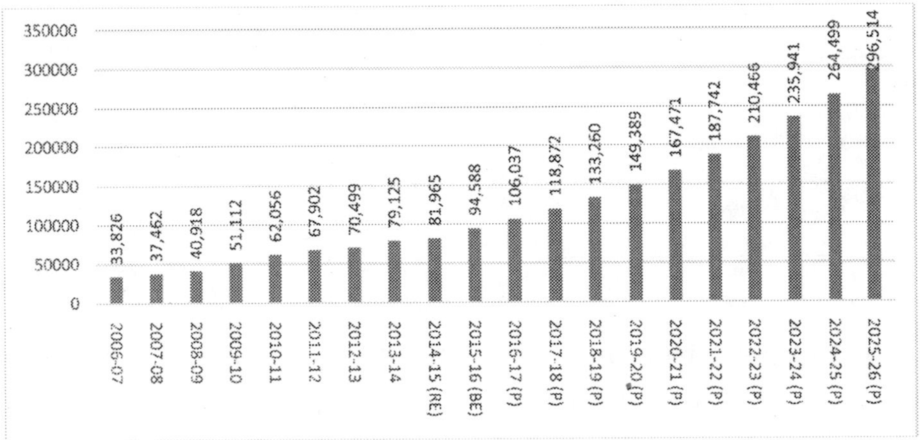

Year	Value
2006-07	33,826
2007-08	37,462
2008-09	40,918
2009-10	51,112
2010-11	62,056
2011-12	67,902
2012-13	70,499
2013-14	79,125
2014-15 (RE)	81,965
2015-16 (BE)	94,588
2016-17 (P)	106,037
2017-18 (P)	118,872
2018-19 (P)	133,260
2019-20 (P)	149,389
2020-21 (P)	167,471
2021-22 (P)	187,742
2022-23 (P)	210,466
2023-24 (P)	235,941
2024-25 (P)	264,499
2025-26 (P)	296,514

Note: RE – Revised Estimate; BE – Budget Estimate; P – Projection.
Source: Author's database.

Private Sector's Contribution to Capital Acquisition

Although the private sector was allowed direct access to defence production in 2001, its contribution to defence production has so far remained marginal (see Tables 4.4 and 4.5).

Table 4.4: Army's Capital Acquisition: Share of Indian and Foreign Vendors

Year	*Capital Acquisition (Rs crore)*	*Indian Vendors (Rs crore and % share)*			*Foreign Vendors (Rs crore and % share)*
		PSUs/OFs	*Private Sector*	*Rest of Industry**	
2011-12	10856.93	7944.06 (73.10%)	515.90 (4.76%)	1899.90 (17.48%)	506.07 (4.66%)
2012-13	10871.79	9297.58 (85.52%)	278.80 (2.56%)	303.74 (2.80%)	991.67 (9.12%)
2013-14	10426.49	8590.10 (82.39%)	199.50 (1.91%)	135.89 (1.30%)	1501.00 (14.40%)

* This pertains to expenditure for which detailed break-up of public/private sector is not maintained.
Source: Rajya Sabha, 'Procurement of poor quality arms and ammunition' Starred Question No. 221, answered on 9 December 2014.

Table 4.5: Air Force's Capital Acquisition: Share of Indian and Foreign Vendors

Year	*Capital Acquisition (Rs crore)*	*Indian Vendors (Rs crore and % share)*		*Foreign Vendors (Rs crore and % share)*
		PSUs/OFs	*Private Sector*	
2011-12	27164.09	11238.05 (41.37%)	667.93 (2.46%)	15258.11 (56.17%)
2012-13	31053.00	8999.46 (28.98%)	2832.59 (9.12%)	19220.95 (61.90%)
2013-14	36917.99	15446.76 (41.84%)	543.68 (1.47%)	20927.54 (56.69%)

Source: Same as Table 4.4.

What has Hindered Private Sector's Participation

By 2014, when Make in India was announced, MoD's Defence Procurement Procedures (DPP) had already undergone eight rounds of major revisions. However, it is the revisions carried out 2006 onwards that created some private sector-specific opportunities, by way of articulating two crucial procurement categories: Make and Buy and Make (Indian). Under these categories the private sector was expected to execute major contracts like the public sector units. The late articulation of these two categories has meant a loss of half a decade before the private sector could be considered for major contracts. The late consideration apart, the opportunities opened through the Make and Buy and Make (Indian) categories also did not materialise due to the procedural difficulties, although several projects were given in-principle clearance by MoD.

In addition to the practical difficulties in getting into big-ticket items, the private sector has also suffered from a lot other difficulties in its one-and-a-half decade journey since 2001. Some of the areas which hurt the industry the most are the process of grant of industrial licence (IL); payment terms, and tax and duty structure followed by the government.

When the defence industry was opened to the private sector, the government made it mandatory for the private companies to acquire an IL. However, there was no clarity with regard to the items against which IL would be granted. There was also undue delay in the licensing process. Against a timeframe of 7-8 weeks, the actual time taken in some cases was more than two years (Table 4.6).

Table 4.6: Select Cases of Delay in Approval of Industrial Licence (As in February 2013)

Entity	*Item*	*Application Date*	*Remarks**
Micron Instruments Pvt. Ltd	Shells, Small arms, Ammunition fuses, etc.	28 December 2006	Comments from MHA received on 20 June 2006 after two reminders. Comments from DDP, DSIR and state government are yet to be received. Second reminder sent to DDP on 7 July 2011.
Bharat Heavy Electricals Ltd (BHEL)	Small arms and components	31 January 2007	Comments from DDP, MHA, DSIR and state government are yet to be received.
Kirloskar Pneumatic Co. Ltd	Design and manufacture of warships, combat vehicles, airborne equipment, arms and armaments, etc.	26 March 2008	Comments from state government and DDP received on 11 June 2008 and 14 October 2009, respectively. Comments from MHA are yet to be received after a reminder on 14 June 2011.
Anjani Technoplast Ltd	Manufacture and assembly of UAV	16 April 2009	Comments received from DDP and MHA on 16 April 2010 and 3 January 2012, respectively. Comments from DSIR and state government are yet to be received.
Tata Motors	Overhaul and upgrade of Armoured Fighting Vehicles/Infantry Combat Vehicles/Main Battle Tanks, etc	8 June 2010	DDP comments were received on 2 March 2012, after three reminders. Comments from DSIR and state government are yet to be received.
NOVA Integrated System Ltd	Electronic Warfare Systems	13 July 2010	Comments from DDP received on 11 August 2011 without any reminder. Comments from MHA are yet to be received after one reminder on 6 June 2011. Comments from DSIR and state government are also yet to be received.

Note: The DIPP upon receiving an IL application seeks comments from the administrative ministries concerned (MoD and MHA) as well as the state governments concerned (where the enterprise plans to undertake manufacturing) and DSIR, Ministry of Science and Technology.

Source: DIPP, Ministry of Commerce and Industry, http://dipp.nic.in/English/Default.aspx

Doing business after winning a contract was not easy either. For a long time, the MoD discriminated against the private sector in terms of exchange rate variation (ERV). As per the Ministry of Finance's 2006 *Manual on Policies and Procedures for Purchase of Goods*, government agencies are empowered to insulate the suppliers from ERV in 'contracts involving substantial import content(s) and having a long delivery period (exceeding one year from the date of contract)'.[7] However, as per the provisions of the DPPs of 2011 and 2013, the private sector is not insulated against fluctuation in the exchange rate in Buy (Indian) contracts, although the benefit was extended to the defence public sector units in 'ab-initio single vendor cases or when nominated as production agency'. Such discrimination has had a huge financial implication for the private sector, considering the massive fluctuations that were prevalent in 2011-12 and 2013-14, during which the Rupee depreciated by more than 26 per cent against the US dollar.[8]

Can the Make in India Initiative Save the Private Sector?

The Modi government has no doubt taken a host of initiatives to incentivise the private sector's participation in defence production. These include a hike in FDI cap, streamlining of IL process, opening up of government-controlled testing facilities, articulation of export promotional measures, extension of ERV benefits to the private sector, and level playing field between the public and private sectors insofar as duty and tax are concerned. But there are many other concerns still pending for the government's attention. Some of these are as follows.

Lack of Conducive Financial Framework

Many countries provide a host of fiscal and other incentives to nurture and develop the defence production sector, which is undoubtedly a strategic sector. For instance, in the early phase of defence industrialisation in South Korea, the government provided a wide range of financial and fiscal incentives, besides raising funds for the industry through a special defence tax (a 10 per cent income and surcharge tax) which remained in force for 15 years till 1990.[9] Israel, a country which boasts an advanced defence industry, continues to incentivise the local enterprises through 15 per cent price preference.[10] In India, the defence industry is hardly considered a strategic sector. The prevailing duty/tax structure potentially bars private sector investment in defence production. See Table 4.7, which summarises the tax and other incentives provided to various industry sectors.

Incentives Demanded by the Private Sector

The incentives demanded by the private sector defence industry broadly relate to cheaper cost of finance, infrastructure status, and deemed export status for certain types of sales. There is a near double-digit interest regime in India compared to substantially low interest rate prevalent in Europe, US and many

Table 4.7: Industry Sector-wise Tax and other Incentives

Sector	*Direct Tax*	*Indirect Tax*			*Incentives*
	Income Tax	*Excise*	*Customs*	*Service Tax*	*Foreign trade policy*
Road infrastructure	No income tax for 10 years	Nil duty (project specific)	Nil duty	Nil duty (project specific)	Deemed export
Power	No income tax for 10 years	Nil duty (project specific)	Nil duty	No exemption	Deemed export
Telecom	No income tax for 10 years	Nil duty (itemised)	Nil duty (itemised)	No exemption	No incentives
Shipping	No income tax for 10 years (area specific)	No exemption	Nil duty (item specific)	No exemption	No incentives
Refinery	No income tax for 10 years (area specific)	No exemption	Nil duty	No exemption	Deemed export
Fertiliser	No income tax for 10 years (area specific)	No exemption	Nil duty (item specific)	No exemption	Deemed export
Defence and Aerospace	No exemption	No exemption	No exemption	No exemption except when Govt.	No incentive

Note: Until 2015, the private sector was required to pay excise and customs duty whereas the DPSUs and OFs were exempted.
Source: Updated version of the table taken from the Dhirendra Singh Committee Report, p. 165.

other countries.[11] To bring about a semblance of parity, the industry has demanded its inclusion in the government's Harmonised Master List of Infrastructure Sub-Sectors[12] and its eventual inclusion in RBI's circular on 'Financing of Infrastructure – Definition of Infrastructure Lending'. The inclusion of defence industry in the infrastructure category would also benefit the sector players in terms of certain tax-related exemptions. As per Section 80-IA of the Income Tax Act, 1961, an infrastructure developer is allowed to deduct 100 per cent profit/gain from computing total income. The benefit can be claimed for any 10 consecutive years out of 15 years beginning from the year of operation of the developed facility.[13]

To provide a level playing field to the domestic manufacturers, the government under the Foreign Trade Policy (FTP) accords deemed export[14] status to select specified cases which are notified from time to time. The status is for 'encouraging import substitution and mainly covers such supply of goods which are otherwise allowed at zero customs duty'. Under the scheme, manufacturers/suppliers are given the benefit of advance authorisation (for duty-free import of input materials), duty drawback of taxes paid on inputs and refund of terminal excise duty paid on final goods, etc. Currently, the defence manufacturers/suppliers are not extended the deemed exports benefits.

In the context of defence, there are two areas which have some relevance from the perspective of deemed export. The areas are: Buy (Global) procurement and the offset transaction of the Indian Offset Partner (IOP). In case of Buy (Global) procurement, Indian companies can also compete with foreign companies. If an Indian company wins a contract in such a procurement category, it amounts to import substitution. Clearly, there is merit in according deemed export status to procurement from Indian companies under the Buy (Global) provision.

The basic objective of the Indian defence offset policy, first announced in 2005, is to strengthen the Indian defence industry. To fulfil this objective, MoD has provided a range of avenues to foreign companies. One is to purchase from the local industry. The purchase can be for own use or for integration in India. For the latter option, it is up to the foreign company to take the help of its Indian supplier. The structure of the existing taxation policy is such that the foreign company does not find it cost-effective to carry out integration in India. Rather it prefers to import the product and re-export to India after integration. In the process, the Indian partner loses out in developing or harnessing a key capability of system integration, which is the basic objective of the offset policy. This could be easily avoided by granting deemed export status to the sales of the Indian partner.

The Union Cabinet on 9 December 2015 granted a host of incentives to promote Indian shipbuilding and ship-repair industry. The measures include, besides the grant of infrastructure status, tax incentives, right of first refusal to the domestic industry in government purchases and financial assistance (of Rs 4000 crore over 10 years) to counter cost disadvantages.[15] These incentives were given to the shipbuilding industry for the following two reasons:

- The industry has the same impact as the infrastructure sector due to higher multiplier effect on investment and turnover (11.6 and 4.2) and high employment potential due to multiplier effect of 6.4.
- It is a strategically important industry due to its role in energy security and maritime defence and for developing heavy engineering industry.

In addition to the foregoing, the Institutional Mechanism on Infrastructure chaired by the Secretary of the Department of Economic Affairs approved on 20 January 2016 the inclusion of shipbuilding and ship-repair under the Harmonised List of Infrastructure Sectors.[16] These reasons, particularly the latter, also equally apply to defence manufacturing. However, no such consideration has been given to this sector so far.

Poor R&D

R&D is probably the biggest weakness in the Indian private sector's foray into defence production. As Table 4.8 illustrates, the number of R&D units and the expenditure, as captured in the government database, are anything but inspiring. With such a minuscule expenditure on R&D, it is natural that the indigenisation content of the items produced by it is not different from that produced by public sector entities. The private sector's minuscule effort in defence R&D is a mere reflection of the poor R&D focus of Indian industry as a whole. In comparison to other advanced countries such as the US, China, Japan and Germany where a major portion of R&D comes from the industry, in India, government agencies are the major contributors. The government is also equally responsible for not incentivising the industry. From the private sector's point of view, the biggest obstacle has so far been the non-operationalisation of Make projects, which were supposed to spur design and developmental efforts by the private sector. Similarly, the non-operationalisation of a 'separate fund', which was first announced in the

Defence Production Policy 2011 to promote R&D in the industry, including the small and medium enterprises, has also contributed to the poor R&D spend.

Table 4.8: Private Sector's Expenditure on Defence R&D

Year	*No. of R&D Units*	*R&D Expenditure*	
		Rs crore	*as % of Sales Turnover*
2005-06	11	7.71	0.37
2006-07	11	6.22	0.26
2007-08	11	7.89	0.26
2008-09	11	9.48	0.28
2009-10	11	12.35	0.32

Source: Ministry of Science and Technology, Government of India.

The private sector also complains that the restrictive income tax provisions pertaining to expenditure on scientific research are also a major hindrance for their poor investment on in-house R&D. As per Section 35 of the Income Tax Act, industry's contribution to national research laboratories/universities or its own in-house R&D investment is allowed a 200 per cent weighted tax deduction.[17] However, the tax benefit is limited to four heads of expenditure: plant and machinery; materials and consumables; utilities and services; and human resource. As noted by the Joint Committee of Industry and Government (JCIG), set up by the Department of Science and Technology (DST) to suggest policy measures to stimulate R&D investment by the private sector, these heads of expenditure do not include the entire R&D value chain, which includes R&D in the laboratory, pilot production, test beds, design and development, standardisation, field trials and pre-commercial trial production.[18] The JCIG had drawn attention that other countries factor the entire value chain for the purpose of providing incentives to industry and had recommended similar measures. The recommendation is yet to find acceptance by the government.

Skill Deficiency

Unlike the public sector units, which are the established players and have a relatively better skilled workforce, the private sector does not yet have the kind of workforce required for a high-end manufacturing sector like defence. According to one estimate, defence along with other strategic sectors such as shipbuilding/repairing and homeland security would require 1.8 million additional skilled workforce over a period of 10 years. To meet this need, the Confederation of Indian Industry (CII) has recently partnered with the National Skill Development Council (NSDC) of the Ministry of Skill Development and Entrepreneurship to set up a Strategic Manufacturing Skills Council (SMSC). The SMSC, which was approved in 2014-15 as one of the 38 industry-led Skill Sector Councils (SSC), intends to train 1.5 million workforce in 50 different job roles while certifying 200 training institutes and 3,320 trainers.[19]

However, the SMSC is already behind in many other sector-specific skill councils, including the Aerospace and Aviation Sector Council which was approved in June 2013. Besides the SMSC's late start, there is also a doubt where it would be able to create a high-end labour force, especially engineers and designers to meet the requirement of the private sector which is expected to undertake complex designing/manufacturing under the Make and Buy and Make (India) projects. As of now, SMSC is geared more towards imparting training to shop-floor level workforce, with maximum six months of training.[20] Evidently, there is an absence of a plan to create a pool of engineers/designers which can only come from dedicated engineering/academic institutions with exposure to defence. The existing academic institutions are not only below the global standards but the research undertaken by them is hardly related to defence. To bridge the gap, the Prime Minister has promised to set up dedicated universities[21] on the lines of ones set up by the Department of Atomic Energy (DAE) and ISRO. However, no action seems to have been taken in this regard.

Delay in Acquisition Process

Although the government has opened a host of big-ticket projects for the private sector's participation, these projects are at the very early stage of the acquisition process. As per the DPP, it takes somewhere between two and three years for a project to be awarded after the in-principle approval is given by the Defence Acquisition Council (DAC), the highest decision-making body of MoD headed by the defence minister. However, it is not the stipulated time scale but the delays and frequent cancellation/retraction of tenders that hurts the industry the most. The Defence Secretary in on record saying that as many as 41 Army tenders were rejected in a matter of less than two years.[22] Tables 4.9 and 4.10 give a glimpse of delays in the procurement cases of the IAF. As may be seen, there is hardly any stage that sticks to the timelines stipulated in the DPP. There is also hardly any movement in all the big projects cleared by the new government. There has also hardly been any movement on the Make projects, 6-7 of which were promised to be processed every year.

Table 4.9: Delay in Acquisition pre-CNC Stage

Stage of Procurement	*Average Time (Weeks)*	
	As per DPP	*Actual Time Taken*
Acceptance of Necessity	–	–
Initiation of draft RFP for collegiate vetting at MoD	4	8
Issue of RFP	4	10
Pre-bid meeting	6	6
Dispatch of pre-bid reply	3	4
Receipt of responses	3	6
Completion of TEC report	12	20
Acceptance of TEC report	4	4
Completion of field evaluation (Trials)	20-45	40
Completion of TOEC	4-8	30
Acceptance of TOEC	4	4
Completion of Trials/Staff Evaluation	4	5
Completion of Trials/Staff Evaluation report	4	4
Acceptance of TOC report (if applicable)	4	5

Note: This is with respect to 37 procurement cases of the IAF.
Source: Standing Committee on Defence, *Demands for Grants 2014-15*, Report No. 4, pp. 16-17.

Table 4.10: Delay in Acquisition post-CNC Stage

Stage of Procurement	*Average Time (Weeks)*	
	As per DPP	*Actual Time Taken*
Contract Negotiation Committee (CNC)	18-26	36
CFA Approval	4-16	13.5
Signing of Main and Offset Contract	02	05

Note: This is with respect to 27 procurement cases of the IAF.
Source: Standing Committee on Defence, *Demands for Grants 2014-15*, Report No. 4, p. 17.

FDI

Post-hike in the FDI cap, there has been a flurry of approvals (Table 4.11). However, flow of funds remains relatively low. Moreover, the majority of FDI proposals are either in the form of FII/FPI investment (which per se do not bring in technology) or for amending the existing shareholding pattern.

Table 4.11: FDI Proposals in the Defence Sector, 2014-15 (As in November 2015)

Sl. No.	*Applicant*	*Country of FDI Inflow*	*Proposal*	*FDI (Rscrore)*
1	Sasmos Het Technologies	Netherlands	Post-facto approval for the foreign investment of Rs 26 lakh received in 2009	Nil
2	QuEST Global Manufacturing Private Ltd, Bangalore	Mauritius	Company having 17.29% FDI under automatic route, wishes to undertake additional activities of the defence sector	Nil
3	Samtel Thales Avionics Ltd	France	To expand existing business activities in the defence sector	Nil
4	Verdant Telemetry and Antenna Systems Pvt. Ltd	FII/NRI	Request for amendment in the approval letter for enhancement of NRI equity	0.23
5	Maini Precision Products Pvt. Ltd	Mauritius	Seeking approval to undertake additional activities in the defence sector and post-facto approval for reduction of foreign equity	Nil
6	Bharti Shipyard Ltd, Mumbai	FII/NRI	To undertake additional activities in the defence sector	Nil
7	Solar Industries India Ltd, Nagpur	FII/NRI	To undertake additional defence activities	Nil
8	IdeaForge Technology Pvt. Ltd	FII/NRI	NRI investment by Sujata Vemuri	Nil
9	Punj Lloyd Ltd, Gurgaon	US	To undertake additional activity of manufacturing of equipment, systems and associated assemblies for the defence sector	Nil
10	Thales India Pvt. Ltd	Hong Kong	Seeking post-facto approval for allotment of partly paid equity shares in December 2005 and converted into fully paid up equity shares in October 2011	Nil
11	Aequs Pvt Ltd (Formerly known as QuEST Global Manufacturing Pvt Ltd)		To seek approval for increasing FDI up to 40% in its capital	40.0
12	Fokker Elmo SASMOS Interconnection Systems Ltd., Bangalore		To transfer 49% of the ownership from residents to non-residents	6.0
13	Dynamatic Technologies Ltd		To amend the initial approval letter to include additional activity of manufacture of unmanned aerial vehicles (UAVs) and related machinery	Nil

(*Contd.*)

Table 4.11: Continued

Sl. No.	*Applicant*	*Country of FDI Inflow*	*Proposal*	*FDI (Rscrore)*
14	Mahindra Telephonics Integrated Systems Ltd	US	To increase FDI from 26% to 49%	42.1
15	Indian Rotorcraft Ltd		To incorporate the helicopter model as AW 119Kx in place of AW 119Ke. To change the foreign investor from Agusta Westland N.V. (Netherlands) to Agusta Westland S.p.A (Italy)	Nil
16	Safran Engineering Services India Pvt. Ltd		Seeking deletion of conditions in the last FIPB approval dated3 February 2010	Nil
17	BF Elbit Advanced Systems Pvt. Ltd	Israel	Seeking approval to increase the foreign shareholding from 26% to 49% by its existing shareholder, Elbit Systems Land and C4l Ltd. Israel	37.8

Source: Author's database.

Foreign defence companies have so far shied away from making any new investment in Indian JVs. In various interactions, the representatives of the foreign companies have voiced their concern about lack of assurance from the Indian government to make the JVs viable. It is pointed out that if a foreign company brings in investment/technology and sets up a factory in India, it must be given an assurance of order to make the inflows financially viable.

Lack of Representation at Defence Ministry

MoD is perceived by the private sector to be biased in favour of the public sector units. Senior MoD officials are on the governing boards of the latter and need to show that they are performing well. From the private sector's point of view what is particularly of concern is the government's continuance of the nomination approach, breaching its own commitment. In November 2010, the then defence minister had publicly committed to stop nomination,[23] especially to the public sector shipyards which are constrained to execute the order book.[24] However, the Defence Acquisition Council on 18 December 2015 decided to award the Rs 9000 crore Fleet Support Vessels contract to HSL.[25] Similarly, MoD on 28 February 2015 nominated the mammoth Rs 32,600 crore project to GSL to manufacture 12 Mine Counter Measure Vessels (MCMVs) through transfer of technology.[26] This certainly does not provide a level playing field to the private sector.

Other Concerns

The private sector also has concerns on two other critical aspects. One issue is the payment terms. While MoD pays foreign companies through irrevocable Letter of Credit (LC),[27] such facility is not extended to the Indian private sector, which gets its payments through the Defence Accounts Department of MoD.[28] LC method of payment is time-bound and does not involve direct interface between the buyer and the seller, whereas the DAD's payment method involves a direct human interface and, more crucially, an element of delay (to the extent of 6-9 months as per one industry representative). Considering that the Indian industry operates in a double-digit interest regime, such delay could add anywhere between 4-6 per cent to the capital cost.

Also, under the Buy and Make (Indian) procurement contracts, there is a mandatory 50 per cent indigenisation requirement. The private sector contends that such uniform requirement across platforms may not be feasible, particularly in aircraft procurement where the domestic capability is the bare minimum. HAL, despite 75 years of existence still depends to the extent of 80-90 per cent on foreign sources. Given this fact, the private sector demands a flexible approach to the indigenisation requirement.

Conclusion

The Indian private sector has come a long way from being a mere supplier of parts, components and raw materials to the public sector defence production units to be recognised as a force to reckon with. Its plans to make huge investments and its success in winning contracts against both the established domestic players and foreign companies and its larger share in defence export demonstrate its competiveness. However, the sector has witnessed a host of difficulties arising primarily out of the government's traditional mindset, non-operationalisation of the Make and Buy and Make (Indian), and taxation- and payment-related concerns. The following steps may be considered.

- Compared to the strategic importance attached to the defence industry by many other countries, India has hardly ever done so. This is amply evident from the prevailing structure of taxation and duties. It is desirable that this sector is given incentives as has been given to other sectors of the economy. Among others, the defence industry may be given the infrastructure status. Price preference and the right of first refusal may also be given to the domestic industry. Deemed export status should also be considered for certain types of contracts, particularly those falling under Buy (Global) categories. In principle the contracts executed by an Indian entity under this category are a substitute for direct import.
- R&D is a big weakness in the private sector's foray into defence manufacturing. While the private sector has to take certain initiatives on its own, there is a need for a big push from the government. While retaining the existing 200 per cent weighted tax incentive for the industry's in-house R&D, the government may like to consider the entire R&D value chain for the purpose of providing the tax incentive. At the same time, the government should also stick to its promise of processing 6-8 Make projects in a year. This would not only spur R&D activity in the private sector but also promote a higher level of manufacturing activity.
- To meet the skilled human resources requirement in the private sector, the government should supplement the planned SSC with dedicated

defence-specific universities on the lines of similar setups by the atomic and space departments.

- The government should stick to its articulated position of awarding no defence contracts on nomination basis. In addition, it should stick to the timelines of the procurement process.
- There is a need to look at the payment terms, including the LC option. It would add to the government's efforts towards ease of doing business and at the same time create a level playing field.
- There is also a need to relook at the uniform indigenisation content requirement in the Buy and Make (Indian) contracts, especially those pertaining to aircraft.
- There is a need to relook at the defence FDI policy. Even after the increase in FDI to 49 per cent, foreign defence companies have not shown much interest in investing in Indian JVs. Lack of assurance seems to be a major reason for the lacklustre response. The government may like to link procurement projects to select JVs.

NOTES

1. '70 pc defence equipment imported, it's shameful, dangerous: Antony', *Indian Express*, 21 July 2009.
2. Pipavav Defence and Offshore Engineering Company Limited, *Annual Report 2010-11*, p. 2.
3. 'Tata Power wins prestigious contract for modernisation of IAF airbases', *Defence Now*, 11 April 2011, http://www.defencenow.com/news/138/tata-power-wins-prestigious-contract-for-modernization-of-iaf-airbases.html
4. Vivek Raghuvanshi, 'Tata wins Indian bid for electronic warfare systems', *Defense News*, 25 October 2011.
5. Vivek Raghuvanshi, 'Domestic firm shares $1B Indian gun tender with Korean partner', *Defense News*, 17 October 2015.
6. 'Mahindra soars into the aerospace segment, acquires majority stake in two Australian companies', http://www.mfe.ag/typo3/index.php?id=118&L=0&L=0
7. Ministry of Finance, Government of India, *Manual on Policies and Procedures for Purchase of Goods*, http://finmin.nic.in/the_ministry/dept_expenditure/acts_codes/MPProc4ProGod.pdf(accessed on 12 October 2015).
8. The average exchange rate of rupee vis-à-vis US$ was depreciated to Rs 61.14 in 2014-15 from Rs 47.92 in 2011-12. Reserve Bank of India, https://www.rbi.org.in/Scripts/PublicationsView.aspx?id=16589 (accessed on 12 October 2015).
9. Yong-Sook Lee and Ann Markusen, 'The South Korean defence industry in the post-Cold War era', in Ann Markusen et al., *From Defence to Development?*, Routledge, London, 2003, p. 229.
10. Israeli Ministry of Economy, 'Industrial cooperation in Israel', http://www.moital.gov.il/NR/exeres/B204AC95-046B-4458-ACF3-41F965386044.htm
11. The median base rates of scheduled Indian public sector commercial banks in the last

quarter of 2011-12, 2012-13 and 2013-14 were 10.75 per cent, 10.25 per cent and 10.25 per cent, respectively. Reserve Bank of India, https://rbi.org.in/rbi-sourcefiles/lendingrate/LendingRates.aspx# (accessed on 14 October 2015). During 2011 and 2014, the bank landing interest rate in the US fluctuated between 3 and 3.3 per cent. The World Bank, http://data.worldbank.org/indicator/FR.INR.LEND/countries?display=default (14 October 2015).

12. The latest Harmonized List notified in October 2013 has five broad categories: Transport (road and bridges and airport, etc.); Energy (oil pipeline, electricity generation/transmission, etc.); Water and Sanitation; Communication; and Social and Commercial Infrastructure (cold chain, soil testing labs, etc.), http://www.finmin.nic.in/the_ministry/dept_eco_affairs/infrastructure_div/HarmonisedMasterList_Infrastructure.pdf (accessed on 13 October 2015).
13. Income Tax Department, Government of India, Section 80-IA, Income-tax Act, 1961-2015, http://www.incometaxindia.gov.in/Pages/acts/income-tax-act.aspx(accessed on 13 October 2015).
14. Deemed exports refer to those transactions in which goods supplied do not leave country, and payment for such supplies is received either in Indian rupees or in free foreign exchange. Ministry of Commerce, Government of India, *Annual Report 2013-14*, p. 49.
15. The cost disadvantage would be countered at the rate of '20 per cent of the contract price or the fair prices, whichever is lower and such assistance is to be reduced at the rate of three per cent every three years and will be given for all types of ships.' PIB, 'Indian shipbuilding and ship-repair industry: a strategy for promoting "Make in India" Initiative', 9 December 2015.
16. PIB, 'Shipyards undertaking shipbuilding and ship-repair to be included under the Harmonized list of Infrastructure Sectors', 20 January 2016.
17. Income Tax Department, Government of India, Section 35, Income-tax Act, 1961-2015, http://www.incometaxindia.gov.in/pages/acts/income-tax-act.aspx (accessed on 17 December 2015).
18. Department of Science and Technology, Government of India, *White Paper on Stimulation of Investment of Private Sector into Research and Development of India*, May 2013.
19. 'CII launches strategic manufacturing skills council', *Business Standard*, 5 July 2015; Ministry of Skill Development and Entrepreneurship, http://www.skilldevelopment.gov.in/ssc.html (accessed on 18 November 2015).
20. Interaction with CII official, 18 November 2015.
21. PIB, 'Text of address by Prime Minister at Aero India Show', 18 February 2015.
22. Standing Committee on Defence, *Demands for Grants 2012-13*, p. 22.
23. PIB, 'Antony hints at major policy changes for defence industry', 10 November 2010.
24. In the debate in the Lok Sabha on 26 February 2016, the defence minister informed that in comparison with Rs 8000-90,000 crore worth of production capacity, the public sector shipyards have an order book of Rs 150,000 crore.
25. Pranav Kulkarni, 'Rs 30,000cr plan to buy Russian air defence missile system cleared', *Indian Express*, 18 December 2015.
26. GSL *Annual Report 2014-15*, p. 10.
27. Letter of Credit is a financial instrument issued by a bank on behalf of the buyer. The instrument allows the seller to recover its price subject to fulfilment of certain conditions.
28. MoD, *Defence Procurement Procedures 2013: Capital Procurement*, pp. 106-110.

5

Defence Research and Development Organisation

If India has been a net importer of arms all through its defence industrialisation process, the lack of a credible defence R&D base is partly to be blamed. For a variety of reasons, ranging from inadequate investment to poor monitoring/accountability and lack of users' interest in indigenously developed products, India's defence R&D has not been able to produce the kind of arms and other equipment required by the armed forces, resulting in India's huge arms imports year by year and poor self-reliance. From the perspective of the Make in India initiative, a strong R&D base has to therefore play a central role, if the goal of 70 per cent self-reliance is to be achieved.

This chapter makes an in-depth analysis of DRDO, the premier R&D wing of MoD, which has near monopoly in India's defence R&D. It also examines some of the problem areas that need to be overcome for establishing a strong technological base for Make in India to flourish.

DRDO: Origin and Growth

DRDO was formed on 1 January 1958 by merging the Defence Science Organisation (DSO) with the Technical Development Establishments of the armed forces.[1] Since then DRDO has been nearly synonymous with India's defence R&D. At its formation, DRDO had only 10 laboratories. Now it consists of 52 research laboratories and establishments spread across the country. It has a workforce of 25,157 including 7476 scientists/engineers (Table 5.1).

Table 5.1: DRDO's Human Resources Strength

Cadre	*No. of Employees*
Defence Research and Development Services (DRDS)	7476
Defence Research Technical Cadre (DRTC)	9398
Armed Forces Officers	377
Administrative and Allied Cadre	6091
Armed Forces (Other Ranks)	1815
Total	25157

Source: PIB, 'Funds Spent on DRDO', 8 May 2015.

DRDO's labs and establishments cater for virtually all possible dimensions of defence technology spanning aeronautics, armaments, combat engineering, electronics, life sciences, materials, missiles and naval system. Headquartered in New Delhi, DRDO works under the Department of Defence R&D and is headed by a senior scientist, known as Director General (DG DRDO), who until recently was also the Scientific Advisor to the Raksha Mantri (Defence Minister) – SA to RM.[2] The head of DRDO, who is also the Secretary, Department of Defence R&D (one of the four departments of MoD), is supported by seven cluster Director Generals (DGs), five Chief Controllers R&D (CCs R&D) and an Additional Financial Adviser (Addl. FA).

Like the organisation itself, DRDO's role in defence R&D has also evolved over a period of time. At the time of its formation, DRDO was mainly an inspection agency. It was only in the 1970s and 1980s that the organisation was geared into design and developmental mode, with government sanctioning a number of high-profile projects including the main battle tank (MBT) Arjun (sanctioned in May 1974), Integrated Guided Missile Development Programme (IGMDP) (July 1983) and Light Combat Aircraft (August 1983).

With the maturity of many of its programmes, DRDO-developed products and technologies are now being increasingly cleared for bulk production and induction into the Indian armed forces.[3] Between 2010 and 2013, as many as 36 different major products designed by DRDO have been inducted into the armed forces. These include a range of missile systems, radars, electronic warfare systems, combat vehicles, unmanned aerial vehicles (UAV), robotic systems, submarine escape suits, and ready to eat meal, among others.[4] As on 1 March 2015, the cumulative production value of all DRDO-developed items (inducted or in the induction process) has touched nearly Rs 174,844 crore (Table 5.2). In addition, many of the DRDO-developed technologies have either been transferred or are ready for transfer to the Indian industry. As of 2015, more than 500 technologies have been transferred to industries.[5]

Table 5.2: Value of DRDO-developed Systems Inducted or Underinduction (Rs crore)

System	*R&D Cost*	*Inducted*	*Under Induction*
Missile Systems	4150.19	23863.25	41725.73
Electronics and Radar Systems	1504.07	10642.70	22826.18
Advanced Materials and Composites	126.53	3504.96	138.84
Armament Systems	108.80	8362.38	4259.44
Aeronautical Systems	12433.68	598.76	18872.04
Combat Vehicles & Engineering Systems	776.02	13692.59	17882.67
Life Sciences Systems	12.51	246.91	286.29
Naval Systems	327.20	1038.76	802.13
Micro Electronic Devices and Computational Systems	195.46	1450.64	4649.41
Total	19634.46	63400.95	111442.72

Source: MoD, *Annual Report 2014-15*, p. 88.

DRDO's Performance: An Overview

As the premier defence R&D agency in India, DRDO is often judged by not only what it designs and develops, but also by the indigenous content of those products– the latter being a sensitive topic among the Indian parliamentarians, policymakers and defence analysts. More often than not, DRDO is asked to furnish statistics to prove domestic content in its developed items. Given the local sensitivities about indigenous content, and the pressure on DRDO to achieve that, it can also be used as one of the indicators of DRDO's performance.

Table 5.3 provides an overview of indigenous content in major DRDO-developed systems. Barring four products, namely the Airborne Early Warning & Control (AEW&C) systems, BrahMos cruise missile, long-range surface-to-air missile (LRSAM) and MBT Arjun, in which the import content is more than 50 per cent, in others the domestic content can be termed satisfactory (considering that India's self-reliance target is 70 per cent). This, in turn, shows not only DRDO's own credibility in developing technology and prototypes, but also its role in partnering and, often handholding, of Indian industry, other S&T institutes and academia for co-development of many technologies and subsystems and final production of the items. As per its official estimate, DRDO is now credited with working with 800 large and small private/public sector industries, and more than 100 academic and S&T institutions across the country[6] – a huge spin-off from India's defence R&D point of view and considering that India had very little defence science and industrial base when DRDO was formed way back in the late1950s.

Table 5.3: Import Content in the major Systems Developed/Being Developed by DRDO

System	*Import Content (%)*	*System*	*Import Content (%)*
Pilotless Target Aircraft (PTA), Lakshya	5-7	Supersonic Cruise BrahMos Missile	65
Remotely Piloted Vehicle (RPV), Nishant	10	Long Range Surface to Air Missile (LR-SAM)	60
Aircraft Arrester Barrier	5	Multi Barrel Rocket System, Pinaka	10
Light Combat Aircraft (LCA)	40	Main Battle Tank, Arjun	55
Airborne Early Warning & Control (AEW&C) System (excluding aircraft)*	67	Radars	10
Combat Free Fall (CFF) System	35	Electronic Warfare Systems	5-30
Parachutes	0	Sonars	5-30
Heavy Drop System	10	Pocket Dosimeter (PDM)	12
Agni Missile	15	Portable Dose Rate Meter	9
Prithvi Missile	15	Roentegnometer	6
Surface to Air Missile, Akash	10	Nuclear, Biological and Chemical (NBC) Recce Vehicle	5
Anti-tank Missile, Nag	30	NBC Water Purification System	5

* Excluding aircraft, the import content amounts to 16 per cent.

Source: Standing Committee on Defence (2012-13), 15th Lok Sabha, *Demands for Grants 2013-14,* Lok Sabha Secretariat, New Delhi, 2013, p. 74; Rajya Sabha, 'Achievements made by DRDO', Unstarred Question No. 1168, answered on 8 March 2016.

From the Indian defence R&D point of view what is more significant is that the expansion of the R&D base has, to a large extent, gone hand in hand with the enhanced manufacturing capability of Indian industry. As has been stated by a former DRDO chief, Dr V.K. Saraswat, the Indian industry, working through DRDO's various programmes beginning with the IGMDP, has improved its capability from that of 'built to print' to 'built to specification', 'built to design' and 'built to requirements'. This has allowed many Indian enterprises to manufacture technologically advanced products which are in conformity with international military standards, and become part of the global supply chain.[7] The latter aspect is also evident from India's huge increase in export of aerospace parts and components in recent years (see Chapter 6, on offsets). With the increasing maturity of the Indian industry, there has also been a spin-off towards DRDO's own activities covered under the 'stores' budget that cater for DRDO's revenue expenses primarily of industrial nature on projects, programmes, schemes and IT-related activities, among others.

As claimed by DRDO, around 80 per cent of its stores budget is spent in local currency, indicating that Indian industry can provide significant support to DRDO's revenue-oriented R&D activities.

DRDO's contribution to defence R&D is perhaps best described by several of its high-profile projects' global comparison. As has been highlighted by DRDO and its chiefs in various forums,

> [India is] one of the four countries in the world to have a multi-level strategic deterrence capability; one of the five countries of the world to have its own ballistic missile defence (BMD) programme and underwater missile launch capability; one of the seven countries to have developed its own main battle tank (MBT) and an indigenous 4th generation combat aircraft; one of the six countries of the world to have developed a nuclear powered submarine; one of the select few countries of the world to have its own electronic warfare and multi-range radar programme.[8]

DRDO's Performance: A Critique

DRDO's foregoing international comparison is however to be read with caution, for not all these projects are mature enough or have passed through the developmental phase for production and deployment. The BMD programme, nuclear submarine and combat aircraft are, for example, still some time away from induction. Moreover, the projects which have passed through the developmental phase for production are not necessarily 100 per cent indigenous. For instance, the power pack, gun control and fire control systems of MBT Arjun and the engine of the LCA are sourced from abroad, indicating the lack of depth in indigenous capability.[9] The LCA's technological shortcomings are further illustrated in the recently published list of 121 systems (pertaining to avionics, electronics, hydraulics, landing gear and propulsion) that the Aeronautical Development Agency (ADA) – an autonomous body functioning under DRDO – wants to indigenise through the participation of Indian vendors.[10] The import content in the products listed in Table 5.3 is a further indication of the technological gap that DRDO is confronted with in its developmental projects.

DRDO's technological gap in frontline military technologies, especially in comparison with advanced countries is perhaps best illustrated in the list of 26 'critical technologies' listed for acquisition from abroad by DRDO through MoD's defence offset guidelines that stipulate a minimum 30 per cent re-investment (through technology transfer and other means) of arms import cost into the domestic industry. The list includes nano technology-based sensors and displays, technology for hypersonic flights, low observable (stealth) technologies, focal plane arrays, gun barrel technologies, and fibre lasers technology (Table 5.4).[11]

DRDO's lack of depth in R&D is also partly illustrated in its IPR portfolio. DRDO is the biggest R&D spending organisation among all the scientific agencies in India – in 2009-10, it accounted for 31.6 per cent of R&D expenditure of major scientific organisations, distantly followed by the Department of Space (15.5 per cent), DAE (14.4 per cent) and CSIR (10 per cent), among other agencies.[12] However, it has lesser IPR to its credit. For instance, in comparison with CSIR which has a portfolio of over 5600 patents, including 2350 abroad,[13] DRDO's IPR portfolio consists of around 1400 patents, copyrights, designs and trademarks.[14]

Table 5.4: List of 26 Critical Defence Technologies for Acquisition by DRDO through Offset Route

Sl. No.	*Name of Technology*
1	MEMs based sensors, actuators, RF devices, Focal Plane arrays
2	Nano Technology based sensors & displays
3	Miniature SAR & ISAR technologies
4	Fibre Lasers Technology
5	EM Rail Gun technology
6	Shared and Conformal Apertures
7	High efficiency flexible Solar Cells technology
8	Super Cavitations technology
9	Molecularly Imprinted Polymers
10	Technologies for Hypersonic flights (Propulsion, Aerodynamics and Structures)
11	Low Observable technologies
12	Technologies for generating High Power Lasers
13	High Strength, High Modulus, Carbon Fibers, Mesophase pitch-based fiber, Carbon Fiber Production Facility
14	Pulse Power network technologies
15	THZ technologies
16	Surface Coated Double Base (SCDB) Propellant
17	FSAPDS Technologies
18	HESH Ammunition technologies
19	Muzzle Reference System
20	Composite Sabot Manufacturing Technology
21	MET projectiles
22	Titanium casting, forging, fabrication and machining
23	Precision Guided Munitions
24	Shock Hardened Sensors
25	Gun Barrel Technologies
26	Advanced Recoil System

Source: DRDO, http://drdo.gov.in/drdo/English/index.jsp?pg=homebody.jsp (accessed on 4 January 2016).

Notwithstanding the technological shortcoming, DRDO often attempts to grab as many R&D projects as possible. However, many a time, it is constrained to complete the projects and achieve the technological deliverables within the sanctioned timeframe and budgetary provision. This has often led to midway cancellation of projects. For example, a 1989 review of all DRDO projects led to closure of as many as 618 projects (out of a total of 989 projects).[15] Although resource crunch at that time was cited as the primary reason behind the short-closure of projects, it nonetheless showed the organisation's inability to develop the technologies of the projects it had pursued originally. It also shows the absence of a strong approval mechanism which would have examined the feasibility of the programme before it was taken up. A 2007 report of the parliamentary committee takes note of the abandonment of several developmental projects (including those of airborne surveillance platform, cargo ammunition and 30mm fair-weather towed air defence gun system) undertaken by DRDO.[16] A 2012 Report of the CAG is also critical of the failure of DRDO in several projects in which progress was dismal.[17]

Apart from midway abandonment of projects, many of DRDO's projects suffer from time and cost overruns (Table 5.5). Almost all of DRDO's flagship projects including MBT Arjun, LCA and Kaveri engine have witnessed significant time and cost overruns, besides eliciting poor user response.[18] The cost overrun of MBT Arjun (the development of which was closed in 1995 as against the originally envisaged bulk production by 1984) was a whopping 1884 per cent.[19] Although Arjun has now been inducted into the Army, the number does not inspire confidence. As against the inventory of over 2000 Vijayanta tanks which the Arjun was supposed to replace, orders for 248 tanks have so far been placed, indicating the user's lack of confidence in the indigenous tank. A 2008 parliamentary committee report also talks of the Army's displeasure with the Arjun, which reportedly 'performed very poorly' in a winter trial.[20] Similar is the fate of the LCA. Sanctioned in the early 1980s for replacement of MiG fighters, the project is yet to get the final operational clearance, over three decades after the project was sanctioned.[21] Like the Arjun, LCA has also got few orders so far. As against 870-odd MiG series of aircraft which the LCA was intended to replace, 40 units have been ordered for production by HAL.[22] The poor user satisfaction is also evident from the IAF's decision to deploy the initial lots of LCA in southern India, far away from the active borders of China or Pakistan.[23]

Table 5.5: Select Cases of Time and Cost Overruns in DRDO Projects

Project Name	*Date of Sanction*	*Original Likely Date of Completion*	*Revised Date of Completion*	*Original Estimated Cost (Rs crore)*	*Revised Cost (Rs crore)*
LCA Phase II	November 2001	December 2008	December 2015	3301.78	5777.56
Kaveri Engine	March 1989	December 1996	December 2009	382.81	2839.00
Long Range Surface-to-Air Missile (LRSAM)	December 2005	May 2012	December 2015	2606.02	No revision
Airborne Early Warning & Control (AEW&C) System	October 2004	October 2011	December 2015	1800.00	2520.00
Naval Light combat Aircraft (LCA Navy Phase-I)	March 2003	March 2010	December 2014*	948.90	1714.98
Air-to-Air Missile System: Astra	March 2004	February 2013	August 2016	955.00	No revision
Nirbhay – Development & Flight Trials	March 2004	February 2013	August 2016	56.93	102.28

*Further revision underway.
Source: Author's database.

Defence R&D: The Problem Areas

Lack of Higher Organisational Structure

The biggest weakness of India's defence R&D (or for that matter defence production) has been the absence of a higher organisational structure which could be made responsible for setting out the R&D (and manufacturing) plan; bringing various stakeholders (users and R&D and production agencies) to a common platform; review of projects in view of its viability; monitoring the progress of indigenous projects and fixing accountability. In the absence of this, crucial decisions with far-reaching implications are being pursued by various stakeholders in a piecemeal fashion, often to cross-purposes. A glaring example of the lack of direction and supervision by a higher authority is the Indian army's recently floated global request for information (RFI), seeking inputs for what it calls Future Ready Combat Vehicle (FRCV). The RFI, issued on 10 June 2015, has clearly upset DRDO, which sees that the FRCV is an attempt to scuttle its own effort to design FMBT.[24] Such difference between two key players is definitely not in the interest of developing indigenous capability in critical defence technology.

Lack of R&D Plan

In the absence of a higher organisational structure, the plan for in-house R&D has been a big missing element in India's defence acquisition process. In fact, the crucial element of R&D is left to be undertaken in a piecemeal manner and is largely viewed as a mere by-product of the procurement process. DRDO, whose core mandate is to design and develop state-of-the-art weapon systems and provide all necessary technical advice in all matters of weapon acquisition, has however been marginalised in the procurement process to the extent of being another stakeholder competing for its fair share of resources in the defence budget. The budget-seeking attitude of DRDO has in fact been institutionalised in MoD's defence procurement procedure (DPP), which until the 2013 revision (which brought out a prioritised order of categorisation) had no provision to enable the armed forces to give priority to indigenous options over the imported ones. Consequently, DRDO's role under much of the DPP's operational life has been confined to contesting those import-oriented proposals if it is of the view that those can be developed or produced indigenously.

It may be noted that unlike India's other sectors of importance for which there are a host of policy statements,[25] there is no policy statement specific to defence R&D, although several documents released in recent years make a passive reference to industrial R&D. Two such documents are the Defence Production Policy released in January 2011 and the Technology Perspective and Capability Roadmap (TPCR) published in April 2013. Both documents not only sideline DRDO but have also little practical meaning for the industry as they are not backed by a concrete R&D or manufacturing plan, which is the minimum necessary condition to enable the industry to commit any investment. This major weakness was highlighted in a 2013 report prepared by the Economic Advisory Council to the Prime Minister.[26]

In the absence of a comprehensive R&D plan, DRDO has on its own prepared a Long Term Technology Perspective Plan (LTTPP) based on its own study and understanding of system requirements as laid down in the armed forces' 15-year Long Term Integrated Perspective Plan (LTIPP). The aim of DRDO's LTTPP is to 'align [its] technology development plan with systems acquisition plan given in LTIPP.'[27] DRDO's plan 'details the technology projects which need to be taken up, resources required in respect of test facilities infrastructure, test ranges and centres of research excellence that would be required.' Notwithstanding DRDO's efforts, there is a cloud of doubt about its efficacy. LTTPP does not seem to have government sanction as enjoyed by LTIPP, which has been approved by the Defence Acquisition Council (DAC). In the absence of government sanction, there is every possibility of non-cooperation by other stakeholders, particularly the armed forces, which may feel that DRDO's efforts are not meeting their requirement. Moreover, without the government's sanction, accountability with respect to key deliverables within a stipulated timeframe and budget also gets diluted. It is also not clear to what extent the DRDO technology plan complements the R&D efforts of others, particularly the DPSUs, OFs and the private sector, which are also pursing their independent R&D, although on a much smaller scale. The lack of clarity on these fronts reduces DRDO's own efforts to a mere wish list.

Lack of Synergy among Stakeholders

The indigenous development of 155mm/45 calibre artillery gun, *Dhanush*, is probably the perfect example of how a synergistic approach involving all the stakeholders can lead to success. The development of the gun, which is based on the Swedish Bofors gun designs acquired in the 1980s, was done by a team that included army, OFs, DRDO and quality assurance and maintenance agencies. According to an official of the OFB, the development of the gun was done in 16 months' time, much shorter that 60 months usually taken for development of such an item.[28] Moreover, with 80 per cent indigenisation, the Dhanush is reportedly '20-25 per cent better than the original Bofors gun in virtually all parameters like range, accuracy, consistency, low and high angle of fire and shoot-and-scoot ability.'[29]

However, such a synergistic approach is rare in India's developmental projects. In fact, MoD is on record that such involvement of all stakeholders 'has been done for the first time in the country'.[30] What typifies many of the projects is lack of synergy among the stakeholders. More importantly, the lack of the users' active involvement in indigenous projects in particular has been a major feature in India's major R&D projects. This has been repeatedly commented upon by CAG about several critical R&D projects, including the LCA and MBT Arjun. In the case of the development of LCA, the auditor observes that the IAF's involvement in various decision-making governing bodies commenced in 2006, some 16 years after the proposal was first suggested to ensure 'closer interaction between the design team and the user for appreciation of mutual perception, including appropriate trade-offs in performance, weight, timeframe, cost, technological complexity and operational considerations of LCA.'[31] In the case of MBT Arjun, the Army's involvement is anything but supportive. Instead of handholding the project, the Army put more stringent quality norms than it placed on the T-90 Russian tank, with which the Arjun's performance was compared. Commenting on the discrimination meted out to the indigenous tank, CAG observed eight instances 'where the Army placed a benchmark of parameters on MBT Arjun which were more stringent in comparison to those placed on T-90 tanks ... precluding a level-playing field' (Table 5.6). The Navy, which is perceived to be more indigenous minded, has also its share of lacklustre involvement in indigenous R&D projects. In a 2014 report, CAG has noted that 12 projects undertaken by DRDO suffered from delays and the reasons were attributed to the Navy's late communication of technical parameters and their frequent changes, among others.[32] CAG also mentions the 'difference of opinion between DRDO labs and the Navy regarding whether a project was successful or not.'

Poor Monitoring and Accountability

As noted earlier, several projects undertaken by DRDO witness time and cost overruns besides abandonment. This, while indicating DRDO's technological shortcoming also demonstrates its poor monitoring and accountability. Usually, DRDO undertakes a project based on its own assessment of technological feasibility. There is hardly any independent external agency that reviews the feasibility of projects and monitors progress. Consequently, when the project does not meet the timelines, exceeds the budget or does not meet the technology requirement, there is no option but to continue with extended time and additional budgetary allocation or short-close the project. The Standing Committee on Defence, which examined several projects dropped/abandoned, had expressed its deep disappointment over the current state of affairs. It had therefore suggested that 'there should be a scientific, technical and concurrent audit of every ongoing project from an independent agency so that such closures are avoided in future.'[33]

Defence Technology Commission

The Rama Rao Committee, constituted by MoD to review DRDO's functioning, in its report (titled *Redefining DRDO*) submitted in March 2008,[34] identified organisational shortcoming as the key weakness in India's defence R&D. To rectify this institutional gap, it suggested the creation of a high-level Defence Technology Commission (DTC) under the chairmanship of the defence minister. To make the DTC an overarching body and the key

Table 5.6: Comparison of Benchmarks for Evaluation of MBT Arjun vis-à-vis T-90 Tank

Activity	*Benchmark for Evaluation for MBT Arjun*	*Benchmark for T-90 Tank*	*Audit Remarks*
Run in terrain	Running of tank in medium and heavy dunal terrain at Mahajan Field Firing Range (MMFR) which imposed running in low gear due to gradient and rolling resistance	Running of tank (automotive trials) at Chaba only	Desert condition at MMFR was tougher than that existed at Chaba
Scientific stress model technique	Firing of 25 Equivalent Full Charge (EFC) after each mobility cycle of 250 km	Firing after completion of automotive trials	Relaxed parameter for T-90 tank
Effect of oil temperature on operational speed	1. Running in first gear until temperature comes down which imposed limitation of speed 2. Provision of software for automatic engagement of first gear to bring down the temperature of transmission oil	1. Lowering of gear was effected to bring down the temperature of transmission oil 2. No such provision	1. Operational constrains due to reduced speed are equally applicable to both the tanks 2. Relaxed parameter for change of gear in case of T-90 tank
Check of lubricants/oils	1. Validation of oil properties after every 250 km run 2. Examination of oil from engine after every 25 hours of engine run	No such checks prescribed	Relaxed parameter for T-90 tank
Obstacle performance	Gradient 355 degree	Gradient 30 degree	Relaxed parameter for T-90 tank
System reliability	Facility for pull-back of gun and strip examination of recoil system at every five years	No such condition prescribed	Relaxed parameter for T-90 tank
Laser range finder	1. Facility for multiple target discrimination 2. Accuracy of range +/- 10 metre 3. Duty cycle 12 ranging in two minutes followed by 4 ranging in 8 minutes	1. No such facility 2. +/- 25 metre 3. No such condition	Relaxed parameter for T-90 tanks
Firing of armour piercing ammunition	Speed of tank and target was 20 km per hour in opposite direction	Speed of the target tested was 10 km per hour	Relaxed parameter for T-90 tanks
Medium fording	Zero level water ingress	2.5 litre water ingress*	Relaxed parameter for T-90 tank

*Permissible limit of water ingress for medium fording was derived with reference to acceptable limit of five litres of water ingress for full-dip fording as mentioned in the trial directive for T-90 tank.

Source: CAG, *Union Government (Defence Services): Army, Ordnance Factories and Defence Public Sector Undertaking*, Report No. 35 of 2014, p. 281.

decision-making institution for all aspects of defence innovation and self-reliance, the committee also suggested that the DTC's other members should include all the senior-most functionaries of the armed forces, ministries of defence and finance, DAE and the Department of Space, and the national security advisor.[35] Membership of the DTC was also suggested to include two eminent personalities in the fields of S&T and industry. The committee believed that such a high-powered body with cross-ministerial/departmental membership and representation from industry and the wider S&T base would bring synergy among the stakeholders and provide the required direction and thrust for India's defence R&D efforts. The DTC would be responsible for articulating defence R&D policy, setting R&D targets and monitoring them. It would also be responsible for enabling DRDO to play a larger role in India's defence procurement, including in technology transfer through the offset route. However, the DTC is yet to be created, the latest information from the government being that a cabinet note has been prepared for its creation.[36]

Poor Human Resource Base

DRDO is also constrained by a poor human resource base, in terms of quantity and quality of scientific cadre and optimisation. Despite its large charter of duties and vast array of technological interest ranging from food research to armaments, missiles, aeronautics and electronics, DRDO has only 16,874 scientific and technical human resources. In comparison, ISRO, which works on a relatively limited area of space S&T, has a workforce of 12,155.[37] Moreover, while ISRO does not face any shortage of human resources,[38] DRDO faces a shortage of 2776 scientists to work on projects whose number as well complexity has increased over the years.[39] As has been admitted by the Defence Minister, 'there has not been any enhancement of scientific human resources since 2001, while the number of projects has grown multi-fold in terms of size and technical complexity keeping in view India's strategic and tactical defence equipment.' In terms of big projects each costing above Rs 100 crore, DRDO is pursuing 44 projects worth over Rs 39,224 crore (Annexure D).

If limited S&T base is a concern for DRDO, what is of greater concern is the poor human resources management. According to a recent report based on insiders, nearly 30 per cent of DRDO's scientific human resources are engaged in 'sundry jobs' that include 'handling administration, accounts, stores, security, building maintenance, canteen, welfare, etc.'[40] Such 'murdering of talent' comes amidst the already heavy presence in DRDO of the auxiliary and administrative workforce. DRDO has the highest ratio of auxiliary and administrative personnel to scientists (Table 5.7), indicating the lack of optimisation of human resources. If DRDO is to achieve the average level of other major scientific agencies (which include the Department of Space and DAE, among others), if not the private sector (which has the lowest proportion of auxiliary and administrative staff to R&D staff), it can save up to 8,774 support staff, including 4,828 personnel from its auxiliary service, the Defence Research Technical Cadre (DRTC).[41]

Table 5.7: Number of Auxiliary and Administrative Staff per R&D Staff/Scientist in DRDO (As in April 2010)

	Auxiliary	*Administrative*
DRDO*	1.3	1.2
Major Scientific Agencies	0.7	0.7
Private Sector	0.6	0.2
Overall R&D Sector	0.6	0.6

*As of 2011.
Source: DRDO and Ministry of S&T, *Research and Development Statistics 2011-12.*

DRDO's limited human resources base is further constrained by a number of other factors such as the high attrition of scientists, low educational profile of the scientific cadre and poor training, which together makes DRDO less dynamic for a qualified and motivated workforce to work in.

As regards attrition, between 2002 and 2006, 1007 scientists left the organisation – an attrition that the government has acknowledged is higher than in the private sector.[42] Although the attrition rate came down from the high of 273 in 2007 to 65 in 2009, such decline can be attributed to the increase in pay of all government employees (including DRDO scientists) post implementation of the Sixth Central Pay Commission recommendations. But once again, the number of resignations has started to increase. For instance in 2011, 86 scientists left DRDO, compared to 63 in 2010.[43] Between 2012 and 2014, 157 scientists have left.[44]

Poor educational profile of its scientists has been a perennial problem for DRDO, affecting some of its high-profile projects. For instance, in an internal review report of 1987 pertaining to the PINAKA Multi Barrel Rocket Launcher (MBRL) project, DRDO identified 'non-availability of adequately qualified human resources as one of the constraints in the smooth progress of the project.'[45] In 1995, CAG observed the persistence of the problem in a review report relating to six DRDO laboratories. In the case of the Armament

Research and Development Establishment (ARDE), a key lab responsible for design and development of combat vehicles, 'about 48 per cent of the strength of officers was unqualified and represented level of education up to B.Sc. or Diploma in Engineering.'[46]

The Rama Rao Committee, mentioned earlier, which reviewed DRDO's functioning, was particularly dismayed by the dominance of first degree holders in DRDO's scientific cadre, with 60 per cent of the scientists having educational degree of Diploma, B.Tech, B.Sc., M.A. and M.Sc. It found that only 10 per cent of DRDO's total scientific human resources had a PhD (3 percent in engineering subjects and 7 percent in science subjects). As many as 43 per cent of the laboratories had less than 2 per cent PhD holders.

More startlingly, the Rama Rao Committee also observed that the majority of DRDO's scientific cadre was not 'research trained', a feature which is also common to other high-end R&D organisations such as DAE and ISRO. Given the classroom-oriented teaching focus in most of the Indian educational institutions, these agencies often struggle to get 'research-ready material' for their R&D programmes. However, while some other agencies have taken certain steps to address this critical issue, DRDO is yet to get its act together. For instance, ISRO, which faced 'severe shortage' of highly talented scientists and engineers to take up the challenges of R&D in space S&T, opened a dedicated institute, the Indian Institute of Space Science and Technology (IIST), which has been running since 2007.[47] With an intake of 150 students per year, the IIST provides graduate, postgraduate and doctoral programmes in areas of space S&T. The students who successfully pass out from the IIST are also required to work for a minimum five years for ISRO. DRDO on the other hand does not have a similar institute. It merely relies on its Defence Institute of Advanced Technology (DIAT) for providing training to the in-house scientists, and that too for a limited 20-week period.[48]

Meagre Budget and Lack of Emphasis on Indigenous R&D

Although India's stated policy is to achieve 'substantive self-reliance in the design, development and production of equipment/weapon systems/platforms required for defence',[49] the resource commitment belies the claim. Compared to the US and China, which spend in excess of 10 per cent of their defence budget on R&D, DRDO's current spending is around 6 per cent.[50] Even the present share in the defence budget came only after the 1980s, before which the allocation on R&D was negligible: about one per cent in the 1960s, rising to about 2 per cent in the early 1980s.[51] This low share in the defence budget together with India's relatively smaller defence budget means that the defence R&D budget in absolute terms is minuscule. In absolute terms, DRDO's 2013-14 budget of Rs 14,358.49 crore (US$1.8 billion)[52] amounts to a mere 3 percent of the US Defense Department's $67.5 billion R&D budget (for 2014).[53]

Moreover, this meagre budget is stretched to the limit. It may be noted over 40 per cent of DRDO's expenditure is spent on strategic products, leaving very little for a vast array of conventional projects.[54] The low share of defence budget for DRDO has an unintended consequence on the type of projects it can take up. This is revealed in the present project portfolio of DRDO (Table 5.8). Of the total 546 projects valued at Rs 85,766 crore, a staggering 89 per cent, in value terms, is accounted for by 153 Mission Mode (MM) projects. These projects are applied research in nature, normally based on technologies that are proven and readily accessible/available,[55] taken on the formal request of the armed forces and given the highest priority. The high priority for the MM projects, however, leaves a meagre amount (less than 10 per cent) to be spent on basic research or on experimental projects, which are categorised as S&T and Technology Demonstration (TD). Although these projects are crucial for generating new technologies for future use and hence vital for India's defence innovation point of view, DRDO's limited budget does not allow much priority to them.

Table 5.8: DRDO's Project Portfolio (As in 2011)

Project Category	*Projects*		*Project Value*	
	No.	*%*	*Rs crore*	*%*
Mission Mode (MM)	153	28	76564	89
Technology Demonstration (TD)	232	42	5934	7
Science and Technology (S&T)	124	23	1383	2
Infrastructure Development (IF)	37	7	1885	2

Source: DRDO, *Annual Report 2012.*

Acknowledging the importance of higher investment in defence R&D, the Standing Committee on Defence in a report presented to Parliament in 1995 had suggested that allocation for DRDO should be progressively increased to 10 per cent of the defence budget by 2000. While making the suggestion, the committee had taken note of the Self-Reliance Review Committee's envisaged plan (to achieve 70 per cent self-reliance by 2005), which was itself linked to a higher level of budgetary allocation to DRDO.[56]

However, DRDO's budget never reached the 10 per cent level during the recommended period, peaking at a much lower level of 6.74 per cent at a much later period in 2008-09. Since then also, there has been a gradual decline, indicating further the low priority defence R&D gets in the annual defence spending.

Table 5.9 provides DRDO's share in India's GDP and the country's total R&D expenditure. Compared to India, advanced countries spend much more. For example in 2012, the US Department of Defense's R&D outlays amounted to 0.45 per cent of GDP and 16.82 per cent of total US R&D expenditure.[57]

Table 5.9: DRDO's Share in India's GDP and Total R&D Expenditure (Amounts in Rs crore)

Year	*GDP*	*Total R&D Expenditure*	*DRDO's R&D Expenditure*		
			Amount	*As % of GDP*	*As % of R&D Expenditure*
1970-71	47638.0	139.64	17.55	0.04	12.57
1975-76	86707.0	356.71	52.13	0.06	14.61
1980-81	149642.0	760.52	83.70	0.06	11.01
1985-86	289524.0	2068.78	321.09	0.11	15.52
1990-91	586212.0	3974.17	689.57	0.12	17.35
1995-96	1226725.0	7483.88	1396.25	0.11	18.66
2000-01	2177413.0	16198.80	3342.34	0.15	20.63
2005-06	3693369.0	29932.58	5283.35	0.14	17.65
2006-07	4294706.0	34238.39	5362.82	0.12	15.66
2007-08	4987090.0	39437.77	6104.55	0.12	15.48
2008-09	5630063.0	47353.38	7699.05	0.14	16.26
2009-10	6477827.0	53041.30	8475.38	0.13	15.98
2010-11	7795313.0	62053.47	10148.92	0.13	16.36
2011-12	8974947.0	72620.44	9937.68	0.11	13.68

Source: Data obtained from MoD, Ministry of S&T and Reserve Bank of India.

The lack of emphasis on domestic defence R&D is also visible in India's annual defence budgeting process, and particularly in the priority attached to resource allocation between the armed forces and DRDO. If the allocation for the armed forces represents an investment on immediate need, the allocation for R&D – which by its very nature is an investment for the future

– is clearly less prioritised. This is evident from Table 5.10, which shows that the extent of underfunding of DRDO during the eight-year period 2006-07 to 2013-14 is consistently higher than of the armed forces as a whole. This could be due to several reasons, including the operational exigencies of the armed forces which sometimes necessitate import-driven defence preparedness to overcome the time-lag and uncertainty associated with indigenous R&D projects. But what is inexplicable is the deliberate attempt by some vested interest groups to marginalise domestic R&D to gain from arms import. As K. Subrahmanyam observes, Indian R&D has often to fight the 'import lobby' and in the process overestimates its deliverables, which in turn leads to delays, cost overrun and failure also.[58] So the challenge for Indian defence R&D is not only to increase the spending but to guard against the vested interests which profit at the cost of India's own technological progress.

Table 5.10: Comparison of Underfunding between the Armed Forces and DRDO (Amounts in Rs crore)

Year	*Projection*		*Allocation*		*Underfunding*		*Underfunding (%)*	
	Armed Forces	*DRDO*	*Armed Forces*	*DRDO*	*Armed Forces*	*DRDO*	*Armed Forces*	*DRDO*
2006-07	88311	6240	83323	5454	4989	786	5.65	12.60
2007-08	96270	6931	89868	5887	6402	1044	6.65	15.06
2008-09	109841	8523	98862	6486	10979	2037	10.00	23.89
2009-10	141879	9516	131154	8482	10726	1034	5.56	12.60
2010-11	158964	11754	135950	9809	23014	1945	14.48	16.55
2011-12	199705	14843	154277	10253	45427	4590	22.75	30.92
2012-13	213413	14463	182100	10636	31314	3827	14.67	26.46
2013-14	262354	16483	192850	10610	69504	5873	26.49	35.63

Note: Projection amount represents the resource requirement projected at the time of budget formulation exercise. Allocation represents funds made available in the budget announced in Parliament.

Source: Author's database.

Monopoly of R&D

Compared to India, other advanced defence manufacturing countries encourage R&D at diverse sources that include dedicated research institutes, universities and industry. The model followed by many of these countries is one of R&D management rather than doing it by one agency. For instance, the Defence Advanced Research Projects Agency (DARPA) of the US, which has been at the heart of several radical innovations including in the areas of stealth, internet, Global Positioning System (GPS) and Unmanned Aerial

Vehicle (UAV) does not do R&D on its own. In fact, DARPA does not own a single lab of its own! Rather, it identifies great talent and ideas from industry, academia, government laboratories and individuals, and awards R&D contracts to be executed on a typical time scale of 3-5 years. DARPA's role is limited to short-listing of projects and managing the programme, which it does through 140-odd programme managers.[59]

Among other countries which are successful in cutting-edge innovation, Israel offers a test case worth examining. The giant strides that this small country has made are attributed to the Office of the Chief Scientist (OCS), which was set up in 1974 under the Ministry of Industry, Trade and Labour. OCS is responsible for executing the government's R&D policy to foster innovation and promote technological entrepreneurship. Like DARPA, OCS also awards R&D contracts to diverse sources and manages them through a small team that comprises 30 full-time employees. OCA's core principle of R&D funding is not to subsidise R&D but partially mitigate risks through government financial assistance. Interestingly, nearly one-fourth of OCS's budget (in 2011) comes through the royalties paid back by companies which have successfully converted R&D funding into marketable products.

Unlike the US or Israel, in India R&D has been monopolised by DRDO. As is generally acknowledged, monopoly breeds inefficiency. The Rama Rao Committee in its report suggested that certain amount of R&D should be promoted outside DRDO, thereby promoting a degree of competition. In specific terms, the committee suggested that DRDO's R&D grants under the four Research Boards should be increased to 10 per cent of DRDO's budget from a mere Rs 30 crore that DRDO was spending then. More significantly, the committee suggested setting up a Board of Research for Advanced Defence Sciences (BRADS) under the Scientific Adviser to the Defence Minister on the lines of DARPA of the US. However, this crucial recommendation has not been accepted by the government, even though it has gone ahead and crated a separate post of Scientific Adviser to the Defence Minister, who was supposed to drive BRADS.[60] DRDO's annual grants through its Research Boards have also not seen an increase as suggested by the committee (Table 5.11). Moreover, whatever little is spent through these boards or on extramural research, there are numerous concerns about its efficacy. CAG has noted that 'there were critical shortfalls in the management and monitoring of the scheme such as improper budgeting process, awarding the project without arriving at verifiable and specific research objectives and not defining the quantitative and qualitative targets to be attained.'[61]

Table 5.11: DRDO's Grants-in-Aid (Rs crore)

Year	*ADA*	*Research Boards*	*Extramural Research*	*Others*	*Total*
2011-12	867.0	56.6	44.1	16.2	983.9
2012-13	402.3	35.4	49.8	29.5	517.0
2013-14	640.5	31.9	60.0	32.3	764.7
2014-15 (RE)	621.0	33.8	40.6	43.4	738.9
2015-16 (BE)	650.0	94.8	65.0	60.0	869.8

Note: ADA – Aeronautical Development Agency. There are four Research Boards, namely, Aeronautical Research and Development Board (AR&DB), Life Sciences Research Board (LSRB), Naval Research Board (NRB) and Armament Research Board (ARMREB).

Source: Author's database.

Poor Innovation Ecosystem

Although DRDO is often criticised for less than expected performance, it is forgotten that DRDO is a mere reflection of India's larger innovation system, which despite having some pockets of excellence (especially in the area of nuclear and space) is largely backward. Given that DRDO depends on this large eco-system for technology, human resources and precision manufacturing, it is only natural for it to reflect this backwardness. In the following paragraphs are discussed some of the broad performance indicators of India's larger innovation ecosystem and how it impacts defence R&D.

Inventiveness in India's basic science, measured by creation of intellectual property, is low in comparison to countries like the US, China, Japan and South Korea. Table 5.12 provides trends of India's patent grants compared with China – a country which in the past two decades has made rapid progress in S&T and moved from what some observers have noted 'R&D obscurity to challenging the US (and likely succeeding) for global R&D leadership.'[62] The trend is shown in three categories: 'resident', 'non-resident' and 'abroad'. In 1997, India's number of patents granted was 49 per cent of China's. By 2011, this was reduced to a mere 4 per cent. Moreover, while China's patents are increasingly accounted for by the 'resident' category (which has surpassed the 'non-resident' category since 2009), India's performance is still overwhelmingly dominated by 'non-resident' patents.

Apart from patent, India's innovation capacity measured in terms of other parameters is also weak. This is evident from a number of composite parameters available in various studies, according to which India's innovation ranking varies between 50 and 70, depending on the parameters used. For instance, as per the joint report published by the

InstitutEuropéend'Administration des Affaires and WIPO, India is ranked 64th (out of 141 countries) in the global innovation index. The report also points out that though India ranks relatively better in terms of market sophistication (rank 46th), knowledge and technology outputs (47th) and creative outputs (34th), it fares poorly in institutional support (125th), human capital and research (131st), infrastructure (78th), and business sophistication (75th).[63]

Table 5.12: Number of Patents Granted: China and India

Year	*China*				*India*			
	Resident	*Non-Resident*	*Abroad*	*Total*	*Resident*	*Non-Resident*	*Abroad*	*Total*
1997	1532	1962	160	3654	546	1161	80	1787
1999	3097	4540	213	7850	633	1527	157	2317
2001	5395	10901	327	16623	529	1020	288	1837
2003	11404	25750	580	37734	615	911	622	2148
2005	20705	32600	870	54175	1396	2924	888	5208
2007	31945	36003	1557	69505	3173	12088	1125	16386
2009	65391	62998	3111	131500	1725	4443	1466	7634
2011	112347	59766	5817	177930	776	4392	2108	7276
2013	143535	64153	10950	218638	594	2783	3794	7171

Note: 'Resident' patent refers to a patent granted in the country to its own resident; 'non-resident' to a patent granted in the country to a non-resident; and 'abroad' to a patent granted in a foreign country.

Source: Data taken from World Intellectual Property Organisation, http://www.wipo.int/portal/index.html.en (accessed on 20 October 2015).

The *Global Competitiveness Report 2012-13,* published by the World Economic Forum, also highlights India's poor competitiveness and ranks the country 59th (out of 144 countries). Table 5.13 provides an overview of India's innovation ranking in terms of six key indicators and with respect to BRICS partners and some major industrialised economies. It shows that India is behind all the select advanced industrialised economies (US, UK and Japan) in every indicator, although it scores better than some BRICS partners in some indicators. Among other indicators, India is ahead of Brazil, China and Russia on the quality of research institutions. However, the research undertaken by such institutions does not necessarily percolate down for commercial use, because of weak linkage with industry. This is partly exhibited through India's poor score on university-industry collaboration in comparison with most BRICS partners. Moreover, none of the Indian research institutions figures in the top-50 global science institutions. According to the SCIMAGO database, which is often cited by the Indian government in various official documents, CSIR, the largest and most diverse S&T organisation under the Ministry of S&T, is currently placed 82nd globally (14th in Asia). CSIR's poor ranking has drawn the ire of parliamentarians, who have (in 2013) urged the policymakers to make an all-out effort to enable it to 'become amongst at least the first 10 global organisations in its field' within the next five years.[64]

India scores better than all the BRICS nations on availability of scientists and engineers. However, in comparison to its population, it has one of lowest densities of R&D personnel. With 137 researchers per million people, India is far behind many countries. Japan, with 5573 researchers per million people has the highest density of researchers among major S&T powers in the world. Comparative figures for other countries are US 4663, South Korea 4627, UK 4181, China 1071, and Brazil 657.[65] India also has a problem of quality of workforce. A 2007 survey by FICCI noted with concern the skill shortages in 20 industry sectors, including engineering/heavy equipment and machinery, IT, biotechnology and pharmaceuticals.[66] This in turn indicates the poor quality of Indian educational institutions, and is a matter of concern given that India has one of the largest pools of universities and technical institutes in the world (33,023 colleges, 523 universities and 40-odd Institutes of National Importance (INI) as of 2010-11).[67]

Table 5.13: Innovation Indicator: Ranking of Select Countries

Country	*Capacity for innovation*	*Quality of scientific research institutions*	*Company spending on R&D*	*University-industry collaboration on R&D*	*Availability of scientists and engineers*	*PCT patents* granted per million population*
India	42	39	37	51	16	63
Brazil	34	46	33	44	113	48
Russia	56	70	79	85	90	44
China	23	44	24	35	46	38
S. Africa	41	34	39	30	122	37
US	7	6	7	3	5	12
UK	12	3	12	2	12	18
Japan	1	11	2	16	2	5

* PCT patent refers to patent granted under the Patent Cooperation Treaty (PCT).

Source: Klaus Schwab (ed.), *The Global Competitiveness Report 2012–2013,* World Economic Forum, Geneva, 2012.

Poor Innovation System: The Crux of the Problem

One of the primary reasons for India's poor innovation index is the less than desired level of investment in R&D and its skewed funding pattern. India's total R&D spending (in purchasing power parity – PPP – terms) for 2014 was estimated to be $44 billion (Table 5.14), amounting to just one-fifth of China's (the second-biggest R&D spender since 2009[68]) and one-ninth that of the US, which leads the global R&D spending with a 30 per cent share. India's current R&D spending, although growing in absolute terms, is not commensurate with its rising economic profile and its own policy goal of stepping up the expenditure level to 2 per cent of GDP. India's global R&D ranking is 7th. The ranking goes further down when compared in terms of R&D intensity (i.e., total R&D expenditure as percentage of GDP). Among the top-10 global R&D spenders, India has the least share at 0.9 per cent of GDP, a marginal increase from 0.7 per cent in 1995-96. In comparison, China has more than doubled its R&D intensity from 0.6 per cent in 1996.[69]

Table 5.14: Top-10 R&D Spenders in the World, 2014

Country	*GERD (PPP US$ Billion)*	*R&D as % of GDP*
US	465	2.8
China	284	2.0
Japan	165	3.4
Germany	92	2.9
South Korea	63	3.6
France	52	2.3
UK	44	1.8
India	44	0.9
Russia	40	1.5
Brazil	33	1.3

Note: GERD – Gross Expenditure on R&D.
Source: Battelle and R&D Magazine, *2014 Global R&D Funding Forecast*, December 2013.

A striking feature of India's R&D spending is that unlike many other advanced countries (such as the US, Japan, South Korea and China) where 60-75 per cent R&D spending is accounted for by the business sector,[70] it is the government which takes the lead in India. However, as observed by a recent document of the Ministry of Commerce, the government-led R&D endeavours 'have had little effect in terms of enhancing the technology depths of Indian firms.'[71] This is because of several factors ranging from poor collaboration between R&D agency and industry, lack of accountability, red tape, and poor human resource base. Currently, the industrial sector in India spends a mere 0.54 per cent of its annual turnover on R&D[72] and accounts for a mere 0.23 per cent of the country's R&D intensity.[73] Nearly half of the industry's R&D spending is concentrated on two areas: drugs and pharmaceuticals and transportation, which have little relevance for defence innovation (Figure 5.1). Industrial R&D spending on defence, which although it ranks fourth, accounts for a mere 6.9 per cent.

Figure 5.1: R&D Expenditure by Leading Indian Industry Groups, 2009-10

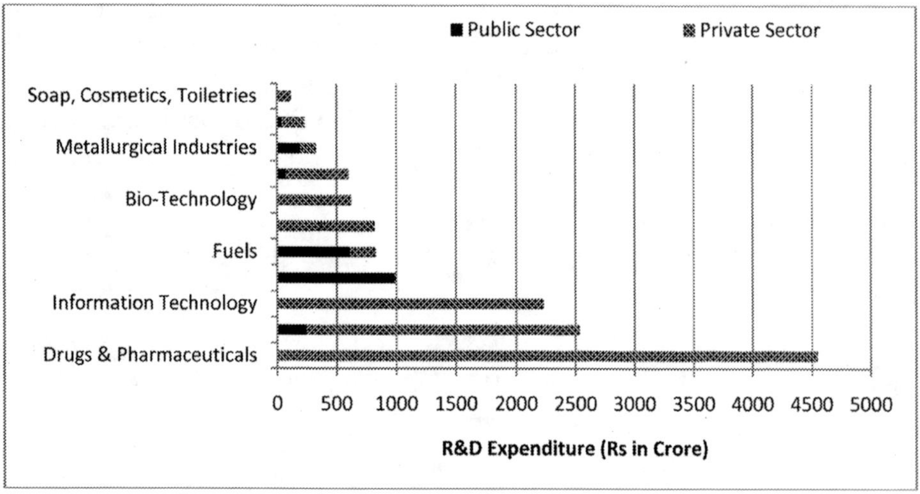

Source: Ministry of S&T, *Research and Development Statistics at a Glance 2011-12*, p. 6.

Conclusion

Various factors ranging from low financial investment to poor supervision and monitoring of projects, lack of credible human resources and users' interest in indigenous products, and poor innovation setup have caused DRDO to perform below sub-optimal level. Given that Make in India intends to spur defence manufacturing, at the core of which lies indigenous design and development, revitalisation of DRDO is a minimum necessary condition to achieve that goal. The following paragraphs make some crucial recommendations in this regard.

There is a need to set up a high-powered mechanism with the task of setting R&D goals, monitoring progress and setting accountability. This body would go a long way in bringing synergy among the stakeholders, which is lacking in the present R&D efforts. Investment in R&D, which is now around 6 per cent of the defence budget, needs to be substantially augmented, to at least 10 per cent. However, all the R&D funds may not necessarily be placed at DRDO's disposal. Alternative mechanisms for funding R&D may be pursued, preferably on the lines of DARPA of the US. The Scientific Adviser to the Defence Minister, which is now an independent post, may be entrusted with the task of heading such a body.

DRDO's human resources management needs a complete relook.

From a long-term perspective, the government may like to set up a defence technology-specific university on the lines of those set up by the departments of space and atomic energy, for developing a strong human resources base for driving defence technology.

Given that there are cross-linkages between civilian and military R&D, DRDO's performance should not be seen in isolation from India's larger innovation setup. At present, India lags not only in R&D spend but also in terms of many other innovation indicators such as patents, quality of scientific research institutions, availability of scientists and engineers and university-industry collaboration on R&D. Alleviating these concerns would go a long way in creating an innovation setup that would be conducive for defence R&D.

NOTES

1. The DSO was established in 1948 to 'advise and assist the defence services on scientific problems and to undertake research in areas related to defence.' MoD, *Annual Report 2014-15*, p. 72.
2. The Modi government has separated the dual position of DRDO chief as Secretary, Department of Defence R&D and Special Adviser to the Defence Minister, with the appointment of Dr G Satheesh Reddy for the latter post. Dr Reddy assumed office in June 2015 for a period of two years.
3. For an overview of DRDO- developed products, see Suranjan Pal and William Selvamurthy, 'Capability-building in defence science and technology: a perspective from the DRDO', *Strategic Analysis*, Vol. 32, No. 2, March 2008, pp. 259-284.
4. PIB, 'Induction of products designed by DRDO in Armed Forces', 8 May 2013.
5. DRDO, List of Technologies Transferred to Industries, http://www.drdo.gov.in/drdo/English/list-of-technologies.pdf (accessed on 19 October 2015).
6. In the early 1990s, the DRDO partnership was limited to 70 academic institutes, 50 national S&T centres and 150 public/private industries. See MoD, *Annual Report 1993-94*, p. 33.
7. See interview with Dr V.K. Saraswat, DG, DRDO, in *Defence ProAc Biz News*, May-June 2013.
8. See Interview with V.K. Saraswat, chief of DRDO, in *Engineering Watch*, March 2013, p. 9.

9. Public Accounts Committee, 13th Lok Sabha, *Action Taken Report on Design and Development of MBT Arjun*, 57th Report, Lok Sabha Secretariat, New Delhi, 2003, p. 15.
10. Aeronautical Development Agency, 'Indigenous Development of Line Replaceable Units (LRU's) for LCA-Tejas', http://www.ada.gov.in/ADA-IND.pdf
11. For the complete list of technologies, see DRDO, http://drdo.gov.in/drdo/English/List_of_Critical.pdf
12. Ministry of S&T, *Research and Development Statistics at a Glance 2011-12*, p. 4.
13. Standing Committee on S&T, Environment and Forests, *Demands for Grants: 2013-2014*, 244th Report, Rajya Sabha Secretariat, New Delhi, 2013, p. 8.
14. DRDO Newsletter, Vol. 31, No. 12, December 2011, p. 3.
15. Standing Committee on Defence, 10th Lok Sabha, *Defence Research and Development: Major Projects*, 5th Report, Lok Sabha Secretariat, New Delhi, 1995, p. 8.
16. Standing Committee on Defence, 14th Lok Sabha, *Defence Research and Development Organisation*, 14th Report, Lok Sabha Secretariat, New Delhi, 2007, pp. 39-40.
17. CAG, Report No. 16 of the Year 2012-13, pp. 54-67.
18. G. Balachandran, 'Development Direction', *Strategic Digest*, January 1984, pp. 13-51.
19. Public Accounts Committee, 13th Lok Sabha, *Design and Development of Main Battle Tank Arjun*, 5th Report, Lok Sabha Secretariat, New Delhi, 2000.
20. Standing Committee on Defence, 14th Lok Sabha, *Demands for Grants 2008-09*, 29th Report, Lok Sabha Secretariat, New Delhi, 2008, p. 75.
21. PIB, 'Final operational clearance for LCA Tejas next year: Antony', 29 May 2013.
22. PIB, 'Delay in manufacturing of Tejas by DRDO', 20 March 2013.
23. 'First LCA squadron to be stationed in Sulur: DRDO', *Zee News*, 21 September 2011, http://zeenews.india.com/news/nation/first-lca-squadron-to-be-stationed-in-sulur-drdo_732796.html (accessed on 17 July 2013).
24. Rajat Pandit, 'Army, DRDO fight it out again over Arjun and futuristic tanks', *Times of India*, 5 August 2015.
25. At the national level, India has at least four major policy documents. These include the Science, Technology and Innovation Policy 2013, Electronics Policy, Cyber Security Policy and National Manufacturing Policy.
26. Economic Advisory Council to the Prime Minister, *Economic Outlook 2013-14*, September 2013, p. 28.
27. MoD, *Annual Report 2014-15*, p. 87.
28. Sudhir Kumar Beri, 'Ordnance factory introduces indigenous version of 155mm gun', *Times of India*, 4 January 2013.
29. 'Dhanush: India's 155-mm artillery gun in trial stages', http://economictimes.indiatimes.com/slideshows/infrastructure/dhanush-indias-155-mm-artillery-gun-in-trial-stages/20-25-better/slideshow/46846409.cms
30. MoD, *Annual Report 2014-15*, pp. 61-62.
31. CAG, Design, Development, Manufacture and Induction of Light Combat Aircraft', Report No. 17 of 2015, p. 27.
32. CAG, *Union Government (Defence Services): Air Force and Navy*, Report No. 4 of 2014, pp. 134-164.
33. Standing Committee on Defence, *Demands for Grants 2015-16*, Report No. 9, pp. 46-47.
34. PIB, 'Recommendations of Rama Rao committee on DRDO', 23 April 2008.
35. Interview with Amiya Ghosh, member, Committee on Refining DRDO, 1 August 2013.

36. PIB, 'Defence Research and Development Organisation', 22 April 2013.
37. ISRO, *Annual Report 2014-15.*
38. PIB, 'Shortage of manpower in ISRO', 3 December 2014.
39. PIB, 'Recruitment of scientists in DRDO', 28 November 2014.
40. Pradip R. Sagar, 'Murdering talent, the DRDO way', *New Indian Express*, 27 December 2015.
41. A similar argument but for an earlier period is made by Ravinder Pal Singh, 'An assessment of Indian science and technology and implications for military research and development', *Economic and Political Weekly*, 29 July 2000, pp. 2762-2775.
42. PIB, 'Exodus of scientists from DRDO', 26 April 2007.
43. PIB, 'Resignation of scientists from DRDO', 5 December 2012.
44. Standing Committee on Defence, Demands for Grants 2015-16, Report No. 9, p. 22.
45. CAG, *Union Government (Defence Services): Army and Ordnance Factories*, Report No. 8 of 1995, p. 20.
46. Ibid., p. 220.
47. PIB, 'Setting up of Indian Institute of Space Science & Technology (IIST)', 26 April 2007.
48. DRDO *Annual Report 2010*, p. 139.
49. MoD, 'Defence Production Policy', January 2011.
50. International Institute for Strategic Studies, *Military Balance 2013*, p. 262; MoD, *Defence Services Estimates 2013-14.*
51. Standing Committee on Defence, 10th Lok Sabha, *Defence Research and Development: Major Projects*, 5th Report, Lok Sabha Secretariat, New Delhi, 1995, p. 4.
52. Conversion of Indian rupee into US$ is based on average exchange rate for the first five months of 2013-14.
53. US Department of Defense, *National Defence Budget Estimates for FY 2014*, p. 8.
54. Standing Committee on Defence, Demands for Grants 2015-16, Report No. 9, p. 20.
55. Nabanita R. Krishnan, 'Critical defence technologies and national security: the DRDO perspective', *Journal of Defence Studies*, Vol. 3, No. 3, July 2009, pp. 91-105.
56. Standing Committee on Defence, 10th Lok Sabha, *Demand for Grants (1995-96)*, 4th Report, Lok Sabha Secretariat, New Delhi, 1995, p. 24; Standing Committee on Defence, 10th Lok Sabha, *Defence Research and Development: Major Projects*, 5th Report, Lok Sabha Secretariat, New Delhi, 1995, p. 6.
57. US Department of Defense, 'National Defence Budget Estimates for FY 2014', pp. 10 and 262; Battelle and R&D Magazine, *2013 Global R&D Funding Forecast*, December 2012.
58. K. Subrahmanyam, *Shedding Shibboleths: India's Evolving Strategic Outlook,* Wordsmiths, New Delhi, 2005, pp. 29-41.
59. William B. Bonvillian, 'Power play: the DARPA model and U.S. energy policy', *The American Interest*, November/December 2006, Vol. 2, No. 2, pp. 39-48.
60. Lok Sabha, 'Committee on Functioning of DRDO', Unstarred Question No. 2087, answered on 11 December 2015.
61. CAG, *Union Government (Defence Services): Army, Ordnance Factories and Defence Public Sector Undertakings*, Report No. 35 of 2014, p. 87.
62. Battelle and R&D Magazine, *2013 Global R&D Funding Forecast*, December 2012, p. 4.
63. Soumitra Dutta (ed.), *The Global Innovation Index 2012: Stronger Innovation Linkages for Global Growth*, Report of the InstitutEuropéend'Administration des Affaires and WIPO, 2012.

64. Standing Committee on Science and Technology, Environment and Forests, *Demand for Grants 2013-14*, 244th Report, Rajya Sabha Secretariat, New Delhi, 2013, pp. 8-9.
65. Hugo Hollanders and Luc Soete, 'The growing role of knowledge in the global economy', in *UNESCO Science Report 2010: The Current Status of Science around the World*, UNESCO, Paris, 2010, p. 8.
66. FICCI, *Survey on emerging skill shortages in the Indian industry*, July 2007.
67. Ministry of Human Resource Development, *Annual Report 2010-11*, pp. 80-94; http://mhrd.gov.in/instiutions_imp.
68. 'OECD Science, Technology and Industry Outlook 2012', http://www.oecd.org/sti/sti-outlook-2012-china.pdf
69. Ministry of S&T of the People's Republic of China, *S&T Statistics Data Book 2001.*
70. For an international comparison of R&D spending, see US Science and Engineering Indicators 2012, pp. 4-47.
71. See, for example, Department of Commerce, Government of India, *Report of the Working Group on Boosting India's Manufacturing Exports for 12th Five Year Plan (2012-17)*, p. 171.
72. Planning Commission, Government of India, *Mid-term Appraisal of 11th plan*, p. 410.
73. PIB, 'Status of scientific research in the country', 4 March 2013.

6

Offsets

Although the Make in India initiative intends to focus on procurement from local industry, offsets, which are applicable to imported arms, would still play a key role for a foreseeable period. This is primarily because of the lengthy period of execution of offset contracts that have already been signed and a long list of pending import-centric contracts that will eventually be signed. In this context, it may be noted that 25 offset contracts valued $4.87 billion that have been signed so far will be fully executed not before 2022. Furthermore, there are 44 more contracts with potential offsets worth $15 billion that would be executed in a phased manner up to 2028.[1] In other words, for the next decade and a half, offset would continue to be a feature in India's defence acquisition even if all the future procurement proposals are executed by the local industry. However, the question is what would be the role of offsets in furthering the interest of Indian defence industry. Or can the Indian offset policy supplement Make in India by way of facilitating inflows of investment and technology transfer and high-end manufacturing work packages to Indian industry? This chapter first analyses the impact of offsets on the Indian defence industry, with a view to see the efficacy of the existing policy framework. Part II examines the design features of the Indian offset policy in the context of some of the offset practices followed by a select number of countries which include Canada, Israel, Malaysia, South Korea, Turkey and the UAE. The cross-country examination is undertaken with a view to learn from others who are supposed to have a longer experience than India in implementing offsets. It may be noted that the Indian offset policy was directly influenced by the South Korean offset policy, which was studied by the Kelkar Committee.

Evolution of Defence Offset Policy

The Indian defence offset policy, an integral part of the Defence Procurement Procedures (DPP), has evolved over a period of time since its first formal articulation in 2005. At the time of first articulation, the policy had little clarity and was rigid in its design. Nonetheless, it sets the basic tone by stipulating a mandatory 30 per cent offsets in arms import contracts valued Rs 300 crore or more – a provision which has remained unchanged for over 10 years despite the policy's revision several times. In 2006, the policy underwent a major revision, bringing out, among others, three broad avenues in which offsets can be delivered by the foreign companies. The avenues allowed them to deliver offsets through either direct purchase of defence products/services from Indian industry, or making investment in defence industrial and R&D infrastructure. The 2006 policy also brought in the much-needed functional clarity by way of stipulating various mechanisms to enable foreign vendors to devise/deliver offsets in a structured way. The major feature of the 2006 revision was, however, the creation of the Defence Offset Facilitation Agency (DOFA), a so-called single-window agency to facilitate offset-related tasks between foreign vendors and the Indian offset partners. In 2008, the policy underwent another round of revision, allowing banking of offsets through which foreign vendors were allowed to accumulate prior credits in anticipation of future contracts. The banking provision also allowed to generate surplus credit from the existing contracts for utilisation in future contracts. The 2008 revision also introduced a list of defence products for the purpose of delivering of offset obligations of the foreign companies.

Some minor changes were made in 2011, before a major change effected in 2013. The 2013 changes allowed transfer of technology and equipment through offset. It also allowed a provision of multiplier of between 1.5 and 3 for incentivising offset inflows into micro, small and medium enterprises (MSME) and for high-end technology acquisition by DRDO. The banking period, which was earlier two-and-a-half years, was extended to seven years. A provision was also made for supervision of offsets by the Defence Acquisition Council (DAC), the highest decision- making body of MoD. Apart from this, an organisational change was effected, by replacing the earlier DOFA with a new structure, Defence Offset Management Wing (DOMW) to be headed by a higher-ranking official in the Department of Defence Production (DDP) of MoD.

PART I

Impact Analysis

Till October 2014, MoD has signed 25 offset contracts valued $4.87 billion. Of the total amount, $1.37 billion worth of offset was to be discharged by March 2014, although the actual reported discharge has been valued at $840 million (or 17 per cent of the total value of offsets signed till October 2014).[2] CAG, which has audited several offset contracts is, however, not very impressed with the way offsets have been implemented. In a report submitted to Parliament in November 2012, it has brought out a variety of weaknesses, including zero value addition, equipment transfer, invalid selection of Indian Offset Partner (IOP) and weak monitoring mechanism.[3]

It is to be noted, however, that though CAG's audit findings on offsets are a useful indicator of the working of India's offset policy, they are not comprehensive enough to throw light on the policy's ultimate success or failure. The audit observations are more of fault-finding rather than seeing holistically the efficacy of the offset policy. For instance, at no point of time has CAG spoken of even a single offset contract that has worked as per the contractual terms. The aim of this chapter is to bridge this gap by examining the extent to which the Indian offset policy has impacted the objectives. While doing so, it recognises the fact that only 17 per cent offsets have been discharged and any meaningful study on the subject is somewhat premature at this juncture. It nonetheless sets a basic foundation by way of establishing an objective methodology, based on which any future study on the subject can be conducted.

Limitation of Data

The impact analysis of offsets, however, suffers from lack of credible data in the public domain. MoD has so far not come out with required details of the offset contracts it has signed. What it has given is some broad financial details, and that too when asked by members of Parliament. These details are in the nature of date of contract signing, value of the main contract and offset amount. What it has so far not revealed is the name of IOPs, the amount and kind of offsets received by each IOP and the detailed timeframe for execution of each offset contract. Lack of information of a more substantive nature hinders a precise economic analysis.

Given the data constraints, this chapter examines certain macro indicators in order to draw some broad references. This analysis is further supplemented by interviews conducted with some leading private sector companies involved in the process. The detailed analysis on these two counts, however, proceeds with a brief outline of the approach of the chapter in analysing the impact analysis followed by a description of offsets that India has singed so far.

The Approach

The chapter follows a multi-pronged approach for analysing the impact of offsets. It begins with an examination of the impact on industry as a whole, followed by an examination of two distinct players in the Indian defence industry: the established public sector and the nascent private sector. While the impact of offsets on these two distinct players is examined through a number of parameters, the impact on the industry as a whole is analysed through the prism of exports and FDI inflows, two key areas of focus since the offset policy's inception in 2005.

Offset Contracts

Of the 25 offset contracts signed so far, the IAF tops the list with 16 contracts, distantly followed by the Navy (six) and the Army (three). Among the foreign companies, the US tops the list with the maximum value of offsets. The biggest chunk of offsets has come through the Foreign Military Sales (FMS) route. The biggest offset worth $1.09 billion came from Boeing from India's purchase of 10 C-17 Globemaster aircraft.

Impact on FDI

Since 2005, the offset policy has retained a key provision by which foreign companies can discharge their offset obligation through FDI. As per the revised guidelines issued on 26 August 2014, FDI cap in the defence sector stands increased to 49 per cent from the earlier 26 per cent.[4] It is to be noted, however, that while foreign companies can claim offset credit for their equity investment in JVs, not all FDIs are necessarily directly linked to offsets. This is because of two reasons. One, the permissible FDI is cumulative one and includes portfolio investment which is not eligible for the purpose of discharge of offsets. Second, FDI can be brought in by companies which do not have (or wish to have in future) direct business with MoD.[5] The impact analysis has to therefore factor in the offset-induced FDI in order to see the precise impact. However, no such offset-induced FDI data are available in the public domain. What is available is the cumulative FDI inflows into the defence sector and a number of approved JV/FDI proposals. Between 2001 (when the industry was opened to the private sector) and October 2014, the government approved 34 JV/FDI proposals, involving mostly the private sector companies that include some of the bigger names such as Tata, L&T, Bharat Forge, Mahindra and ABG Shipyard. However, in terms of inflow of funds, there is hardly any inflow into the defence sector, although there has been an increase post-revision of FDI cap to 49 per cent. Table 6.1 shows FDI inflows into select sectors, including defence, up to August 2014, when the revised defence FDI policy was announced. As the data show, of 62 distinctly identified sectors, defence industries rank 61 with a meagre flow of Rs 24.36 crore ($4.94 million).

Table 6.2 maps the FDI inflows post-increase in FDI cap. Although the volume of inflows in eight months post-increase in FDI cap is significantly higher than the cumulative inflows in the preceding years (of more than a decade), there is no evidence of such inflows being influenced by offsets. There is not a single inflow which is brought in by companies having offset liability with MoD.

Table 6.1: Select Sector-wise FDI Equity Inflows into India (April 2000-August 2014)

Rank	*Sector*	*FDI Inflows*		*% of Total FDI Inflows*
			Rs crore	*(US$ Million)*
1	Services Sector	192,090.45	40,546.07	17.66
2	Construction Development	111,223.10	23,751.76	10.35
3	Telecommunications	80,621.20	16,499.09	7.19
4	Computer Software and Hardware	61,914.18	13,191.22	5.75
5	Drugs and Pharmaceuticals	61,443.39	12,500.42	5.44
41	Vegetable Oils and Vanaspati	2241.30	441.76	0.19
52	Timber Products	440.51	86.41	0.04
61	Defence Industries	24.36	4.94	0.00
62	Coir	22.05	4.07	0.00

Note: Services sector includes financial, banking, insurance, non-financial/business, outsourcing, R&D, tech. testing and analysis.

Source: Ministry of Commerce and Industry.

Impact on Exports

The DPP from 2008 onwards has provided a list of eligible items for the purpose of the discharge of offset obligations. The list has been expanded over the years to include both defence and civilian items. For the purpose of this chapter what is significant is that the items eligible for offset discharge broadly fall under four categories for which the Indian Trade Classification (Harmonisation System) – ITC (HS) - Codes have recently been announced (Table 6.3). Suffice to mention that these are the precise HS Code-wise categories under which various defence items are now subject to industrial licence.[6]

It is to be noted, however, that ITC (HS) codes as mentioned in Table 6.3 are broad-based and inclusive of non-defence items also. For instance, codes 8801 to 8805, which come under HS Code 88 (aircraft, spacecraft and parts thereof) also include civilian aerospace items. In other words, there are no comprehensive defence item-specific HS codes. This is, however, likely to change with the new foreign trade policy promising to 'create ITC (HS) codes for defence and security items for which industrial licences are issued.'[7]

Table 6.2: Approved JVs post-increase of FDI Cap (August 2014-March 2015)

Indian Company	*JV Company*	*Proposed Foreign Investment*	*Investment Inflow (Rs crore)*
Hats Off Helicopters Training Pvt Ltd	CAE Inc., Canada	Post Facto Approval for the issue of 5,84,205 equity shares of Rs10/- each to CAE Inc., Canada	37.82
Ideaforge Technology Pvt. Ltd.	NRI Investment	0.1704	
Punj Lloyd Ltd.	FII & NRI Investment	Foreign Shareholder NRI IPO Allottees Repatriable Investment 22.79%+NRI 2.52%+ FII 7.68%-Addition of activities	
Quest Global Mfg. Pvt. Ltd.	Aequs Mfg. Investment (P) Ltd., Mauritius	FDI 49% from existing 17.29%	40.0
Fokker Elmo Sasmos Interconnection Systems Ltd.	Fokker Elmo BV, Netherlands	FDI 49%	6.0
Star Wire Ltd.	Aubert & Duval France	FDI 5%	12.28
Total			96.1

Source: Rajya Sabha, http://rajyasabha.nic.in/ (accessed on 15 March 2015).

Table 6.3: ITC (HS) Codes for Category of Defence Items Requiring Industrial Licence

ITC (HS) Code	*Category*
8710	Tanks and other armoured fighting vehicles
8801 to 8805	Defence aircraft, space crafts and parts thereof
890610	Warships of all kinds
9301 to 9307	Arms and ammunition and allied items of defence equipment; parts and accessories thereof

Source: Ministry of Commerce and Industry, 'List of Defence Items Requiring Industrial Licence', Press Note 3 (2014 Series), 26 June 2014.

It is also to be noted that India's trade statistics as captured by ITC (HS) codes do not include defence goods 'as a matter of principle'.[8] By this principle, all the offset-induced exports as captured by these codes are essentially non-defence items.

Column 2 of Table 6.4 provides the export value of items that fall under the ITC (HS) Codes as mentioned in Table 6.3. As may be seen, there has been a hefty growth in exports to $6.3 billion in 2014-15, which is more than the cumulative value of offsets signed so far. Significantly, much of the growth coincides with the period after the promulgation of the offset policy. This may indeed sound incredible, but needs a closer examination before a reference can be drawn. It must be noted that of the total exports, exports under HS Codes 8801-8805, which broadly cater to 'aircraft, spacecraft and parts', account for an overwhelming share – 98 per cent in 2014-15 (Column 3 of Table 6.4). This is not surprising given that except for Codes 8801-8805, others mostly pertain to defence-specific items which are not captured by the trade database.

The significant jump in exports of 'aircraft, spacecraft and parts' raises a vital question: Does it mean that the Indian aerospace industry has come of age? Not necessarily, especially from the point of view of export of the major platform. As pointed out by an official of the Directorate General of Commercial Intelligence and Statistics (DGCIS), the agency of the Ministry of Commerce responsible for collection, compilation and dissemination of India's trade statistics and commercial information, some of the exports under this category are 'temporary and non-revenue earning in nature', although their precise figure is not publicly available. Explaining further, the official intimated that such exports include, among others, the satellites taken out of the country by ISRO for launch from foreign launch pads. The major portion, however, constitutes civilian aircraft and related components sent abroad for scheduled maintenance, repair and overhaul.

Table 6.4: ITC (HS) Code-wise Exports

Year	*Exports under ITC (HS) Codes 8710, 8801-8805, 890610 and 9301-9307 ($ Million)*	*Exports under ITC (HS) Codes 8801-8805 ($ Million)*
2004-05	52.0	49.8
2005-06	65.6	63.1
2006-07	86.9	77.6
2007-08	698.8	693.3
2008-09	1522.1	1467.0
2009-10	1064.7	1030.3
2010-11	1895.2	1766.4
2011-12	2351.6	2275.2
2012-13	2256.3	2210.2
2013-14	4674.6	4585.3
2014-15	6268.4	6159.6

Source: Ministry of Commerce and Industry.

In order to further probe the point mentioned by the DGCIS official, an attempt is made to examine the major components and direction of exports under the broad HS Codes 8801-8805. Table 6.5 provides the 2014-15 value of exports under the two heads 8802 and 8803, which together account for 99.1 per cent of exports under the heads 8801-8805. As seen in Table 6.5, exports under 8802, which is in the nature of platforms, are mostly to countries other than the ones which have offset obligations with MoD. On the other hand, majority of exports under 8803, which cater for mostly parts

Table 6.5: Select Country-wise Exports under ITC (HS) Codes 8802 and 8803, 2014-15 (in US$ million)

Country		*Under Code 8802*	*Under Code 8803*
Countries without Offset Liability	China	130.89	26.86
	Ireland	336.55	0.72
	Romania	137.39	0.12
	Singapore	244.51	86.43
	Sri Lanka	1744.01	1.17
	UAE	1037.60	31.24
Countries with Offset Liability	France	38.57	127.37
	Israel	...	39.91
	Italy	0.68	7.97
	Russia	...	97.82
	Switzerland	...	0.10
	UK	146.43	202.32
	US	156.19	333.81
Total		4603.90*	1497.79*

* Figures include exports to other countries not mentioned in the table.
Source: Ministry of Commerce and Industry.

and components, are accounted for by countries having offset liability with India. The question is to what extent the export of the parts and components is influenced by offsets. As seen in Table 6.6, growth of exports to countries having offset liability with MoD coincides with the period post-announcement of offset policy. In other words, offset policy seems to have promoted a huge growth in export of aerospace parts and components.

Table 6.6: Exports under ITC HS Code 8803 to Countries with Offset Liabilities (US$ million)

Year	*France*	*Israel*	*Italy*	*Russia*	*Switzerland*	*UK*	*US*	*Total*
2002-03	15.3	5.2	1.3	12.1	0.5	11.1	10.2	55.8
2003-04	15.8	2.3	1.5	3.0	0.2	24.7	6.8	54.3
2004-05	15.0	0.9	2.1	4.2	0.1	7.9	5.0	35.2
2005-06	16.9	1.4	4.7	10.3	0.4	6.8	3.6	44.1
2006-07	23.6	2.4	2.4	16.4	0.0	13.4	5.6	63.9
2007-08	98.0	30.7	13.4	45.6	0.0	35.9	83.9	307.5
2008-09	142.8	36.6	11.7	72.9	6.9	84.2	265.3	620.2
2009-10	140.1	22.0	9.2	46.0	2.2	98.4	156.3	474.3
2010-11	221.6	62.7	10.5	98.5	8.7	150.7	508.7	1061.5
2011-12	158.5	38.2	6.1	61.9	72.4	315.6	237.9	890.6
2012-13	170.7	51.5	7.5	193.5	87.7	239.9	279.9	1030.7
2013-14	165.6	44.3	10.3	74.0	43.1	115.2	343.6	796.0
2014-15	127.4	39.9	8.0	97.8	32.9	202.3	333.8	842.1

Source: Ministry of Commerce and Industry.

Impact on Public Sector Defence Production Units

Table 6.7 provides select statistics of DPSUs and OFs over a 10-year period beginning with 2004-05, the year before the formal offset policy was announced. As may be seen from the table, while the aggregate employment in DPSUs and OFs is in continuous decline, the other indicators – value of sales (VoS) and value of exports – show a near continuous increasing trend. However, the question is: to what extent are these changes attributable to the offset policy?

The answer to this question lies in the details, which need careful examination. It is noteworthy that though offsets to the tune of $4.8 billion have been signed, the actual flow into DPSUs and OFs would be less, although the precise estimation is difficult. As pointed out by CAG, a host of offsets, including several high-value ones, are in the form of equipment transfers and therefore do not contribute to the aforementioned parameters of the DPSUs and OFs. Moreover, given that offsets are open to both private and public sectors, the actual share of DPSUs and OFs in total discharged offsets would be even lesser.

Given these factors, the extent to which offsets would influence the key parameters of DPSUs and OFs is limited. This is particularly true with respect to one indicator: value of sales (VoS), the annual value of which (particularly in later years) is larger than the cumulative offset inflows since 2005. In other words, the large disparity in VoS and offsets makes the latter an extraneous factor to the former. This is also true in case of employment. Its decrease is largely due to the continuous reduction in the industrial workforce in OFs, which itself is the result of an accounting change effected in the late 1980s to bring cost consciousness in OFs.[9] Suffice to mention, between 2004-05 and 2011-12, the human resources strength of OFs has been reduced by 22,745 (19 per cent), with the industrial employees accounting for 72 per cent of total decrease.

Given the size differential, offset may have been an extraneous factor to influence the VoS of DPSUs and OFs, but it needs closer examination to see any linkage with these enterprises' exports, which is not only smaller in size but, as noted earlier, an area of clear-cut focus of the offset policy since its inception in 2005. To see any linkage, an attempt is made to look at export performance at the macro level and also of the two biggest exporters, HAL and BEL, which together account for nearly three-fourths of the exports of all DPSUs and OFs together. The underlying rationale is to see the extent to which offsets have contributed to exports and through that the overall sales. It is assumed that if offset has led to increased exports, it must be reflected in the form of rising share of exports in total sales.

As can be seen in Table 6.7, exports of DPSUs/OFs have more than doubled in a period of 10 years. However, as a percentage of total turnover, there is hardly any increase. The figure remains almost static at 1.8 per cent between 2004-05 and 2012-13, for which data for the entire public units are available. This suggests that the offsets have not yet been a key factor in the total exports of DPSUs and OFs.

The picture at the individual enterprise level is somewhat different. In the case of BEL, there has been growth in exports, both in absolute terms and as a percentage of VoS. What is more significant is that a part of the growth is led by offsets. For instance, in 2012-13, of the total exports of $32.8 million, offset-led exports accounted for 23 per cent. Moreover, of the total accumulated export orders of $200 million booked by the end of 2014-15, 22 per cent ($44 million) is accounted for by offset orders.

Table 6.7: Key Performance Parameters of DPSUs and OFs

DPSUs/OFs#	*VoS (Rs Cr)*	*% increase in VoS*	*Exports (Rs Cr)*	*% increase in Exports*	*Employment*	*% increase in Employment*
2004-05	17435.2	6.2	307.43	–27.7	192776	–2.7
2005-06	19916.8	14.2	318.76	3.7	189670	–1.6
2006-07	22046.7	10.7	439.38	37.8	186332	–1.8
2007-08	23678.1	7.4	628.15	43.0	184376	–1.0
2008-09	27237.1	15.0	854.38	36.0	180575	–2.1
2009-10	33995.9	24.8	477.76	–44.1	175164	–3.0
2010-11	36537.9	7.5	653.66	36.8	173465	–1.0
2011-12	40494.0	10.8	730.01	11.7	169556	–2.3
2012-13	40956.2	1.1	770.64	5.6	168310	–0.7
2013-14	41001.0	0.1	768.50*	1.7*	68972*	–4.2*

Note: VoS – Value of Sales; # DPSUs do not include HSL, which came under the administrative control of MoD in 2010; * Figure is exclusive of OFs.

Source: Author's database.

In the case of HAL's exports, although there has been a growth in absolute terms, there is a decline in terms of percentage of VoS (Table 6.8). This suggests that HAL's whole focus lies in the domestic front, with overall exports taking a backseat, and offsets playing almost a negligible role. In fact, the only major offset that it has received directly as a result of MoD's contracts is a mere $4.7 million order from Boeing for providing weapons bay door for the P8-I long-range maritime reconnaissance and anti-submarine warfare aircraft for the Indian Navy.[10] HAL's negligible role in offsets combined with a similar situation for DPSUs and OFs as a whole thus indicates the limited impact of offsets in promoting a key area of exports.

Impact on the Private Sector

The Indian private sector may be a late entrant to the Indian defence industry, but is its most enthused player. Anybody who has been to any of the defence-related seminars organised in recent years would have witnessed the active participation of private players, both big and small. Moreover, the industry associations, particularly the Confederation of Indian Industry (CII), FICCI

Table 6.8: Exports as Percentage of Turnover of HAL and BEL (Amounts in Rs crore)

	HAL			*BEL*		
	VoS	*Exports*	*Exports as % of VoS*	*VoS*	*Exports*	*Exports as % of VoS*
2004-05	4533.8	150.1	3.3	32112.1	36.9	0.1
2005-06	5341.5	186.2	3.5	3536.3	52.7	1.5
2006-07	7783.6	270.5	3.5	3952.7	41.4	1.0
2007-08	8625.3	341.1	4.0	4102.5	57.1	1.4
2008-09	10373.4	436.6	4.2	4623.7	72.3	1.6
2009-10	11456.7	204.7	1.8	5219.8	99.4	1.9
2010-11	13115.5	237.4	1.8	5529.7	161.7	2.9
2011-12	14204.2	348.3	2.5	5703.6	187.9	3.3
2012-13	14323.6	382.8	2.7	6012.2	166.1	2.8
2013-14	15127.9	440.0	2.9	6174.2	246.2	4.0
2014-15	15621.6	499.4	3.2	6694.6	358.5	5.4

Note: VoS – value of sales.
Source: Author's database.

and Associated Chambers of Commerce of India (ASSOCHAM), which were relatively insignificant players in the deference sector earlier are now quite actively pursuing the interests of the private industry through whatever institutional mechanisms they have to interact with the defence establishment. The question is: to what extent have the offsets stimulated the private sector's interest in defence production? One way of finding this enthusiasm is by looking at the year-wise issuance of Letters of Intent (LoI)/ILs by the government. As may be seen from Table 6.9, the number of LoI/ILs granted has suddenly jumped after the detailed offset policy was announced in 2006, indicating a strong correlation between offsets and the private sector's interest in defence production.

It is to be noted, however, that the mere increase in the private sector's interest as manifested through a hefty growth in LoI/ILs does not necessarily mean that offsets have led to actual defence production in the Indian private sector. It is quite possible that LoI/ILs are bagged by companies in the hope of getting offset business in future which may not happen in due course. This seems to be the case for a large number of companies which are yet to begin production even after getting a licence for it. Of the 251 LoI/ILs issued to 150 companies till January 2015, 101 (67 per cent) are yet to commence production.

Table 6.9: Letters of Intent/Industrial Licences Issued to the Indian Private Sector

Year	*LoIs/ILs Issued*	
	No.	*Cumulative*
2002-03	12	12
2003-04	03	15
2004-05	07	22
2005-06	06	28
2006-07	09	37
2007-08	36	73
2008-09	46	119
2009-10	8	127
2010-11	28	155
2011-12	23	178
2012-13	12	190
2013-14	20	210
2014-15 (Till Jan 2015)	41	251

Source: Author's database.

The bigger question is: what is the contribution of the 49 companies (which have commenced production) to India's overall defence production and the role of offsets in that? In the following paragraphs an attempt is made to probe this question.

On the aspect of defence-specific production or sales of the Indian private sector, it is to be noted that official information is hazy. MoD, which compiles various data for DPSUs and OFs in its annual report, does not do so for the private sector. Most of the private sector companies, especially the bigger ones, on their part also do not publicise the defence-related information. A part of the reason is that defence business of the major private companies is clubbed into their larger civilian segments. For instance, the defence and nuclear business of L&T falls under the company's heavy engineering segment, and no separate accounting is presented exclusively for the former. Similarly, Tata, which conducts its defence business through 14 group companies, does not present consolidated defence revenue separately. Among the very few major companies which present some aggregate figure is Astra Microwave Products Limited, a Hyderabad-based company engaged in design and manufacturing of radio frequency (RF) and microwave super components and sub-systems. In 2013-14, the company's defence segment accounted for 90 per cent of its revenue of Rs 544.2 crore.[11]

The lack of official information across the private sector notwithstanding, there are several market survey reports about the volume of defence business of the Indian private sector. According to one estimate, the current defence revenue of the entire private sector, including from overseas orders, is around $2 billion.[12] Among the big companies, Tata, which has a defence order book of Rs 8000 crore, generated revenue of Rs 2500 crore in 2013-14.[13] L&T's revenue from defence is believed to be Rs 1200 crore.[14] Dynamatic Technologies, a Bangalore-based company with three business verticals – aerospace, auto parts and hydraulic pumps – generated a business of Rs 1589 crore from the aerospace sector in 2013-14.

The moot question is: what is the influence of offsets on the private sector's defence production or sales? Like in the DPSUs and OFs, one way of finding out is to examine the volume and growth of exports made by the private sector. The underlying rationale is that if offsets have contributed to the private sector's production and sales, it should be visibly reflected in exports. Unfortunately, unlike for the DPSUs and OFs, the export data for the private sector are limited. Table 6.10 provides the value of defence exports for six years up to 2015-16 for which data could be obtained. As the table suggests, there has been a nearly 15-fold increase in exports, indicating the possibility of a growing influence of offsets.

Table 6.10: Defence Exports by the Indian Private Sector

Year	*Exports (Rs crore)*
2010-11	29.1
2011-12	137.5
2012-13	138.1
2013-14	286.0
2014-15	132.17
2015-16 (Up to 30 September 2015)	441.06

Note: The export figures are based on the non-objection certificate issued by MoD.
Source: Author's database.

It is to be noted, however, that the private sector's interest in offsets goes beyond immediate exports. Given that the private sector is a late entrant to defence production, many companies view offsets as a medium of not only getting business but also gaining expertise through technology transfer, working with global majors, besides getting international market visibility. Given this, it is important to know to what extent the Indian offset policy has helped the Indian private companies. In order to probe this, a questionnaire was sent to a number of leading private sector companies, of which eight companies responded. These companies are: Alpha Design Technologies Pvt Ltd, Astra Microwave Products Ltd, Dynamatic Technologies Ltd, Elcom

Group, L&T, MKU Pvt Ltd, Precision Electronics Ltd and Tata Power SED.[15] The views of the companies were sought on eight specific questions. The response of the industry is summarised below.

Of the eight companies, six said yes to receiving offsets. Of the remaining two, one company is in the advanced stage of negotiation with foreign companies but has not yet received any offsets. The other one, which despite having a significant international exposure (with 90 per cent turnover coming from exports) in homeland security products has not got any offsets so far. Of the six companies which have received offsets, in four companies, the amount of offsets as a percentage of turnover is minuscule (less than 5 per cent). In one company the share is increasing to around 15 per cent whereas in another, the share is over 50 per cent. There is almost unanimity that the said offset-related business would not have occurred without a formal policy in place, signifying the importance of MoD's offset policy in generating some defence business.

However, the quality of offset received by most companies is not significant from the point of view of capability enhancement of the Indian defence industry. The majority view of the industry is that most of the offsets are in the nature of build-to-print (BTP) in nature with little value addition done by the Indian partners. Most of the companies are also of the view that offsets have so far not been a catalyst for technology transfer.[16] Moreover, offsets are received with strings attached, in that the Indian partners are made to honour IPR of the foreign partners and abide by the non-competitive agreement that restricts the freedom of export.

PART II

Lessons from International Practices

Offsets: Threshold, Percentage and Multiplier

As a common practice, countries often define the threshold limit of the main arms contract beyond which offsets are mandatorily applicable. Countries also define the precise offset requirement by way of specifying a certain percentage of the main contract value to be mandatorily ploughed back to the domestic industry. Beyond this, countries also have a multiplier provision in their offset policy. While the threshold limit determines the scope of offsets, the latter two provisions (offset percentage and multiplier) determine the size of the offsets that can flow from the main contract. Table 6.11 summarises these conditions for a select number of countries studied in the chapter. As can be seen, except for Canada, India has the highest threshold limit. This means, unlike most other countries which demand offsets in contracts valued as low as $5-15 million, Indian industry cannot benefit from such smaller contracts unless the contact value reaches $55 million.

India has also the lowest offset percentage requirement among the listed countries. This means, given the value of an arms contract, the size of offsets that the Indian industry can get is lower than that for the other listed countries. However, this may not be true if one is to factor in the multiplier which ranges between 1.5 and 9 for these select countries. Given the wide variation in the value of the multiplier, the actual transaction value of offset can logically be different for countries having different offset percentage requirement. For instance, 100 per cent offset with a multiplier of 9 (as is the case with Canada) in a procurement contract valued, say at $900 million, results in lower offset transaction value ($100 million) than a similar contract with 60 per cent offset with a multiplier of 5 (as is the case of UAE). In the case of UAE, the actual value of offset transaction would be $108 million.

Table 6.11: Offset: Threshold, Percentage and Multiplier

Country	*Threshold Limit (US$ million)*	*Offset Requirement (%)*	*Multiplier*
Canada	100*	100	4-9
India	55	30	1.5-3
Israel	5	50	1.5
Malaysia	15	100	No multiplier**
South Korea	10	50	No multiplier
Turkey	No threshold***	70	2-8
UAE	10	60	1.5-5

Notes: * Canada, however, has the option of asking offsets in contracts valued between $2 million and $100 million. The demand for offsets in such cases is determined by three factors: '(1) Is the procurement strategic to Canadian industry? (2) Are the potential bidding companies of interest to Canadian industry and are they capable of fulfilling [offset] obligation? and (3) Is the project a smaller part of a larger one?'

** Although Malaysia does not allow multiplier as a general rule, it however considers it in 'exceptional circumstances such as when the programme acquired can lead to high-end technology acquisition or maximisation of FDI into Malaysia.'

*** In its revised policy of 2011, Turkey abolished its earlier threshold limit of $10 million, virtually giving it the power to ask for offset irrespective of the value of the contract.

Source: Author's database.

From the foregoing discussion, it appears that a lower offset percentage requirement with a lower multiplier is technically the same as a proportionately higher offset percentage requirement with a higher multiplier. However, this logic hides a critical dimension that goes beyond the simple mathematical calculation. It is noteworthy that a multiplier is used for specific areas of activities such as investment in R&D (as is the case in Israel), platform exports, technological cooperation and enabling technology specifically asked (Turkey), and high-end technology transfer (India). However, in most cases, the vendors have the discretion to choose those activities for fulfilling their offset obligations. In practice what one notices is that very few vendors choose these specific areas, because the nature of transactions is considered to be too beneficial to the buyers. This is the reason why a multiplier has been of little relevance in offset transactions at the global level. This is amply illustrated in the 17th BIS Report, which notes that out of 12,100 offset transactions made between 1993 and 2012, only 12 per cent transactions had a multiplier of greater than one. The average value of the multiplier was a mere 1.2.[17]

Since the multiplier is of lesser use, what becomes significant from a buyer's point of view is the percentage of offset requirement that determines the size of offsets that can flow to the domestic industry. This is perhaps the reason why countries like Malaysia and South Korea do not have a multiplier provision, yet have a high offset percentage requirement. India on the other hand persists with a 30 per cent offset requirement ever since the policy was first announced in 2005.

Hybrid Input-Output Model for Calculation of Offset Credit

Many countries including India allow investment as one of the means for discharge of the supplier's offset obligations. However, few countries bother to see if such investment, for which the foreign vendors earn offset credits, is having any real impact on the domestic economy. In this regard, the UAE's revised offset policy brought out in 2010 is an exception. This policy has incorporated a 'hybrid' model for the calculation of offset credit that virtually puts the onus on the foreign suppliers to ensure that a part of the offset inflows brings real benefits to the UAE economy.[18] As per the model, total offset credit is divided into two categories: inputs credits and output credits. A foreign company earns input credits when it makes an investment in UAE. The investment can take place in three broad forms: industry enablers, knowledge empowerment and equity contribution. The maximum that the foreign company is allowed to earn input credit is 30 per cent of its total obligations.

In other words, minimum 70 per cent credits are to be earned through output credits, which are given when such investment leads to export sales, net profit of the ventures in which investment is made and generates incomes (salary) for UAE nationals. Evidently, the UAE model of calculating offset credit ensures that the flow of investment leads to measurable outcome rather than being an end itself. This model could be useful for other countries which want foreign investment but have no clue how to ensure measuring outcome flowing from such investments.

Value Addition

Many countries apply the principle of value addition for the purpose of estimating the true value of offset credit which can be claimed by the foreign vendors. The value-add principle ensures that the foreign vendors get their due offset credit for the local content they are able to achieve in the buying country. Normally, the value of offset credit is equal to the value addition of a product, although some countries allow 100 per cent credit beyond a certain localisation level. For instance, Norway's 2004 policy provides 100 per cent offset credit if 80 per cent localisation or more is ensured by the foreign vendors.[19]

Many countries have formulated detailed guidelines for estimating value addition in offset transactions. Canada's Industrial and Regional Benefits (IRB) policy, which seeks offset benefits from the government's defence and security procurement, provides two methods – Net Selling Price and Cost Aggregate– to estimate the Canadian Content Value (CCV). The underlying principle of both methodologies is to ensure that 'only the Canadian labour and materials of a particular work package is counted toward an IRB contractor's obligation; all foreign overhead, labour and materials for any particular transaction is excluded from CCV.'[20]

In India value addition is determined 'by subtracting (i) value of imported components, i.e. import content in the product and (ii) any fees/royalty paid' from the final purchase/export price of the eligible products.[21] It is to be noted, however, that unlike Canada, which applies the value addition principle for both products and services, the Indian policy is restricted to products. In other words, under the Indian offset guidelines, foreign vendors can claim full credit for services-related transactions which may have 100 per cent import content. This not only gives an undue advantage to the foreign supplier but also skews the playing field to the disadvantage of the manufacturing sector.

Principle of Additionality and Causality

As Hartley and Martin rightly note, an offset agreement 'oblige[s] the foreign supplier and its sub-contractors to buy goods and services over and above what they would have bought from firms in the purchaser's economy in the absence of the offset agreement.'[22] In other words, offsets involve transactions that are in addition to the transactions made under the normal market forces and are purely caused by the new contractual obligations. The idea of offsets is therefore to create new market opportunities which would not have been possible without an offset contract. However, many countries, including India which does not have any provision in its offset guidelines to this effect, often overlook the principle of additionality and causality while awarding offset contracts. Consequently, the foreign vendors are free to claim credits for the transactions (say for purchase of goods and services) which they normally do as part of their commercial activities under the normal market forces.

Compared to India, Canada, Malaysia and UAE emphasise additionality and causality in their offset contracts. From the additionality point of view, the Malaysian policy categorically states that 'all new proposals or activities must reflect visible increment of value-add on top of the basic/mandatory needs of the main procurement contract through direct offsets and present offset recipient's capability/capacity through indirect offsets in order to be considered for offset credits. For the purpose of causality, the Malaysian policy states that 'all offset programmes must result directly from the procurement contract.'[23] The UAE policy also talks of 'expansion of existing business' and 'causality (causing business to happen)' as the minimum criteria for offset activities in order to be considered for credits.[24]

Compared to Malaysia and the UAE, Canada offers a better scientific approach to additionality and causality. From the additionality point of view, Canada applies the following methodology for the purchase of goods and services which are made from the existing Canadian vendors:

- The average of three-year purchases immediately preceding the date of identification of offset transaction by the Canadian offset authority;
- Offset credit would be awarded in each of the reporting periods, based on those purchase values which exceed the three-year average.

This methodology for calculation does not, however, apply if the product/service being purchased:

- Involves a direct work;

- Is substantially different from what was previously purchased;
- Involves a different end use (market sale, application, etc.) than what was previously purchased; or
- Follows a competitive process to re-select the Canadian supplier.

To establish the causality factor, Canadian policy provides detailed guidelines that among others require the bidder to submit documentary evidence including 'internal emails, official correspondence, meeting notes, corporate presentations or other complete or redacted documents, to prove that transactions are influenced by the offset requirement.' While the responsibility for demonstrating causality lies with the bidder, the acceptance of such claim is with the Canadian offset authorities. Among other factors, the Canadian authorities assess the causality claims based on the following three key factors:

- *Market share*: What is the market share held by an offset recipient for a particular product or service?
- *Business history*: What is the nature, intensity and longevity of any existing business relationship between the offset supplier and the offset recipient?
- *Intellectual property*: Are there any intellectual property considerations that impact on the offset provider's choice of the offset recipient?

Banking and Offset Trading

Among the seven countries studied in this chapter, except for the UAE, others have a banking provision in their offset policies, although they differ in terms of the kind of transactions allowed for banking, the extent to which banking is allowed, the validly period of banked credits and the flexibility in the use of banked credit (Table 6.12). Except for South Korea, which allows banking only for the excess transactions generated by vendors from their ongoing offset programmes, others allow banking in anticipation of future procurement programmes as well as in the event of over-achievement of credits from the ongoing programmes. The freedom to bank is unlimited in all countries except for Canada, which requires the vendors to identify a future procurement project against which the banked credits would be used; and stipulates a cap for banking amount. Vendors are allowed to bank a maximum 15 per cent of their bid price of a future contract they wish to participate in it. In case of over-achievement, the vendors are allowed to bank a maximum of 10 percent of total obligation value of an ongoing offset project, subject to a maximum of $100 million.[25] Canada also follows a stringent methodology for the validity of banked offset credit. Unlike others who allow the entire value of banked credit to remain valid for a certain fixed period (3-7 years), Canada follows a 'depreciation schedule' that reduces the value of banked credit over a period of time. 100 per cent of the value of the banked credit remains valid for the first three years, followed by 75 per cent of value between the third and fourth years and 50 per cent of value between the fourth and fifth years; the validity lapses after the fifth year.

Table 6.12: Offset Banking and Trading

Country	*Validity of Banking Period (Years)*	*Trading*
Canada	5	Not permitted
India	7	Permitted with the scope of the same contract between the main contractors and its Tier-I sub-contractors
Israel	Not less than 5	Permitted among the supplier's corporate divisions and subsidiaries
Malaysia	5	Permitted subject to a limit of 50 per cent of the new obligations
South Korea	3	The banked offset credit of subcontractors can be utilised by the main contractors provided the former participate in the 'identical main acquisition programme'
Turkey	5	Permitted to a limited extent
UAE	No provision	No provision

Source: Author's database.

The freedom to use banked credit differs from country to country. Israel and Malaysia have a liberal policy that allows the vendors to use the entire banked credit for future use. Canada, India and South Korea on the other hand allow a limited use of banked credit. Canada puts a 'limit of 50 percent of the total obligation that can be met using banked transactions.' India allows full use of banked credits, but requires minimum two contracts for utilising the entire banked credit. In South Korea, the 'ratio upon which the contractor may utilise the banked offset value against the obligations will be determined within 50 per cent by the Defence Acquisition Programme Administration (DAPA).'

Trading of banked offset credit does not seem to be a favoured option among countries. For instance Canada, which allows banking for upto five years, clearly prohibits trading of banked transaction between the companies.[26] Malaysia on the other hand allows trading, but subject to a limit of 50 per cent of the new obligations.[27]

Offset Obligations on Domestic Enterprises

In an emerging trend, some countries such as Canada, India, Turkey and the UAE subject their own companies to offset conditions when the product offered by the domestic companies includes a certain percentage of import elements. The idea is to prevent the local companies from acting as front organisations of foreign companies; and force them to develop sub-suppliers of parts and components through compulsory subcontracting. However, there is a difference in the way various countries stipulate offset requirement for their own countries. Among the countries which require their own industry to provide offsets, Canada is a useful case study. The Canadian policy does not distinguish between foreign and domestic companies as far as procurement contracts are concerned. The IRB, Canada's official offset policy, categorically states that 'any company that wins a specific Government of Canada procurement that has an Industrial and Regional Benefits (IRB) requirement must fulfil the Industrial and Regional Benefits (IRB) obligation.'[28] Since Canada stipulates 100 per cent offsets, the local companies winning contracts are also required to place business activities in the domestic industry valued at 100 per cent of the contract value. Like any other foreign companies having offset obligations, the Canadian companies are also required to meet the same set of criteria in order to become eligible. For instance, the Canadian company has to demonstrate that its offset proposals are compatible with the criteria of causality, incrementality and Canadian Content Value (CCV).

As per the Defence Offset Guidelines, Indian companies participating in Buy (Global) contracts valued at Rs 300 crore or more are required to provide offset if the indigenous content of their offered product is less than 50 per cent.[29] However, unlike Canada the Indian policy does not provide a clear framework for the local companies to discharge their offset obligations. Of the seven different avenues that the DOG provides for discharge of offset obligations, the local industry can at best use only one avenue (i.e. executing export orders) to discharge its obligations. Suffice to mention that unlike the foreign companies which can earn offset credit for investment in Indian enterprises or for the purchase order placed on Indian companies, the Indian companies cannot take credit for such types of transactions. Evidently, the Indian companies having an offset liability have a disadvantage vis-à-vis their foreign counterparts.

Apart from the offset avenue-related disadvantage, the Indian companies also face discrimination on account of the indigenisation requirement. As mentioned earlier, Indian companies participating in Buy (Global) procurement contracts are subject to offset liability if the indigenous content is less than 50 per cent. The offset liability is to be discharged at the rate of 30 per cent of the foreign exchange component of the procurement contract. From the outside it appears that Indian companies have lesser obligations than the foreign companies. However, a deeper examination would show that the Indian company has to bear a larger burden than its foreign counterpart. Unlike the foreign companies which are free to supply the final product based on parts and components sourced from anywhere in the world, the Indian company has to undertake a certain level of indigenisation, which is nothing but direct offset that it has to bear apart from the offset liability arising out of the import content. Moreover, the direct offset, indicating the level of indigenisation, is to be proved at the time of field evaluation trials.[30] On the other hand the entire 30 per cent offset liability of the foreign supplier can be discharged indirectly in the areas totally unrelated to the procured item, and the time period for discharge can exceed two years beyond the warranty period of the main procurement contract.

The discrimination of time period apart, the degree of indigenisation associated with direct offsets combined with the offset liability arising out of import content skews the playing field against the domestic suppliers. The distortion is so much that except for zero indigenisation (a theoretical possibility in which case the Indian company is a mere trader), at all other levels of indigenisation, the burden on the Indian company is more than 30 per cent, which is the total offset obligation for the foreign company. This is illustrated in Table 6.13, which shows the nature of the burden on the Indian companies at varying rates of indigenisation.

Channelling Offset

While discharging the offset obligations, the foreign companies tend to choose certain business activities which may be cost-effective for them but are of little value from the buyer's point of view. This occurs primarily due to the design of policy that gives complete freedom to the foreign companies in choosing offsets. To guard against this, countries like Turkey, Canada and South Korea have reserved a right to ask specific offsets. Turkey, which is more concerned about boosting arms exports, specifically asks foreign vendors through the request for proposal (RFP) to buy local-made defence items through the offset route.[31] Turkey's focus on arms exports through offsets seems to be yielding rich dividends. In 2012, its total arms exports were valued at $1.2 billion, placing the country among the world's 20 biggest arms

Table 6.13: Burden on Indian Companies under Buy (Global) Contract

Indigenous Content (%)	*Offset Liability, % (30% of Import content)*	*Total Burden, % (indigenous Content plus Offset liability)*
0	30	30
10	27	37
15	25.5	40.5
20	24	44
25	22.5	47.5
30	21	51
35	19.5	54.5
40	18	58
45	16.5	61.5
49.9	15	65
50	0	50
>50	0	>50

Note: It is unlikely that an Indian company offering a product with less than 30 per cent indigenous content would be issued a Buy (Global) tender to respond. In that case the indigenous content between 0 and 30 per cent (as shown in column 1 of the table) is a mere theoretical possibility.

exporters. It is believed that around 80 per cent of the arms exports are offset-induced.[32]

In its policy improvement carried out in December 2011, Canada has for the first time stipulated an Enhanced Priority Technology List (EPTL), for which a minimum 5 per cent offset is to be reserved. The List, to be stated upfront in the RFP, is intended to encourage the development of advanced technologies in the aerospace and defence sectors.[33]

In South Korea, offsets are channelled in two ways: influencing the source selection and reserving the right to nominate local companies to partner with the foreign companies. The source selection is influenced by way of stating upfront in the RFP the offsets required in each acquisition. The required offsets are divided into a number of categories, with each category having an assigned numerical value. The categories then become the basis for selecting the winner. Currently, South Korea has six categories of offsets, as given in Table 6.14. DAPA has also the provision of giving 10 points provided the foreign company agrees to give state-of-the-art technology that can be utilised in the R&D projects. As regards choosing the Korean Industry Participant (KIP) who would partner with the foreign company for discharge of offset obligations, in those cases where the foreign vendors are allowed to suggest

KIP, DAPA has the final say. By reserving the right to select KIP, DAPA ensures that the right kind of domestic industry players get the opportunity which is in the interest of the Korean industry.

Table 6.14: South Korean Offset Category and Weighted Value

Category	*A*	*B*	*C*	*D*	*E*
Weighted Value	6	4	3	2	1

Source: Defence Acquisition Programme Administration (DAPA), Republic of Korea, *Defence Offset Programme Guidelines*, January 2012, p. 9.

Establishing Long-term Relationship through Offsets

Many countries use their offset policies to force foreign companies to resort to business activities in the buyer's country through legally binding contracts, violation of which warrants penalties. However, many a time such legally binding offset-induced activities are of short duration and are not necessarily beneficial for the buyer's country in the long term. This is because the business arrangement is not often based on competitiveness to sustain the viability of the offset-induced projects after the transaction period is over. A case in point is Malaysia, which witnessed closure of certain projects after the supplier's offset obligation was over. Two such projects related to Malaysia's foreign purchase of modular suspension bridge and ACV300 armoured personnel carriers (APCs). As part of the modular suspension composite bridges, an offset investment of $1.5 million was spent on a Malaysian firm, CTRM, by way of training its workers and investing in the factory's jigs and fixtures. CTRM's role was to provide carbon composite launch rails for the bridges. However, once the offset period was over, CTRM received no further orders and consequently it was forced to shut down its factory. In the case of APC procurement, the deal involved off-the-shelf procurement of 146 APCs from a Turkish firm followed by licence production of 65 vehicles completely knockeddown (CKD) by a local firm, DEFTECH. A total of $17.5 million offset credit was claimed by the Turkish supplier for providing licence and for its investment in infrastructure, jigs, tools and a test track at the Pekan facility. Like in CTRM's case, the Pekan facility also did not receive much work to sustain its activities beyond the offset period.[34]

To prevent recurrence of such experience, Malaysia now emphasises on long-term viability of offset-induced projects. Its revised policy, announced in March 2011, categorically states that offset 'programmes proposed must be economically and operationally sustainable after the [offset] discharge period.' Post the 2011 revision, it is now the responsibility of the vendors to justify to the Malaysian offset authorities the sustainability of the projects they propose to undertake through the offset route.

The offset policy followed by Israel emphasises heavily on establishing long-term partnership with foreign companies. To build such partnership, its policy focuses on two broad principles: proactive guidance by the Israel offset authority and competitiveness of Israeli industry to work with foreign companies. Unlike offset authorities of many countries, the Industrial Cooperation Authority (ICA) – the offset agency under the Ministry of Economy – takes extra care in facilitating offset-related interaction between the domestic industry and foreign companies. The idea is to identify areas of cooperation and the best Israeli companies which can work on offset projects efficiently. Some of the roles that ICA plays include:

- Assistance to overseas companies in identifying and locating suitable Israeli manufacturers and partners for JVs, outsourcing, R&D and other modes of cooperation and strategic partnerships with Israeli industry
- Providing information about Israeli industry
- Conducting surveys related to Israeli industry
- Coordinating visits by representatives of Israeli industry to foreign companies
- Coordinating visits by representatives of foreign companies to Israel in order to survey local industry
- Organising conferences between foreign companies and Israeli industry.

Israel acknowledges that any long-term relationship with foreign companies cannot sustain without the best Israeli company being in the loop.[35] Accordingly, it allows a competition within the domestic industry so as to allow the best company to partner in an offset project. Israel's stated policy seems to be yielding long-term value for the domestic industry. As stated by the outgoing chief of Israel's offset authority, 'on each $1 of [offset] obligation, we tend to secure about $3 or even $4.'[36]

ICA's model for establishing long-term partnership, especially through a proactive role in cementing the domestic industry's long-term relationship could be a lesson for other countries which, despite having a dedicated offset authority, are often found constrained to play the role of a true facilitator. For instance, India's DOFA, or its successor, DOMW, are never heard of performing the functions that ICA does.

Offset Swapping

In an emerging trend, South Korea is one of the few countries which allows offset swapping. The swapping is allowed to support the domestic industry with offset obligations in a foreign country. Either the domestic industry or the foreign partner having an offset obligation in South Korea can approach DAPA to consider a swapping proposal.[37]

Beyond Defence: Offset Policy at the National Level

Some countries, including India, operate offset policy in the narrow prism of defence procurement only. In other words, the offset requirement is not applicable for the non-defence sector. South Korea and Israel are among those countries whose offset policy is applicable for procurement at the national level for both defence and civil procurement. In the case of Israel, the offset requirements, enshrined in its official Industrial Cooperation (IC) guidelines, are applicable for any procurement by the state, government corporations and public agencies when their value of purchase of foreign goods or services exceeds $5 million. Moreover, Israel is in the process of bringing municipal authorities under the offset purview. This would subject contracts for sewage treatment projects, water treatment, power systems, etc. to mandatory IC conditions.[38]

Israel's (and for that matter any country's) offset policy at the national level, however, brings out a critical issue which merits some explanation. The issue is related to the international norms set out by WTO. Israel is a signatory to the WTO's Government Procurement Agreement (GPA).[39] The GPA, which is in force since January 1996, is a legally binding agreement among the signatory members (42 as of 2013) to promote cross-border government procurement of goods and services. The Agreement prohibits discrimination against foreign suppliers in government procurement. Article 16 of the GPA specifically forbids use of offsets for 'qualification and selection of suppliers'. However, an exception is provided under Article 23 on national security grounds, which allows virtually unrestricted use of offsets in military contracts.

GPA is plurilateral in nature, meaning its applicability is limited to the GPA signatories. In other words, GPA is not legally binding on the remaining 117 members of WTO (including India[40]) who are not signatories of GPA.

It is also to be noted that though Article 16 of GPA prohibits offsets in government procurement, it still gives special exemption to the developing counties to 'negotiate [at the time of accession] conditions for the use of offsets, such as the requirements for incorporation of domestic content.' However, such offset 'requirement shall be used only for qualification to participate in the procurement process and not as criteria for awarding contracts.'[41]

Although Israel is a developed country it has managed to retain the rights to demand offset in civil contracts also. Israel's offset rights seem to have been allowed under the window of negotiation provided for negotiation for each party within the GPA group. The negotiation allows a party to negotiate the list of the government agencies and the goods and services which are open to bidding by all GPA members. Since the list is agreeable to all the parties, asking offsets from others also means giving the same rights to others. Keeping this in view, Israel's offset threshold for civil contracts within the GPA framework is different from the threshold limits for non-GPA members and for military contracts. These are mentioned below:

- Defence and security purchases require an undertaking of at least 50 percent of the foreign content value.
- Civil procurements from countries that are signatories to GPA will be subject to a requirement of 20 percent of the foreign content value.
- Civil purchases from non-GPA countries are subject to Industrial Cooperation amounting to 35 percent of foreign content value.

Israel's dynamic threshold limits for offsets could be a useful tool to learn from for countries like India, which aspires to become a member of GPA, and is contemplating a national offset policy.[42] When it becomes a member of GPA, its offsets requirement as enshrined in MoD's DPP would be insulated by article 23 of GPA on the national security grounds. And being a developing country it could bargain at the time of accession as to the list which it wants to subject to international bidding with offset requirement.

Implementation and Monitoring

One of the trickiest issues associated with offsets is related to management of offsets, particularly with respect to implementation and monitoring. Loopholes in these two areas could be counterproductive, as is found by CAG, which undertook a critical study of 16 offset contracts (valued Rs 18,444.6 crore) signed by India between 2007 and 2011. CAG observed invalid selection of Indian Offset Partners (IOP); zero value addition by the IOP; award of the offset contract in violation of the stipulated provisions; and weak monitoring of offset projects. Interestingly, CAG's observations were attributed largely to weak management of offsets.[43]

To manage offsets, Canada has set up an IRB directorate within the Aerospace, Defence and Marine Branch of Industry Canada. The directorate is the single-window agency for managing offsets. The management responsibility includes deciding the applicability of offsets, evaluating the offset proposal, and giving credit for offsets discharged. Evidently, the power to implement and monitor is at one place, even though the main procurement contract is signed by another agency.

Israel has also an organisational structure similar to that of Canada for managing offsets. Its Industrial Cooperating Authority (ICA), which is under the Ministry of Economy, is the nodal agency for management of offset. Under the Israeli law, the ICA is authorised to ensure that the foreign procurement (valued at $5 million or more) undertaken by any government entity is in compliance with the mandatory offset requirement. Although it is not directly responsible for signing the contract, it has the responsibility, as a first step in managing offsets, to vet the offset undertaking form which is part of the tender document. Post-signing of the main contract, the ICA is completely responsible for enforcement of the foreign vendors' contractual obligation. The ICA's functions include communication with the foreign suppliers; receiving periodic reports from the vendors and assigning credits based on the progress in implementation; and granting extension of time period if required.[44] Evidently, the ICA acts as a single-window agency for everything related to offsets.

Turkey and South Korea have also dedicated agencies for offsets, namely the Undersecretariat for Defence Industries (SSM in Turkish abbreviation) and DAPA of South Korea. Unlike the IRB and ICA, SSM and DAPA are not confined to their defence ministries; their role goes beyond offsets to include defence industrial development, acquisition and R&D management. Being the single agency for the entire range of tasks including offsets, these agencies are believed to be more agile and faster in decision-making.

In India, there is no single agency for managing offsets. DOFA or its successor DOMW, which functions under MoD's DDP, performs a part of the functions, the others being diffused among the service headquarters and the Acquisition Wing of the Department of Defence. Evidently, there is no single point of accountability.

Conclusion

Despite the limitations of data, the balance of evidence as brought out in this chapter suggests a mixed impact of offset policy on the Indian defence industry. On the positive side, the offsets seem to have made an impact on certain types of exports, which include the exports of civilian aerospace items (particularly parts and components), defence exports of the private sector and exports of BEL. On the negative side, offset has not been a catalyst in influencing FDI inflows, a key objective of the policy. Offset has also not been a catalyst in bringing ToT or meaningful manufacturing to the industry. The impact on exports is largely confined to parts and components of civil aerospace items, not the platforms. Considering that manufacturing and technology are the heart of an industry like defence, it is imperative that MoD focuses its policy accordingly. This aspect assumes importance given that over $3 billion worth of signed offsets are yet to be discharged.

NOTES

1. Dhirendra Singh Committee Report, p. 114.
2. Standing Committee on Defence, *Demands for Grants (2014-15)*, Report No. 2, Lok Sabha Secretariat, New Delhi, 2014, pp. 27-28.
3. CAG, Report No. 17 of 2012-13, pp. 17-25.
4. Ministry of Commerce and Industry, 'Press Note No 7 (2014 Series)', 26 August 2014.
5. It is to be noted, however, that in such a case, the foreign company can utilise the banking provision allowed in the offset policy for future discharge.
6. DIPP, 'List of defence items requiring industrial licence', Press Note No.3 (2014) Series, 26 June 2014.
7. Ministry of Commerce, 'Highlights of the Foreign Trade Policy 2015-2020', pp. 15-16.
8. Ministry of Statistics and Programme Implementation, *Statistical Year Book India 2015* (Chapter 18). According to an official of the DGCIS, interviewed on 22 April 2015, if the exporter/importer mentions that the trade is for defence purpose, the trade is not captured in the database; if the exporter/importer certifies that the trade is not for defence purpose, the data are captured in the database.
9. Amiya Kumar Ghosh, *India's Defence Budget and Expenditure Management in a Wider Context*, Lancer Publishers, New Delhi, 1996, p. 222.
10. Boeing, 'Boeing teams with Hindustan Aeronautics Limited for P-8I Weapons Bay doors', News Release/Statements, 11 February 2011, http://boeing.mediaroom.com/2010-02-11-Boeing-Teams-With-Hindustan-Aeronautics-Limited-for-P-8I-Weapons-Bay-Doors.
11. Astra Microwave Private Ltd, *Annual Report 2013-14*, p. 33.
12. Tommy Wilkes, 'Indian firms tool up for defence orders on Modi's "Buy India" pledge', *Reuters*, 20 August 2014, http://www.reuters.com/article/2014/08/20/us-india-defence-idUSKBN0GK2AQ20140820
13. Suman Layak, 'Top Guns', *Economic Times Magazine*, 20-26July 2014.
14. Cuckoo Paul, 'L&T: armed but commissioned', *Forbes India*, 29 September 2014, http://forbesindia.com/article/boardroom/lt-armed-but-not-commissioned/38703/1
15. The author would like to thank Nitin Arora of Emkay Global Financial Services Ltd for his valuable assistance. Due to the sensitivity involved, many companies did not want

explicit use of their names. The views presented in the paper are therefore not ascribed to any particular company.

16. Interestingly, an official of a large company interviewed mentioned receiving technology through the non-offset route. He further mentioned that when a successful business case is presented, there is likelihood of obtaining technology, irrespective of the offsets.
17. Bureau of Commerce and Security, US Department of Commerce, *Offsets in Defence Trade*, 17th Study, February 2013, pp. 4, 21.
18. Offset Programme Bureau of United Arab Emirates, *Defence Contractor Offset Guidelines*, http://www.idp.ae/en/agreements/Offset%20Policy%20Guidelines.pdf
19. Norwegian Ministry of Defence, *Guidelines for Establishing and Implementing Offset in connection with Procurement of Defence Material from Foreign Suppliers*, September 2004, p. 4.
20. Industry Canada, 'IRB Eligibility Criteria', http://www.ic.gc.ca/eic/site/042.nsf/eng/h_00043.html
21. MoD, *Defence Procurement Procedure 2013*, p. 46.
22. Stephen Martin and Keith Hartley, 'UK firms' experience and perceptions of defence offsets: survey results', *Defence and Peace Economics*, Vol. 6, 1995, p. 124.
23. Malaysian Ministry of Finance, *Policy and Guidelines on Offset Programmes in Government Procurement* (2nd Edition), March 2011, p.4.
24. UAE Offset Programme Bureau, Defence Contractor Offset Guidelines, 2010 to 2011 Edition, p. 9.
25. Industry Canada, 'Banking of industrial and regional benefit transactions', http://www.ic.gc.ca/eic/site/042.nsf/eng/00035.html
26. Industry Canada, *Industrial and Regional Benefits: Model Terms and Conditions*, Version 3.0, 2013, p. 31.
27. Malaysian Ministry of Finance, *Policy and Guideline on Offset Programmes …*, n. 23, p. 8, http://mides.mod.gov.my/index.php/info/pekeliling/pekeliling-offset; DAPA, Republic of Korea, *Defence Offset Programme Guidelines*, January 2012, p. 18.
28. Industry Canada, 'Frequently Asked Questions', http://www.ic.gc.ca/eic/site/042.nsf/eng/00015.html#q14
29. MoD, *Defence Procurement Procedure 2013: Capital Procurement*, p. 46.
30. It is to be noted, however, that the DPP is not clear as to how and when the Indian companies would show the indigenous content.
31. Undersecretariat for Defence Industries, Ministry of National Defence, *Industrial Participation/Offset Guidelines*, April 2011, p. 9.
32. Carola Hoyos and Antoine Amann, 'Turkey builds domestic defence industry', *Financial Times*, 9 October 2013, http://www.ft.com/intl/cms/s/0/837ef75a-1980-11e3-afc2-00144feab7de.html.
33. Industry Canada, 'New Approach: Enhanced Priority Technology List', http://www.ic.gc.ca/eic/site/042.nsf/eng/00062.html
34. Kogila Balakrishnan, 'Evaluating the role of offsets in creating a sustainable defence industrial base: the case of Malaysia', *The Journal of Defence and Security*, Vol. 1, No. 1, 2000.
35. Israeli Ministry of Economy, 'Industrial Cooperation in Israel', http://www.moital.gov.il/NR/exeres/B204AC95-046B-4458-ACF3-41F965386044.htm
36. Barbara Opall-Rome, 'Israel's offsets soar; more local firms earn a share', *Defense News*, 19 January 2013.
37. DAPA, *Defence Offset Programme Guidelines*, n. 27.

38. Israeli Ministry of Economy, 'Guidelines for Industrial Cooperation in Israel',http://www.moital.gov.il/NR/exeres/85C96324-328D-40FC-9E8A-78B6CC5F6E7E.htm
39. WTO, 'Parties and observers to the GPA', http://www.wto.org/english/tratop_e/gproc_e/memobs_e.htm
40. India has an observer status in GPA.
41. See Article XVI of WTO, 'Agreement on Government Procurement',http://www.wto.org/english/docs_e/legal_e/gpr-94_e.pdf
42. Amit Sen, 'Govt mulls offset policy for purchases from foreign firms', *Hindu Business Line*, 18 November 2013.
43. Report of CAG for the year Ended March 2011, *Union Government (Defence Services): Air Force and Navy, Compliance Audit*, No. 17 of 2012-13, pp. 17-25.
44. Israeli Ministry of Economy, 'Industrial Cooperation in Israel', http://www.moital.gov.il/NR/exeres/B204AC95-046B-4458-ACF3-41F965386044.htm

7

Review of Policy Recommendations

Post-Kargil conflict, India has set up a number of committees to look into various aspects of national defence, including indigenous defence production and self-reliance. The author is aware of at least 10 committees/taskforces which have delved into the latter aspect (Table 7.1). However, common to the fate of the reports of many government-appointed committees on national security, their recommendations have hardly been implemented in time or in their totality. Worse, several of these reports are not put in the public domain, thus preventing a wider public debate. In the following paragraphs, an attempt is made to review the policy recommendations of the various committees on self-reliance. The review is based on the author's interaction with some of the members of the committees and/or on information available in the public domain. It is restricted to the 6 committees including the Dhirendra Singh Committee which was appointed by the Modi government to make suggestions for promoting the Make in India initiative in the defence sector.

Group of Ministers

In pursuance of the Kargil Review Committee (KRC) Report, the then Prime Minister set up a Group of Ministers (GoM) in 2000 to review national security in its entirety and the KRC recommendations in particular. Four Task Forces – one each on intelligence apparatus, internal security, border management and management of defence – were constituted to assist the GoM. The Task Force on Management of Defence, headed by Arun Singh,

Table 7.1: Select Committees on National Security post-1999

Report	*Chairman*	*Year of Submission*	*Status of Report*
Reforming the National Security System*		2001	Declassified
Towards Strengthening Self Reliance in Defence Preparedness; Revitalising Defence Public Sector Undertakings and Ordnance Factories	Vijay L. Kelkar	2005	Partly declassified
Improving Defence Acquisition Structures in MoD	N.S. Sisodia	2007	Classified
Redefining DRDO	P. Rama Rao	2008	Yet to be declassified
Defence Expenditure Review	V.K. Misra	2009	Yet to be declassified
National Security	Naresh Chandra	2012	Yet to be declassified
Defence Modernisation and Self-Reliance	Ravinder Gupta	2012	Yet to be declassified
Restructuring of HAL	B.K. Chaturvedi	2012	Yet to be declassified
Committee of Experts for Amendments to DPP 2013 Including Formulation of Policy Framework	Dhirendra Singh	2015	Declassified
Selection of Strategic Partners**	V.K. Aatre	2015	Declassified

Note: * This is the report of the Group of Ministers (GoM) consisting of then four cabinet ministers of home affairs, defence, external affairs and finance.
** For critical review of Aatre Task Force, see Annexure B.

former minister of state for defence, made a number of vital recommendations, including the creation of the post of Chief of Defence Staff, which were made part of the final report after being processed in several Inter-Ministerial Group meetings and detailed discussions with the chiefs of the armed forces, DRDO and Department of Defence Production. On the defence industry and self-reliance front, the task force emphasised three key aspects: long-term planning and coordination among various stakeholders; efficiency of defence R&D; and entry of private sector in defence industry.

Defence Minister's Council on Production

The GoM assessed that India's defence industry, on which 'huge investments' have been made over the years, is constrained in delivery due to the absence of planning and coordination among various stakeholders. It, therefore, recommended setting up a high-level Defence Minister's Council on Production (DMCP), which would be responsible for laying down 'the broad objectives of long-term equipment policies and planning on production and simplification of procedures' to facilitate domestic industry participation. The council would comprise all the stakeholders of the defence establishment including the Chief of Defence Staff (CDS), a new post recommended to replace the existing Chief of Staff Committee (COSC) which was found to be 'ineffective in fulfilling its mandate'. Other members from the defence establishment which the task force recommended to be part of the council included the chiefs of the three services, Defence Secretary, Secretary (Defence Production), Scientific Adviser to the Defence Minister, Vice Chief of Defence Staff (VCDS), and Financial Adviser (Defence Services). To ensure that the DMCP reflected the broader S&T areas, particularly from the nuclear and space domain, the membership was also recommended to include the secretaries of the Department of Space, DAE and Department of S&T. The membership was also visualised to include eminent industrialists from the private sector so as leverage its expertise toward building a stronger national defence industry. The GoM recommended the Directorate of Planning and Coordination in the DDP to undertake the additional function of being the Secretariat for the Defence Minister's Council.

New Procurement Management Structures and Systems

As part of the implementation of the report of the GoM, MoD set up what it called a 'new Procurement Management Structures and Systems'. However, what came to define this new management structure and system was a tiered system for procurement planning and a number of hierarchical organisations to execute the plan. The main organisational structure that came into existence was the Defence Acquisition Council (DAC) headed by the Defence Minister, with other members being the three Service Chiefs, Defence Secretary, three secretaries of Defence Production, DRDO and Defence Finance, Chief of Integrated Defence Staff and Director-General, Acquisition (DG Acq). Under the DAC are three boards: Defence Procurement Board (DPB), Defence Production Board and Defence R&D Board headed by the Defence Secretary, Secretary (Defence Production) and Secretary, Defence (R&D), respectively. The DAC is responsible for giving in-principle approval to the 15-year Long Term Integrated Perspective Plan (LTIPP), five-year Services Capital Acquisition Plan (SCAP) and all major capital acquisition projects. The decisions of the DAC are to be executed by the three boards depending on the nature of the proposal. Among the three boards, the DPB approves the Annual Acquisition Plan (AAP) (a subset of SCAP) and deals with all matters concerning capital acquisition. The DPB is assisted in its functioning by the Director General Acquisition, who is supported by a dedicated Financial Advisor (Acquisition) and a number of joint secretary-level officials drawn from the civil and military bureaucracy (Figure 7.1).

The DPB and Defence R&D Board come into the picture when the acquisition proposal entails an element of indigenous development and manufacture. The DPB, headed by Secretary Defence Production, overseas activities in the capital acquisition related to the industrial component of indigenous manufacture, whereas the Defence R&D Board, headed by Secretary DRDO looks into the developmental and technology aspects of indigenous manufacturing.

Figure 7.1: Organisational Structure for Defence Capital Acquisition

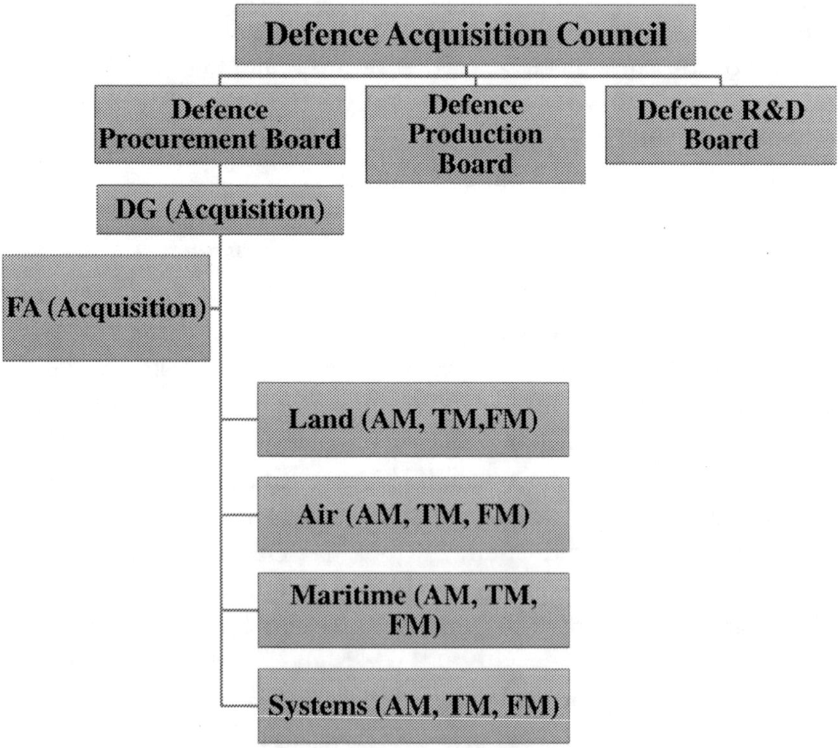

Defence Acquisition Council

Defence Procurement Board

Defence Production Board

Defence R&D Board

DG (Acquisition)

FA (Acquisition)

Land (AM, TM,FM)

Air (AM, TM, FM)

Maritime (AM, TM, FM)

Systems (AM, TM, FM)

Note: AM – Acquisition Manager; TM – Technical Manager; FM – Finance Manager.

It is to be noted, however, that the new management structure/system is not what the GoM visualised. What it visualised was a dedicated structure and clear-cut procedures for boosting indigenous production. What was established was, however, an elaborate structure and procedures for procurement dominated by the Defence Procurement Procedures (DPP) and the DPB under which functions the all-powerful office of DG (Acquisition). Compared to DPB, two other boards (DPB and Defence R&D Board), which were supposed to spur indigenous arms production, have been sidelined to the extent of their virtual non-existence. It may be noted that unlike for procurement for which there exist various plan documents (such as LTIPP, SCAP and AAP), there are no concomitant plan documents for production and R&D boards to execute. Consequently, the focus on in-house production has been a missing link in the new management structure and system.

Private Sector Participation

The GoM was of the firm opinion that the Indian private sector, which has made giant progress post-economic liberalisation, can be harnessed towards building a strong domestic defence industrial base. For this, it recommended that the DDP in consultation with all concerned should examine the issue further. Among others, measures to provide a level playing field to the private industry were to be examined urgently. To provide a fillip to private sector participation in the defence industry, the GoM made a specific recommendation to rationalise the defence export policy. The group was of the strong view that a proactive export policy would not only generate employment opportunities, but would go a long way in achieving economies of scale that would benefit the large defence industrial cause. Such exports could also be used selectively for furthering India's relationship with target countries. The GoM also noted that the DDP, which was already engaged in an exercise to review the export policy in consultation with other ministries concerned, particularly the Ministries of External Affairs, Finance and Commerce and private industry, should complete the exercise in six months' time. However, it took nearly 15 years for MoD to finally articulate a Defence Exports Strategy and a set of guidelines for granting no objection certificate to the industry for exports.

R&D

The GoM recommended that collaborative ventures with private sector participation would be required to be institutionalised to instil a spirit of competitiveness and result orientation in both R&D and production. Specific areas where the participation of the private sector was desirable would need to be identified and time-bound action taken.

Regarding DRDO, the GoM observed:

> DRDO needs to focus more on core technologies, in which expertise is neither available within the country nor can be procured from alternative sources. At the same time, on a case to case basis, short term R&D on

> parts, components and sub-assemblies can be undertaken by the PAs [production agencies] and in certain cases also by the Services. DRDO could provide necessary expertise/guidance to facilitate their successful completion by the PAs and Services, on an 'as required' basis. In due course of time, some of the PAs can be considered for designation as nodal agencies for development and production of platforms, with the required technical support being provided by DRDO. There is need to rationalise DRDO laboratories and to create a close knit interface between specific laboratories on the one hand and production agencies/service entities on the other. A group to be headed by Secretary DDP&S and comprising Scientific Adviser to Raksha Mantri and three Service Chiefs should examine this rationalisation and make its recommendations expeditiously to the Defence Minister for his consideration.[1]

These recommendations have, however, not been implemented yet, with DRDO retaining monopoly on every aspect of defence R&D and the industry not gearing towards R&D.

Kelkar Committee

Three years after the GoM submitted its report, the government constituted another committee under Vijay L. Kelkar, then an adviser to the Finance Minister. Unlike the GoM whose mandate was broad national security, the mandate of the Kelkar Committee was specific to the defence industry. The terms of reference were to suggest measures to facilitate Indian industry's participation in the defence procurement process, harmonise the interest of the armed forces, MoD and the industry (both public and private), and to increase defence exports, include offset provisions in procurement contracts, and strengthen DPSUs and OFs to assume the role of system integration. The committee included representatives of diverse backgrounds, including members from the private sector, think tanks, armed forces and MoD.

The Kelkar Committee submitted its report in two parts in 2005. Part One, titled *Towards Strengthening Self-reliance in Defence Preparedness,* contained 40 recommendations, including the following:[2]

- Preparation of a 15-year long-term plan forming the basis for the acquisition programme
- Sharing of long-term capital acquisition plan of the armed forces with the domestic industry
- Identification of entry points for the private sector in the acquisition process

- Identification of Raksha Udyog Ratna (RUR)/Champion from the private sector
- Policy framework to promote participation of small and medium enterprises (SMEs) in defence production
- Setting up a dedicated and professional agency to undertake defence acquisition
- Defence R&D opportunity both with DRDO and the industry
- Provision of offsets for procurement contracts valued at Rs 300 crore or more
- Re-examine the concept of negative list for defence exports and setting up of an export marketing organisation.

The committee carried out an 'Impact Analysis' of its recommendations. Taking 2003-04 as the base year in which the domestic share in total procurement budget was 58 per cent, the committee was of the firm view that the reform measures proposed by it would lead to progressive increase in the domestic share to 90 per cent in a period of five years. The committee identified three major economic benefits – higher manufacturing output, additional generation of employment and savings through relatively reduced procurement cost of indigenous products – that would accrue to the wider economy. The details of the economic benefits as identified by the committee are as follows:

- Higher defence production would accelerate the growth of the overall manufacturing sector by 8-14 per cent
- Increase of employment by 120,000-200,000
- Savings of 30-50 per cent as a result of import substitution and cheaper cost on account of spares and maintenance. In absolute terms, this would translate into saving of more than Rs 4,000 core per year.

Part II of the Kelkar Committee report, *Revitalising Defence Public Sector Undertakings and Ordnance Factories*, contained 19 recommendations, including the following:

- OFs
  - o All OFs should be corporatised under a single corporation (corporatisation does not necessarily mean privatisation)
  - o The corporation should be accorded *Navratna* status
  - o The corporatisation could be on the lines of Bharat Sanchar Nigam Ltd
  - o The existing dispensation by the government to the OFs should

continue for a period of three years to help them steer the changed process internally

- DPSUs
    - o HAL and BEL should be accorded *Navratna* status
    - o BEML and MDL may be accorded *Mini-ratna* status by relaxing the eligibility criteria
    - o Except MIDHANI, all other DPSUs may be allowed to invest in foreign companies with the objective of obtaining hitherto non-available technology
    - o DPSUs should explore the possibility of mergers and acquisitions in order to achieve economies of scale and remain globally competitive.

The report of the Kelkar Committee has so far drawn the maximum attention of MoD, with several recommendations having been implemented or accepted for further action. Recommendations which have not been accepted for implementation mostly pertain to Part II of the report.

The major recommendations which have been implemented include: entry point for the private sector in the acquisition process; articulation of guidelines for shared development cost in Make projects and introduction of offset clause in arms import. The major recommendations which have been accepted for further consideration include: sharing a public version of the armed forces' capability perspective plan with the industry, guidelines for selection of Raksha Udyog Ratna (RUR), review of DRDO by an independent committee and constitution of a committee to recommend restructuring of the acquisition organisation. Acting upon the RUR recommendations, the government came out with a set of guidelines for selecting RURs. A committee was also constituted (in May 2006) to identify a number of private companies which could be accredited RUR status. The recommendations of the committee have not, however, been implemented.

Restructuring the Acquisition Wing of MoD

The Kelkar Committee also recommended examining the possibility of restructuring the acquisition wing of MoD on lines similar to the direction générale de l'armement (DGA), the French defence procurement organisation. DGA is a highly professional and integrated body with a staff strength of about 9800, 50 per cent of whom are engineers and managers. With a procurement budget of €11.5 billion for 2014, DGA is responsible for the entire cycle of project management, including the tasks of design, procurement and test-evaluation of systems. It is also responsible for promoting export orders (€8.06 billion in 2014) on behalf of French industry.[3]

The Kelkar Committee was of the view that a professional organisation on the lines of DGA would go a long way in establishing synergy among various stakeholders (armed forces, civilian bureaucracy in MoD, R&D agency and industry). The committee was also of the view that such synergy is necessary to provide an optimum 'materiel solution' once the capability requirements of the armed forces are finalised. From the industry point of view, the synergy among the stakeholders provides an opportunity to participate in solutions from the very beginning after a capability gap is identified. This in turn provides adequate time for long-range developmental and production planning for indigenous solutions, wherever feasible. The proposed outfit could be named as the Indian Defence Acquisition Organisation (IDAO), the committee said.

Sisodia Committee[4]

Following the Kelkar Committee recommendation, MoD set up a committee under the chairmanship of then Director General, IDSA, N.S. Sisodia, who in his previous posting in MoD was in charge of DPSUs and was the authour of the first DPP articulated in 1992. Although the Sisodia Committee's report focused more on the structure and procedures of defence acquisition, it also contained vital recommendations, including some innovative suggestions on promoting the domestic defence industry's participation in the procurement process. Some of the domestic industry-centric recommendations are discussed in the following paragraphs.

Involvement of Industry in the Defence Acquisition Process

The Sisodia Committee was of the view that the involvement of the domestic industry in the defence acquisition process from its earliest stage is a necessary condition for greater self-reliance. The entry point for the industry in the process is the finalisation stage of the long-term defence capability plan (covering a 15-yer period) when the industry can be invited to suggest a range of options to meet a capability gap. Prior consultation with the industry, the committee argued, would sensitise planners about what could be available domestically and what needed to be bought from outside to thwart a likely threat in the future. Informed decisions including regarding lifecycle costs could also be taken on the basis of a broad-based cost-benefit analysis of various options. If an indigenous solution was found feasible and cost-effective, the capability plan could accordingly be prepared to give an opportunity to the domestic industry.

In addition to involving industry players in the consultation process while preparing the capability plan, the committee also recommended that a public version of the capability plan be shared with wider industry and defence and scientific communities. It argued that the sharing of long-tem plan with industry would provide adequate time to the players concerned to plan and invest in the required infrastructure.

Involvement of Industry in Formulation of QRs

Qualitative Requirements (QR) have been a source of concern in India.[5] QRs, which constitute the starting point of the country's defence procurement, are often formulated by aggregating the best features of many weapon systems available in the global market. Consequently, the requirements are often projected beyond the minimum capability requirements of the armed forces and even the industrial might of global players. The domestic industry hardly gets a chance to participate in the process of acquisition of weapons having such demanding QRs, even though they have the capability to meet the minimum requirements. To give a fillip to the domestic industry in the acquisition process, the Sisodia Committee made a strong pitch for the industry's involvement during the preparation of QRs.[6] The committee argued that efficiency in QR formulation would not only lead to faster and better procurement, it would also promote greater self-reliance by realistically projecting the requirements keeping in view the domestic industry's potential. Like in the capability plan, the industry could be invited to offer suggestions about the domestic industrial capabilities to meet the minimum inescapable requirements of the armed forces. Informed decisions could be taken based on the interaction with the domestic industry.

Re-designation of DDP

The Sisodia committee was of the view that the existing Allocation of Business Rules of DDP was not consistent with its responsibility, which has been expanded with the entry of the private sector since 2001. The committee argued that since the private sector has an important role to play in defence production, its interest should also be protected by DDP. To create a level playing field between the state-owned enterprises and the private sector, the committee recommended that DDP should be re-designated as Department of Defence Industry. The re-designation was to be accompanied by concrete measures to reflect DDP's expanded role. One of the measures suggested was to assign the present additional secretary in the revamped DDP the task of looking after the private sector's interests. The committee also suggested that the designation of joint secretary-level officials in DDP, who are in charge of the PSUs concerned, should also be changed to reflect their wider role. For instance, JS (Shipyard), who looks after the four MoD-owned shipyards, should be changed to JS (warship production) to extend his purview to the private shipyards also. Similarly, JS (HAL) could be re-designated as JS (Aircraft Production).

Defence Industrial Policy Statement

Drawing upon the experience of advanced countries such as the UK and Australia, which periodically announce defence industrial policy statements, the Sisodia Committee recommended a similar exercise to be undertaken by MoD. The committee expressed the view that a high-level policy statement would go a long way in clarifying the government's intention in nurturing the domestic industry in view of the changing environment. The UK MoD, for instance, brought out a revised industrial strategy statement, Defence Industrial Strategy (DIS) in 2005 to reflect the global security environment post-Cold War, and the evolving transnational nature of the defence industry.[7] The DIS emphasises two aspects: the need to retain sovereign capability in certain key areas and sourcing the rest from a wider global market. The DIS thus provides the industry early policy clarity and informed decisions can be made by the industry to meet the government's objectives.

Rama Rao Committee[8]

As a follow-up action on the Kelkar Committee recommendations, the government set up a committee in February 2007 under the chairmanship of Dr. P. Rama Rao, former Secretary, Department of S&T, to review and suggest measures to improve DRDO's functioning. The committee was mandated to review the organisational structure and to recommend necessary changes in the institutional, managerial, administrative and financial structures for improving the functioning of the premier R&D organisation. The committee submitted its report on 7 February 2008.

The committee noted that despite notable success in the strategic programme (nuclear and missiles in particular), DRDO's role in defence procurement has remained as insignificant as ever. This is evident from the overwhelming share of import and licence production in Indian defence acquisition. The committee also noted that over the years, DRDO's mandate – as stipulated in the government's *Allocation of Business Rules of 1961*[9] – in rendering scientific advice to the authorities concerned had been diluted, leading to, among others, an import-driven procurement process. The committee urged a demonstration of leadership similar to that displayed during India's independence struggle to enable DRDO to focus on its mandate and attain technological independence for the country. It highlighted the need for an unambiguous self-reliance policy articulated by higher authority and quantitative targets to achieve that. There were many missing links in indigenous defence R&D, including lack of synergy among the three key branches of the defence establishment (i.e. DRDO, industry and users), DRDO's rigid financial, organisational and management structure, thinner distribution of scarce resources on non-core areas, and incentive-free human resources policy pursued by DRDO.

To overcome the problems facing DRDO, the Rama Rao Committee made a number of recommendations, including the creation of a Defence Technology Commission (DTC) with the Defence Minister as its head; decentralisation of DRDO management; making DRDO a leaner organisation by merging some of its laboratories with other government-funded institutions with similar disciplines; engagement of a human resources expert to revamp DRDO's human resources; and setting up of a commercial arm of DRDO. The committee also recommended creating a Board of Research for Advanced Defence Sciences (BRADS) to function like DARPA of the US. The committee expressed the belief that BRADS would be at the core of stimulating advanced research by accessing and utilising the best available human resources across the country and outside. The committee also recommended the continuation of design and development of combat aircraft by the Aeronautical Development Agency (ADA), which is an autonomous society under DRDO; continuation of the Kaveri aero-engine programme; development of MBT Arjun, Mk-II and Akash Mk-II programmes by DRDO; and selection of industry partners by DRDO through a transparent mechanism.[10]

An in-house committee was constituted under the chairmanship of the Defence Secretary to 'examine' the recommendations of the Rama Rao Committee report regarding their acceptability. This committee's report was approved for implementation by the Defence Minister on 12 May 2010. The committee's recommendations, especially those pertaining to the creation of DTC, are still in the bureaucratic process. The proposed DARPA-likebody, which was first mooted by the Kelkar Committee and then suggested by the Rama Rao Committee in the form of BRADS, does not find a place in the Defence Secretary-led report.

V.K. Misra Committee

In 2009, MoD set up the Defence Expenditure Review Committee (DERC) under the chairmanship of V.K. Misra, former head of the Finance Division of MoD, to recommend measures to curb wasteful expenditure in defence.[11] The committee's report is yet to be declassified, but certain details have been made public by MoD and the media. In a written reply to Parliament in November 2010, the Defence Minister informed that one of the mandates of the DERC was to recommend measures to achieve higher self-reliance by 'tapping the strength of the vibrant private sector'.[12]

According to media reports, the DERC has suggested a host of specific measures for not only strengthening the private sector but also to bring about reforms in the broad defence industrial sector, including DPSUs, OFs and DRDO. Among others, the DERC has made the following recommendations:[13]

- The private sector should be encouraged to become tier-I players. The government should also encourage it through various measures, including government support to takeover foreign defence firms.
- FDI in the Indian defence industry should be increased to 49 per cent across the board and to 74-100 per cent on a case-by-case basis. This was the first time that an MoD-appointed committee recommended an increase in FDI in the defence industry. Previously, the Ministries of Finance and Commerce had argued for such an increase.
- A time-bound disinvestment plan may be worked out for each DPSU so as to promote transparency, accountability and efficiency
- A Defence Advisory Committee may be set up in MoD.

The DERC also fully supported the recommendations of the Rama Rao Committee on strengthening defence R&D. It also recommended peer review of major DRDO projects every one and a half year interval.

Dhirendra Singh Committee

In a significant departure from its accustomed ways, MoD has made public the report of the 10-memebr Experts Committee that was set up in May 2015 to evolve a policy framework for facilitating Make in India within the purview of DPP.[14] The report was put in the public domain even before the government has taken action on its key recommendations.

The committee included members from all the key stakeholder institutions: the armed forces, various wings of MoD (DDP, Department of Defence and DRDO), and the industry. Chaired by Dhirendra Singh, a former Director General (Acquisition), the committee had also the benefit of the expertise of another former DG (Acq.) – Satish B. Agnihotri – who has had hands-on experience of DPP-2013, the latest procurement manual in vogue for capital acquisition. The committee interacted with a vast range of stakeholders including industry (both domestic and foreign), various wings of the defence establishment, thinks tanks and others. The 263-page report was submitted to the government within three months of the committee's convocation.

The report has seven chapters, as follows: Defence Materiel; Defence Industry; Make in India; DPP; Trust and Oversight; Beyond DPP; and Enabling Framework and Summary of Observations and Recommendations.

Key Recommendations

The report contains 43 recommendations. Of these, the committee identifies 15 as pertaining directly to Make in India while the remainder relate to DPP. However, given that many of the DPP provisions have a direct impact on indigenous arms production, the industry-related recommendations (both direct and indirect) are therefore more than what the committee has identified. Some of the key recommendations that would have an impact on Make in India are as follows:

Strategic Partnership Model

The signature recommendation of the committee pertains to various models for the private sector. After taking into account the unique nature of defence equipment and the configuration of the global defence industry, the committee has arrived at three models for the Indian setup – Strategic Partnership, Developmental Partnership and Competitive Partnership. The choice of the model should be based on 'strategic needs, quality criticality and cost competitiveness'.

Strategic Partnership (SP) is somewhat akin to the Raksha Udyog Ratna (RUR) concept, first mooted by the Kelkar Committee. The RUR concept failed to take off apparently due to objections from trade unions affiliated with DPSUs and reservations expressed by some industry players on the manner in which the Prabir Sengupta Committee had identified a dozen or so companies as RURs. Like the RUR concept, the SP model also visualises selective identification of a few big private players and nurturing them through preferential treatment, which would entail co-opting them for Buy and Make and government-to-government procurement programmes.

The committee has identified the following six segments for SP with the private sector:

1. Aircraft: fighter, transport and helicopter and their major systems.
2. Warships of stated displacements, and submarines and their major systems.
3. Armoured fighting vehicles and their major systems.
4. Complex weapons which rely on guidance systems to achieve precision hits, which may include anti-ship, air defence, air-to-air, air-to-surface, anti-submarine, land attack.
5. Command, control, communication and computers, intelligence, surveillance, target acquisition and reconnaissance.
6. Critical materials (titanium alloys, aluminium alloys, carbon composites, nickel/cobalt alloys, etc.).

The committee has categorically suggested that just one or two private players would be identified in each segment. In order to prevent 'conglomerate monopoly', it has further suggested that only one SP should be permitted in one segment, and once it is chosen in a particular segment it should not be considered directly or indirectly (through cross holdings in another company) in the other segments.

Industry-friendly Procurement System

A major focus of the Expert Committee is on streamlining the acquisition process and structure so as to create more opportunities for the local industry. The committee argues that for Make in India to succeed, the procurement system must recognise the unique and strategic nature of defence equipment, which is characterised by high-technology content, stringent quality standards, limited vendor base, low production rate, rapid obsolescence and restricted mobility across borders. For the local industry to prosper, there is a need to take it into confidence in every possible procurement step, beginning with the planning process. The committee has suggested that the relevant information as contained in various plans and other documents be shared with the industry with the sole objective of enabling it to make a concrete decision on investment or technology partnership. It has suggested the revision of the current Technology Perspective Capability Roadmap (TPCR) so as to reflect the type and nature of the equipment required by the armed forces in the next 15 years. The committee has also suggested that schemes amenable to Make projects be shared with the industry along with the details of other schemes as contained in the five-year Services Capital Acquisition Plan (SCAP).

The committee is of the view that for the Indian industry to contribute meaningfully to Make in India, the procurement system needs to move towards indigenous design, development and production or Make projects. It argues that since Make projects involve a long-gestation period, the decision on such projects must precede that of other categories by at least one plan period (five years) or more. Such pre-positioning of Make projects would give much-needed leeway to the industry and the services to iron out any issue that may arise at the developmental stage without significantly disturbing the planned induction schedule. The eligibility criteria for soliciting expression of interest (EoI) from the industry should be liberal to include not only the big players but also all the 'innovative and agile industry' including from the Micro Small & Medium Enterprises (MSME) sector. Moreover, the industry executing the Make project should be given tax incentives by way of allowing its developmental cost (of 20 per cent) as being qualified as R&D expenditure.

For the local industry to grow, the current approach of the procurement system towards single vendor situations needs a relook. Single bid situation is an emerging reality, particularly in cases involving Buy and Make and Buy and Make (Indian) projects. Rejecting such proposals for the sake of competition not only delays acquisition, but hampers the interest of the local industry which is now expected to play a much larger role under Make in India. Aligning with the concept of SP, the committee therefore recommends suitable changes in DPP to reflect the emerging reality.

There has been an increase in the last two years of the share of Buy (Indian) and Buy and Make (Indian) categories (see Table 7.2). The committee attributes this to a critical change brought in DPP-2013, which provides a higher preference to these categories over others. To build on the progress, the committee has suggested a 'decision flow chart' to be incorporated in the

DPP that would guide the procurement authorities to arrive at suitable procurement categories in a more credible way and consistently.

Commenting on the existing procurement structure, which was set up in pursuance of the implementation of the 2001 report of the GoM, the committee notes that 'time is ripe for a second set of reforms'. It argues that the existing structure neither has the mandate nor the expertise to further the interest of the local industry, which is expected to play a larger role under Make in India. A specialised organisation, physically separate from MoD, would go a long way in bridging this gap. The committee also suggests that the functionaries posted in the organisation should have a longer tenure and be well trained for which a detailed curriculum should be prepared by the Headquarters Integrated Defence Staff (HQ IDS).

Table 7.2: Category-wise Acceptance of Necessity (AoN)
(Rs crore)

Year	*Buy (Indian)*	*Buy & Make (Indian)*	*Make (Indian)*	*Buy & Make*	*Buy (Global)*	*Total*
2010-11	60835	16710	15845	19450	40547	153387
2011-12	28561	2032	0	5747	20500	56840
2012-13	18689	385	1004	13460	27114	60652
2013-14	21001	2733	0	3504	371	27609
2014-15	38318	72750	0	0	6759	117827
Total	167404	94610	16849	42161	95293	416317

Emphasis on Greater Indigenisation

The Experts Committee is of the view that Make in India should not 'become assemble in India with no IPR and design control and thereby perpetuating our dependence on the foreign suppliers.' To guard against such a situation, it has emphasised on progressively increasing the indigenisation content, to be ensured not only through DPP-driven procurement but also by entities like DRDO, DPSUs and OFs. The committee has specifically suggested that these need to imbibe an indigenisation culture and reflect it in their sourcing of parts, components and raw materials and also the final product. To ensure greater indigenisation through the DPP route, the committee has suggested an incremental upward revision of the local content requirement stipulated in various procurement categories in successive DPPs. For DPP-2016, the committee has recommended that the ingenious requirement under Buy (Indian) and Buy and Make (Indian) should be increased to 40 per cent and 60 per cent, respectively, from the present 30 per cent and 50 per cent. And for Make (Indian) projects, the indigenisation content should be increased from the present 30 per cent to 40 per cent.

In cases where the domestic capability is minimal and where the local industry is likely to face difficulties in achieving the stipulated local content, the committee has given the flexibility to the procurement authorities to lower the local content requirement. And in systems in which local capability is relatively developed, the authorities would have the option of enhancing the indigenisation requirement.

Human Resource Development

The committee has made a number of vital recommendations for enhancing human resources in India's defence industrialisation process. These include setting up a defence manufacturing sector skill council, initiating a joint MoD-industry sponsored internship programme, a provision to enable skill development through the offset route, setting up of tool rooms around defence industry clusters, and a university programme for military engineering. To address the human resources issues affecting India's defence R&D establishments, the Rama Rao Committee had suggested the creation of a dedicated defence technology university on the lines of the ones set up by the Department of Space and DAE. The Prime Minister had also promised in his Aero India 2015 address to 'set up special universities ... to cater to our defence industry, just as we have done in atomic energy and space'. The committee has neither referred to the Prime Minister's address nor to the Rama Rao Committee report.

Conducive Financial Framework

The committee has laid much emphasis on creating a conducive financial framework for the private sector, to do business in the defence sector. It has taken note of the concerns voiced by the private sector on various aspects of taxes, duties, payment terms, exchange rate variation and cost of capital, which render its products uncompetitive vis-à-vis the products of public sector companies as well as foreign vendors. The committee has also taken note of the discrimination towards the defence manufacturing sector vis-à-vis other sectors such as power, telecom, refinery, etc., which enjoy a host of tax benefits and other incentives. One of the glaring discriminations meted out to the local entities is in the domain of offsets, according to the committee. It has observed that the current taxation policy prevents the development of in-house system integration capacity through the offset route as foreign companies do not find it cost-competitive. The committee has suggested that deliveries by the Indian Offset Partners (IOP) may be covered under the list of 'declared goods' and also given the 'deemed export' status, which will provide the necessary incentive to foster local capability in the high-end spectrum of defence manufacturing. The committee has also suggested various other incentives for the local industry, including the benefit of 300 per cent weighted tax deduction for its contribution towards Make projects.

Other Recommendations

The committee's other recommendations include provisions:

- To prepare a competency map of local capability and a registry of Indian industry to facilitate decision-making.
- To allow foreign companies to discharge offset obligations through subscription to defence-specific venture capital funds.
- To consolidate the four DPSU shipyards (MDL, GRSE, GSL and HSL) into one corporate entity to take advantage of the single management of a large entity.
- To issue tenders to Indian companies having IL in the relevant domain.
- To allow private sector companies access to public-funded R&D infrastructure and testing and proof firing ranges.
- To provide liberalised funding to MSME though MoD's proposed Technology Development Fund (TDF).
- To develop a robust quality assurance and standardisation system.
- To set up an independent body to ensure single-window clearance for defence exports.
- To create a single-window mechanism to provide regulatory and other clearances to the industry to do business under the Buy (Indian) and Buy and Make (Indian) projects.

The committee has also endorsed the recommendations of past committees with regard to corporatisation of OFs and setting up of an export arm of DRDO on the lines of the Antrix Corporation of ISRO.

Besides, the committee has recommended the formulation of a 10-year roadmap for the local industry, giving specifically measureable targets to achieve. The task of formulating the roadmap is assigned to the DDP. The outcome of such an exercise is, however, in doubt as there is no high-powered institutional mechanism to enforce the objectives of the roadmap.

Recognising the absence of an institutional mechanism as a major handicap in India's defence industrial growth, the GoM had suggested the creation of a Defence Minister's Council on Production (DMCP), with its membership drawn not only from the top leadership of the defence establishment but also from other high-end S&T ministries/departments as well as local industry. The DMCP was visualised to lay the long-term roadmap and ensure that every possible roadblock for its implementation was removed. However, like the RUR concept of the Kelkar Committee, and the idea of a dedicated technology university of the Rama Rao Committee, the idea of DMCP has not been referred to by the Dhirendra Singh Committee.

What Next?

While making a host of recommendations, the Dhirendra Singh Committee has been cautious in assessing their impact on the domestic industry. It has therefore set 2027 as the target year by which the elusive goal of 70 per cent self-reliance can be achieved. Incidentally, the target year coincides with the term of the current Long Term Integrated Perspective Plan (LTIPP) 2012-27 of the armed forces. Evidently, if the armed forces are to be inducted with 70 per cent indigenous equipment by 2027, the recommendations of the committee have to be implemented in right earnest and in the least possible timeframe. The government has done the sensible thing by placing the complete report in the public domain, thereby opening its subsequent actions on each of the committee's recommendations to public scrutiny. All eyes would now be on MoD as to how it proceeds with the committee report. In this regard, DPP-2016, which would have the opportunity to incorporate most of the recommendations, would be a key to see the government's seriousness.

NOTES

1. 'Reforming the National Security System', Recommendation of the Group of Ministers, February 2001 , p. 111.
2. Standing Committee on Defence (2008-09), 14th Lok Sabha, *Indigenisation of Defence Production: Public-Private Partnership*, 33rd Report, Lok Sabha Secretariat, New Delhi, pp. 78-88.
3. Frédéric, 'French defence exports rose 17% in 2014', *Jane's Defence Weekly*, 12 February 2015.
4. The section is largely based on an interview with N.S. Sisodia, Chairman, Defence Acquisition Committee.
5. For a detailed overview of the QR-related problems, see Laxman Kumar Behera, 'India's defence acquisition system: need for further reforms', *The Korean Journal of Defense Analysis*; CAG, *Defence Services, Army and Ordnance Factories, Performance Audit Report* No. 4 of 2007, pp. 10-12.

8

An Agenda for Make in India

The Make in India initiative, launched by the Modi government, has no doubt provided a fresh lease of life to India's moribund defence industry, which for several reasons has remained a gross underperformer, leading to India's high arms import dependency. Under the ambit of Make in India, the government has undertaken several reform and other 'ease of doing' business measures. These include relaxation of the FDI cap, streamlining of industrial licensing, articulation of defence export promotional measures and a degree of tax reforms, among others. Most of these measures are confined to the private sector. There is hardly any measure taken to revitalise the state-controlled entities, which despite their lacklustre performance would remain key players in India's self-reliance drive. Moreover, the private sector remains hobbled by several challenges. The following paragraphs summarise the key issues and reforms that the government needs to pursue in a time-bound manner, to give a fillip to this vital sector and make the Make in India initiative a truly transformational slogan.

Set up a Make in India Council within MoD

A fundamental weakness of India's tryst with self-reliance has been the absence of a strong overarching institutional mechanism to set out policy goals, bring on-board various stakeholders (the users, the R&D agencies and the industry) to a common platform, monitor the progress of indigenous projects and fix accountability. This gap has been pointed out by both the Group of Ministers

6. QRs are a set of technical/operational specifications that a weapon system is requ have/achieve.
7. UK Ministry of Defence, *Defence Industrial Strategy: Defence White Paper*, July 2(2.
8. This section is largely based on an interaction with Amiya Ghosh, former Financial A Defence Services, MoD, and member of the Rama Rao Committee.
9. Details of Allocation of Business Rules are available at Cabinet Secretariat, Govern of India, http://cabsec.nic.in/showpdf.php?type=allocation_download
10. PIB, 'MoD announces major DRDO restructuring plan', 13 May 2010.
11. Standing Committee on Defence (2009-10), 15th Lok Sabha, *Demands for Grants 2 11*, 12th Report, Lok Sabha Secretariat, New Delhi, 2010, p. 18. For the compositic the DERC and its mandate see 'Discussion with Defence Expenditure Review Comm (DERC), Centre for Land Warfare Studies, 16 January 2009.
12. PIB, 'Defence Expenditure Review', 15 November 2010.
13. Josy Joseph, 'Panel proposes FDI hike in defence sector to 49%', *DNA*, 29 Decem 2009.
14. The report of the committee is available at the MoD website, http://www.mod.nic. forms/Sublink1.aspx?lid=2228&Id=0

(GoM) and the Rama Rao Committee, which have suggested the creation of such a high-powered institution under the chairmanship of the defence minister. However, such an institution is still to see the light of day, although the government has established the Defence Acquisition Council (DAC) under which are two boards: Defence Production Board and Defence R&D Boards. The two boards are more or less dysfunctional and the DAC, as the name suggests, is geared more towards acquisition rather than focusing on defence industrialisation. Consequently, several high-value projects are undertaken in an adhoc manner with little oversight from the top. The Future Ready Combat Vehicle (FRCV) is the latest example of this adhoc decision-making and shows how a project of national importance can be in direct conflict with the indigenous design and developmental efforts.

Make in India has provided a fresh opportunity to relook the need for an overarching institution. The government may like to convert the DAC into a Make in India Council with the added responsibility of approving the long-term R&D and manufacturing policy and plan, besides revitalising the existing boards for timely execution.

Articulate an R&D and Manufacturing Plan

The armed forces have a system of drawing defence acquisition plans that cover three distinct time periods: 15-year Long Term Integrated Perspective Plan (LTIPP), five-year Services Capital Acquisition Plan (SCAP) and two-year roll-on Annual Acquisition Plan (AAP). These plans are approved by MoD, giving a degree of sanctity to the projects listed in the plan documents. In contracts to these plans, there are however no concomitant period-wise comprehensive R&D and manufacturing plans encompassing DRDO, DPSUs, OFs, private sector and other S&T centres which are approved by the government. Consequently, a situation is created by which the domestic R&D and manufacturing entities become clueless as to which and when projects listed in the acquisition plans would finally come to them. Given that defence R&D and manufacturing involves a long gestation period besides investment decision, advance planning and technology tie-up, it is imperative that MoD articulates an approved R&D and manufacturing plan. At the same time, it is also vital that plans are communicated to the domestic entities well in advance so as to enable them to get ready when the tendering process begins.

Appoint an Additional Secretary within the DDP for the Private Sector

In its existing setup, the Department of Defence Production is confined to state-owned enterprises although its area of interest, as mandated in the amended Allocation of Business Rules of the Government of India, encompasses the entire defence industry, including the private sector. The DDP's confined role is due to the continuation of an administrative system where the officials look after the DPSUs and OFs, with senior officials being on their governing boards. This has led to a conflict of interest wherein the DDP is often accused of protecting government-owned enterprises, much to the annoyance of the private sector. The frustration of the private sector has been reinforced even under the Make in India environment when MoD, breaking its own commitment, awarded two big projects worth Rs 40,000 crore to the public sector shipyards.

With frustration increasing, the private sector has of late demanded a shift of administrative responsibility of the entire defence industry to the Prime Minister's Office which is perceived as being successful in managing the space and atomic energy sectors. Given that the private sector has a vital role in armament production, the DDP's existing setup needs to be redefined. Among others changes, the DDP needs to have dedicated officials headed by an additional secretary to look after the private sector.

Reform the OFs and DPSUs

The DPSUs and OFs have so far been the dominant players in Indian defence production but have not been able to meet the growing requirements of the armed forces, with the gap between India's defence procurement (both revenue and capital) and supplies of these entities rising to over 50 per cent. Besides, there are a host of concerns regarding their functioning. In terms of productivity, R&D, technology absorption and new product design and development, value addition, capacity utilisation, price and quality of products, they have a long way to go. So far, there was no pressing need to overcome these concerns as they had near monopoly over defence production. However, with Make in India focusing on a major role for the private sector and competition in the tendering process, DPSUs and OFs would have no choice but to drastically improve their functioning to stay relevant. At the same time, the government also needs to examine their management and other concerns for their long-term benefit.

The OFs, the biggest and oldest departmentally run organisation, needs to be corporatised, as suggested by the Kelkar Committee. Although corporatisation is not the ultimate panacea (as seen in the context of the DPSUs which are corporate entities), it is nonetheless the first step for further reforms that can be undertaken through systematic disinvestment of their equity and, if necessary, ultimate privatisation. In addition to corporatisation, some of the factories, which have lost relevance due to high overhead cost and the availability of efficient and alternative capacity in the private domain, need to be shut down or handed over to the private sector on a public-private partnership basis. This will not only make the OFB a lean and mean organisation but also give a huge push to the private sector, which will have a readily available infrastructure and skilled human resources to jump start its defence production.

For the DPSUs, a roadmap needs to be drawn out by which all the unlisted entities would be listed in the stock market, so as to bring in an enhanced level of governance and transparency. BEL and BEML, which are listed in the stock market, may at the same time be disinvested further with the objective of bringing the government's equity in them to 51 per cent. At the same time, a roadmap may be prepared to completely privatise these entities in the future.

Revitalise DRDO

With little R&D carried out in the industry and other agencies, DRDO has been synonymous with India's defence R&D. The organisation despite its pockets of excellence (especially in the areas of nuclear and missiles) has not been very successful in providing a range of equipment to the armed forces. At present it faces a number of challenges, including lack of policy direction, absence of an approved R&D plan, low investment, poor human resources management and a poor ecosystem not conducive to achievement. Addressing these challenges holistically would be a key to revitalise DRDO. The following specific suggestions are made in this regard:

- Increase DRDO's share in the defence budget to 10 per cent.
- Allocate at least 10 per cent of DRDO's budget (i.e. one per cent of overall defence budget) for promoting R&D on the lines of DARPA of the US or OCS of Israel.
- Set up a defence technology-specific university to cater for long-term specialised human resources requirements of DRDO.

- Set up a comprehensive review of human resources with reference to the multiplicity and increased complexity of DRDO projects. At the same time, ensure that DRDO brains are assigned to the work they are best at.
- Create a mechanism for increased number of higher appointment of senior armed forces officials in DRDO.
- Institute third-party review system for each of the major DRDO projects to ensure greater accountability.

Provide Conducive Financial and Procurement Framework to the Private Sector

The private sector has come a long way since 2001, when the defence industry was liberalised. It has shown not only a great deal of interest in the sector by way of getting ILs and forming JVs, but also has shown capability in winning contracts against both the domestic and foreign players. However, the journey of the private sector has been anything but smooth. The difficulty in getting ILs, lack of level playing field vis-à-vis foreign companies and established state-owned entities, import/DPSU/OF-centric procurement and non-operationalisation of Make and Buy and Make (Indian) projects have been some of the major hurdles. Although Make in India has so far attempted to allay some of these concerns, there are still many financial and procurement-related obstacles that need to be overcome. The following are recommended in this regard:

- Provide infrastructure status to investment by the private sector as has been given recently to the shipbuilding and ship-repair industry.
- Provide price preference to the domestic manufacturers vis-à-vis foreign companies.
- Provide the right of first refusal to the domestic enterprises.
- Include defence manufacturing under the Harmonised List of Infrastructure Sectors.
- Grant deemed exports status to sales under Buy (Global) and offsets.
- Extend the present 200 per cent weighted tax deduction benefit to the entire value chain of R&D covering R&D in laboratory, pilot production, test beds, design and development, standardisation, field trials and pre-commercial trial production.
- Extend the LC-based payment system to the private companies, as is given to the foreign companies.

- Abolish nomination approach of awarding contracts to DPSUs and OFs.
- Process 6-8 Make projects every year, as promised. Also ensure that the timelines stipulated in the DPP are adhered to.

Streamline Defence Offset Policy

The defence offset policy, which is in vogue since 2005, has so far been a major disappointment. The policy has inherent design weaknesses and is poorly implemented and monitored. Compared to the policy followed by many countries such as Canada, Israel, Malaysia, South Korea and Turkey, the Indian offset policy gives too much leeway to the foreign companies. Its biggest weakness is the freedom given to foreign companies to choose offsets that they want to deliver. Obviously, they have so far chosen offsets which do not add to the capability enhancement of the local industry. Considering that offsets worth several billion dollars are yet to be delivered, there is an urgent need to tighten the policy framework apart from strengthening the implementation and monitoring aspects. Among others, the policy should clearly focus on technology acquisition and high quality and sustainable manufacturing work for the industry, which would go a long way in strengthening the indigenous capability.

Curb Indirect Import

Licence production has so far been a key feature in India's defence industrialisation process, with major projects such as Su-30 MKI, AJT Hawk, Scorpene submarine and the T-90 tank being currently undertaken by the state-owned enterprises. This approach does not seem to have enhanced India's self-reliance, since the enterprises concerned have been unable to indigenise the parts, components and raw materials, for which the DPSUs and OFs alone have spent a whopping Rs 78,740 core in the last five years ending 2013-14. This huge import not only puts a question mark on the capability of the Indian defence industry but also defies the very logic of self-reliance. One of the reasons why DPSUs and OFs are overwhelmingly dependent on foreign sources is their lack of accountability in ensuring indigenisation either through their own efforts or through a well-calibrated indigenous supply chain development. Although MoD has recently unveiled certain guidelines to enable them to develop an indigenous vendor base, the guidelines do not fix any target or accountability as to when and by how much indigenisation would be achieved. Considering that curbing indirect import is as important as curbing direct import (given that both can be disrupted in a time of crisis), it is imperative that certain targets and accountability are fixed. The proposed Make in India Council, in addition to laying out the R&D and manufacturing plan, may also layout a comprehensive roadmap for curbing indirect imports in a given timeframe.

Involve the Industry in the Formulation of Qualitative Requirements (QRs)

QRs, which form the basis for procurement, are often prepared by aggregating the best of the features taken from the equipment available in the world market. The process does not allow trade-offs between what is realistic/feasible through the available industrial/technological means and the minimum requirement of the armed forces. The absence of trade-offs puts the domestic industry at a disadvantage, since the high-pitched technical requirement either bars its participation or, in case of participation, contributes to delay and uncertainties by way of chasing the unrealistic goals. To prevent this, it is imperative that the industry is consulted while formulating the QRs.

ANNEXURES

ANNEXURE A

DPP-2016: An Overview

After a prolonged delay, MoD released the revised DPP on 28 March 2016 (see http://www.mod.nic.in/forms/Mainlinks.aspx?lid=1545&Id=56). The document, coming into effect from 1 April 2016, is applicable to all projects which are given in-principle approval or Acceptance of Necessity (AoN) thereafter. (With government's specific approval, the new DPP is also applicable for cases in which AoNs have been given earlier but formal tenders had not been issued.)It is, however, to be noted that document, running into 100 pages, is not complete: a key chapter on strategic partnership and all the annexures, appendices and schedules are expected to be released later. Nonetheless, the revised document, the first under the Modi government, has set the tone for a new procurement regime with a clear intention to boost the Make in India initiative in the defence sector, and to speed up the procurement process. While articulating the new features, DPP-2016 draws heavily from the report of the Committee of Experts set up by the Modi government under the chairmanship of Dhirendra Singh, to suggest a policy framework for facilitating Make in India in defence and further streamlining the procurement process. Among others, DPP-2016, running into 100 pages, envisages an array of features that include: a preamble to the document which articulates the peculiar nature of defence acquisition and the imperatives of self-reliance in defence production; a brand new procurement category, favouring purchase of locally designed, developed and manufactured products; higher yet flexible indigenisation content requirement in the existing Buy (Indian) and Buy and Make (Indian) procurement categories; a comprehensively revamped Make procedure; an institutionalised set of steps for processing the request for information (RFI); and certain measures to deal with procurement in single-vendor situations.

Key Provisions

Buy (Indian-IDDM) Procurement Category

To provide a greater thrust to Make in India in defence production, DPP-2016 has introduced a new procurement category, Buy (Indian–Indigenously Designed, Developed and Manufactured – or Buy (Indian – IDDM)). In terms of prioritisation, the new category, which would also be used for procurement of all locally designed and developed items under the revamped Make procedures, is placed above the existing Buy (Indian) category which itself is placed above the other categories, namely Buy and Make (Indian), Buy and Make and Buy (Global), in that order. Under the new category, indigenously designed equipment with 40 per cent indigenous content (IC) or equipment not necessarily designed in-house but having a 60 per cent IC, is intended for procurement from the local industry. The intent is clearly to promote in-house design capacity and higher localisation, two critical aspects which, if implemented in the right spirit, could deepen the role of domestic industry, especially the private sector, in domestic defence production.

The responsibility to prove an indigenous design rests with the industry, while the final say would be that of the government. To examine the industry's claim, DPP-2016 provides for a committee system comprising scientists from DRDO and members of the Service Headquarters (SHQs) concerned. The guidelines, on the basis of which the committee would verify the claims, will be promulgated later. The newly provisioned committee, however, has a challenging task ahead. This is because typical defence technologies are not patented nor do DRDO/SHQ have full knowledge of the designs of military equipment developed by other countries. Given these constrains, it looks like the committee would rely mostly on the industry's say so.

Higher yet Flexible Indigenous Content Requirement

DPP-2016 has enhanced the indigenous content requirement under the existing Buy (Indian) category from the earlier 30 per cent to 40 per cent. But for cases which require different indigenisation requirement, it provides flexibility to the procurement authorities to stipulate either higher or lower indigenisation content, depending on the merits of the projects. This flexibility, which is also extended to Buy and Make (Indian) procurement, will go a long way in meeting a key demand of local industry, which has long complained that the rigidity in IC is oblivious of the ground reality. The industry was particularly vocal about the critical aerospace items, in which local capability is bare minimum and achieving even 20 per cent IC is a difficult task at the present state of India's defence industrial development. HAL, for example, depends for up to 80-90 per cent on foreign sources for input materials.

Revamped Make Procedures

One big disappointment in DPP's recent operational history has been the complexity, leading to ineffectiveness, of Make procedures which were first articulated in 2006 with a view to promote in-house research, design, development and production of 'high-technology complex systems' by the domestic industry, especially the private sector. DPP-2016 has attempted to plug certain loopholes by way of making a number of changes, beginning with the planning process. The structure of the Annual Acquisition Plan (AAP), which is a subset of the five-year Services Capital Acquisition Plan (SCAP) and the guiding document for procurement, has undergone a change to include, for the first time, a number of Make projects which have already been given in-principle approval or are to be considered for in-principle approval by the higher procurement authorities. Besides, the existing Technology and Perspective Plan (TPCR), which has been criticised for being too vague, is now given a new life by requiring it to reflect the 'details of the acquisition plans for a period of 15 years, for use by the industry.' These two developments on the planning front are likely to lead to a greater visibility of Make projects and, more importantly, accountability on the part of the procurement authorities. Apart from this, changes have also been made in respect to the responsibility of SHQs, classification of Make sub-categories, funding pattern for prototype development, and clarity as to who would be eligible for undertaking Make projects.

Compared to its predecessors, DPP-2016 has attempted to make the SHQs own and, being responsible for, Make projects. In this regard, the SHQs would now be entrusted with the task of identifying potential Make projects and undertaking feasibility studies of each identified project in consultation with other stakeholders (earlier, the responsibility for both activities was entrusted to the Headquarters Integrated Defence Staff (HQ IDS)). Under the new Make procedures, the SHQs, including the Coast Guard, are also required to establish a permanent Make-Project Management Unit (Make-

PMU) comprising a two-star serving officer as the head and officers drawn from various ranks/branches/specialisation as members. Make-PMU is intended to instil a sense of ownership among the armed forces whose direct involvement is critical in any successful development of military items. In a move to ensure continuity in decision-making, the head of Make-PMU is required to have a minimum three-year tenure, whereas other officials are required to have a longer tenure. The head and the members are also required to serve as key members in the important multi-disciplinary Integrated Project Management Team (IPMT), which has the key responsibilities of preparing of Project Definition Document (PDD), issuing the Expression of Interest (EoI), short-listing the developmental agencies, and monitoring the progress of prototype development. Under the revamped Make procedure, the power to constitute the IPMT is vested with DDP (under the earlier procedures, the responsibility was with the Director General (Acquisition)). It seems that DDP, which has long been criticised for its limited role in defence indigenisation efforts, is now trying to acquire a larger role under DPP-2016.

DPP-2016 has divided the Make projects into two categories – Make-I (government funded) and Make-II (industry funded) – besides giving a decisive say to the Micro, Small and Medium Enterprises (MSMEs), which had long craved for government's attention for their role in the defence indigenisation efforts. In Make-I projects, the government would take the lead in funding prototype development by industry. In Make-II, which is largely confined to import substitution, industry will bear the full cost of development. For Make-I, DPP-2016 envisages government funding commitment of up to 90 per cent (it was 80 per cent under the earlier Make procedures) for prototype development, with a further provision that 20 per cent of the developmental cost would be paid in advance. In order to bring in a degree of accountability and to follow best commercial practice, the new procedure provides for mandatory issuance of request for proposal (RFP) within two years of successful development, failing which the balance 10 per cent funded by the industry would be reimbursed to it. For the MSMEs, the new procedure provides the first right to undertake prototype development up to Rs. 10 crore under Make-I and up to Rs. 3.0 crore under Make-II. Only when the MSMEs are not interested, the projectscan be opened up to the bigger industry players.

DPP-2016 has restricted the participation in the Make programme to 'only Indian vendors including Association of Persons (AoP)', to be detailed in an appendix, to be published in due course. Pending its release, it is believed that entities with majority resident Indian holding would be eligible for Make projects. This would ensure that decision-making and the crucial IPR of the Make designs would stay in the hands of resident Indians. It is also believed that eligibility criteria would include a minimum five years of operational experience (three years for the MSMEs) besides a credit rating of B++ issued by credit rating agencies of repute.

Institutionalising the RFI Process

DPP-2016 has institutionalised the request for information (RFI) process which was followed flexibly under the earlier DPPs. Although the new measure has increased the number of procurement steps involved in Buy and Buy and Make schemes by one more to 12, it has nonetheless brought much-needed clarity that has far-reaching implications on source of procurement, indigenisation, the degree of competition, and more importantly, the timeliness of procurement. Besides articulating the objectives and format of the RFI process, DPP-2016 also stipulates the specific inputs that the procurement authorities would seek through the institutionalised step. In addition, in a departure from the past, the RFI is now required to be formulated by the SHQ concerned in consultation with other relevant stakeholders, including DRDO, DDP and HQ IDS (earlier the SHQs were responsible for preparing the RFI). This would be ensure that any alternative views that the other stakeholders might have on a particular proposal would be taken into consideration at the outset of the procurement stage, rather than leaving to later stages which could lead to delays.

Introduction of L1-T1 Methodology for Award of Contracts

In a clear departure from the past, DPP-2016 has introduced what is widely known as the L1-T1 methodology for selecting suppliers under the Buy and Buy and Make schemes. L1-T1 methodology, in essence, means that the final bidder would not necessarily be selected on the basis of lowest price quoted (the so-called L1 methodology), but in a combination of price and superior technology offered. L1-T1 is intended to buy equipment with Enhanced Performance Parameters (EPP) – a newly introduced feature – which are a notch higher than the Essential Parameters required to be mandatorily met by all the suppliers participating in MoD tenders. L1-T1 is also intended to provide an additional incentive to equipment suppliers who have products with much superior features.

For the purpose of evaluation of the final bidder, vendors offering approved EPP would get an additional credit score of maximum 10 per cent, with each parameter not exceeding a score of 3 per cent. To put it alternatively, the commercial quote of a vendor offering EPP would be suitably deflated by a credit factor ranging between e” 0.9 and < 1.0, to arrive at the bid selection. As an illustration, if a vendor quotes $1.0 billion for a product with EPPs attracting a maximum 10 per cent credit score (or a credit factor of 0.9), the commercial quote for the purpose of evaluation would be $900 million ($1.0 billion x 0.9). The vendor would, however, get $1.0 billion if it wins the contract.

But the L1-T1 methodology has some drawbacks as well, which is why MoD has so far been reluctant to adopt it despite repeated demands from several quarters. Apart from the complexity and implementation-related challenges that L1-T1invites, it has also a clear financial ramification. L1-T1, in a crude sense, allows certain war equipment with more features than the minimum inescapable parameters (best captured in the EPs). This would force MoD to pay more for features that are not critically important. Moreover, by keeping L1-T1open to foreign companies, MoD would also incur extra foreign exchange. It would have been prudent to limit L1-T1for selection of bids from among the local industry.

Provision for 'Single OEM, Multiple Bids' and 'Multiple Bids through Single Indian Vendor'

DPP-2016 has incorporated two provisions – 'single OEM, multiple bids' and 'multiple bids through single Indian vendor'. The first case is likely to arise in Buy and Make (Indian) category in which a single foreign original equipment manufacturer (OEM) offers the same product through multiple bids in collaboration with a number of Indian companies. In such a situation, the new provision allows the authorities to continue with the procurement process, provided that the Defence Acquisition Council (DAC) decides that changes in the RFP condition will not invite participation of any more foreign vendors. The second case is likely to arise under the Buy and Make procurement category, in which multiple bids are submitted by foreign vendors through collaboration with one Indian company. Such a case is now acceptable under DPP-2016. The main argument for accepting such a case as not a single-vendor situation is that the technical and commercial arrangement of one foreign vendor would vary from that of others.

Provision of Procurement in Single Bid Situation

In a major departure from its predecessors, DPP-2016 has allowed the procurement process to continue in certain situations where only one bid is received in response to an RFP. The continuation of the process is, however, subject to the approval of the DAC, which must certify that there is no scope for change of the RFP conditions.

Reduced Validity and Sanctity of AoN

In a move to cut down the procurement timeframe under the Buy and Buy and Make schemes, DPP-2016 makes two subtle changes, one by reducing the validity of the AoN from earlier one year to six months, and the other by making the validity period sacrosanct. The reduced validity of AoN would mean that the RFP has to be issued within six months time (from the date of sanction of AoN), failing which the SHQ would 're-validate the case and seek fresh AoN with due justification for not processing the case in time.' Making the AON validity sacrosanct, the new provision makes it mandatory for the SHQs to re-issue any retracted RFP within the original validity of AoN. Earlier, the validity of AoN for the re-tracked RFP was increased by one year from the date of retraction, causing unpredictable delay and lack of accountability in the procurement process.

Essential Parameters A and B

In a move to increase vendor participation, DPP-2016 has divided into two parts (A & B) the non-negotiable Essential Parameters (EP) that the Indian armed forces want a particular equipment to possess. EP-A would capture some of the features of the 'contemporary equipment available in the market, and form core of Services Qualitative Requirements (SQRs)' for the purpose of testing and validation at the time of crucial Field Evaluation Trial (FET) stage. EP-B, on the other hand, may not be available at the time of FET but can be developed/achieved by the vendor after entering into a contract. To ensure that a vendor does not renege from its commitment of meeting EP-B, it is required to provide an additional bank guarantee of up to 10 per cent of the contract value. EP-B, whose inclusion in the RFP is necessarily to be approved by the DAC, must be met prior to the commencement of delivery of the contracted item. The incorporation of EP-B will not be part of the RFP if at least two vendors claim to possess the same at the RFI stage.

Definition of Indian Vendor

DPP-2016 defines an Indian vendor as an Indian entity (which could include incorporation, ownership model, and proprietorship among others) which is established under the Companies Act or any other applicable regulations. The DPP divides Indian vendors into two categories: one for defence products requiring industrial licence (IL) and the other not requiring IL. (DIPP has already announced a list of defence products which are subject to IL.) Companies in the first category can participate in almost all defence tenders (subject to certain restrictions under the Make procedure), whereas companies in the second category are restricted to participate in tenders involving non-licensable items only.

The definition of Indian vendor paves the way for JVs, in which the FDI component can go up to 100 per cent (up to 49 per cent through automatic route and beyond that through the Foreign Investment Promotion Board (FIPB) route), to be treated as Indian vendors. However, as explained earlier in the context of Make procedure, JVs in which the foreign equity is more than 49 per cent would not be eligible to participate in the Make programme.

Hike in Offset Threshold Limit

DPP-2016 has raised the offset threshold limit to Rs. 2,000 crore (approximately US$305 million) from Rs. 300 crore. It is surmised that MoD's difficulty in implementing the existing offset contracts could be the main factor for hiking the threshold. Nonetheless, the hike is untenable not only from the point of view of practices followed by other countries, but also in view of the Make in India initiative. The offset threshold is as low as $5-15 million in many countries that include Israel, Malaysia, Turkey and UAE. Moreover, countries generally lower the offset threshold over a period of time based on experience gained.

The hike in threshold would mean that fewer arms import contracts would now be eligible for offsets. This would be a big setback to the local industry, particularly the manufacture of parts and components which have exploited the existing offset policy for boosting their export performance, and in the process set up capability which could have been further exploited for Make in India.

Other Provisions

DPP-2016 also includes the following new provisions:

- Provision for Equipment Policy Committee (SEPC) to hire experts including from academia and industry for the purpose of 'review, rationalisation and finalisation of SQRs.' (The list of experts is to be maintained by HQ IDS and SHQs.) This is likely to help expedite the procurement process, particularly of the Army which often suffers from delay in acquisition due to deficiency in SQR formulation.

- No IC requirement from Indian companies in a Buy (Global) contract if offset is waived off in the contract. This is intended to provide a level playing field between the foreign OEMs and Indian companies.
- Provision for change of name of vendor at any stage between RFI and execution of contract, to enable unhindered progress in procurement.
- In certain cases specifically stipulated in the RFP, the cost of low-value items is to be reimbursed to vendors qualified at the FET stage. This is intended to incentivise wider participation, especially by the smaller companies which may have reservations due to high-cost participation in extensive field trials.
- The cost of Buyer Nominated Equipment (BNE) procured from the OFB would not be taken into consideration for the purpose of selection of L1 vendor. This is intended to insulate the L1 vendors from arbitrary hike in price by OFB post-submission of a commercial bid.
- In certain Buy and Make programmes, in which foreign OEMs are allowed to select their Indian Production Agency (PA), the RFP would stipulate the eligibility criteria for selection. This would bring transparency in the selection process.
- The scope of Fast Track Procedures (FTP) has been expanded to apply to items 'where undue/unforeseen delay, due to reasons beyond the control of acquisition setup, is seen to be adversely impacting the capacity and preparedness of the regular and special forces.'

An Assessment

The introduction of Buy (Indian-IDDM) procurement category, the revamped Make procedure, structural change in the AAP, and higher and flexible indigenous content requirement in certain procurement categories are some of the new provisions in DPP-2016 that are likely to deepen the involvement of the domestic industry in defence production. Also, the reduced validity of AoN and its sanctity, together with the measures to undertake procurement in single-vendor situations, are likely to arrest some of the delays in the acquisition process. However, much of the effectiveness of these changes would depend on how the new measures are implemented by the SHQ, MoD, DRDO and HQ IDS, which together constitute India's larger procurement setup. In this respect, DPP-2016 has done little to strengthen the current institutional mechanism, which is now more than 15 years old. Despite some notable successes, the procurement setup has been constrained to own up responsibility and drive procurement at a desired pace. The biggest issue that the procurement machinery faces is its decentralised nature, resulting in lack of coordination, diffused accountably and delay. It would have been prudent if DPP-2016 had reflected some of the structural changes in the procurement setup to complement the changes made in the procedures.

ANNEXURE B

Strategic Partnership: An Overview of the Aatre Task Force Report

MoD made public on 19 April 2016 the report of the Aatre Task Force (see http://www.mod.nic.in/forms/Mainlinks.aspx?lid=1545&Id=56). The report, running into 120 pages, deals with detailed criteria for the selection of Strategic Partners (SPs) from within the Indian private sector, which will be given preferential treatment for executing certain types of high-value, strategic defence items. The public release of the report, which comes barely three weeks after MoD released a portion of DPP-2016, is yet another bold attempt by the Modi government to push Make in India in the defence sector.

The V.K Aatre-led Task Force was constituted in September 2015 in pursuance of the recommendation of the Dhirendra Singh Committee to suggest a policy framework to drive Make in India in defence, and align it with the necessary changes in the provisions of the DPP. The committee suggested a 'Strategic Partnership model for creating capacity in the private sector on a long-term basis.' It also suggested setting up a Task Force to 'lay down the criteria in detail for selection of SPs' in certain critical segments of military items in which the identified SPs would play a role equivalent to that of DPSUs and OFs. The committee reasoned that given the high-cost and technology-intensive nature of the defence items, combined with the sporadic demand and limited market access, the producers of major military items cannot be left to the vagaries of open competition without making a compromise on long-term capability creation. The Aatre Task Force submitted its report in December 2015.

The Dhirendra Singh Experts Committee had suggested one or two SPs each in six different segments, namely: (1) Aircraft fighter, transport and helicopters and their major systems; (2) Warships of stated displacements and submarines and their major systems; (3) Armoured vehicles and their major systems/weapons; (4) Complex weapons which rely on guidance systems to achieve precision hits, which may include anti-ship, air defence, air-to-air, air-to-surface, anti-submarine and land attack; (5) Command, control, communication and computers, intelligence, surveillance, target acquisition and reconnaissance (C4ISTR); and (6) Critical materials (titanium alloys, aluminium alloys, carbon composites, nickel/cobalt alloys, etc.

The Aatre Task Force, on the other hand, has listed 10 segments in two groups from which SPs would be selected (see Table 1). One segment suggested by the Experts Committee but found missing in the Task Force Report is C4ISTR, for which it has suggested the Developmental Partnership model for creating capability. As per the Task Force's reasoning, each segment in Group I is in the nature 'system of systems' which is not the case with Group II segments. For Group I, the Task Force has suggested selection of only one SP in each segment, whereas the number can go up to two in Group II segments. In other words, the Task Force visualises a maximum of 13 SPs (seven in Group I and six in Group II). It may be noted that 13 SPs may not necessarily be 13 different parent companies. Two different companies under the same parent company can apply for SP in two groups. This means that a maximum 10 different parent companies can obtain 13 SPs status.) Incidentally, the number of SPs recommended for selection is the same as the number of companies identified under the Raksha Udyog Ratna (RUR) scheme, which was first suggested by the Kelkar Committee report of 2005 but never implemented.

For consideration for selection as SPs, the Task Force lays down a three-step stringent process, involving both financial and technical norms. For Group I, the financial norms include a consolidated turnover of Rs. 4,000 crore (approximately $612 million) for each of the past three years, consolidated capital assets of Rs. 2,000 crore in the last financial year and a consolidated revenue growth of minimum 5 per cent in at least three of the past five years. For Group II the corresponding norms in regard to consolidated turnover and capital assets are Rs. 500 crore and Rs. 100 crore respectively. For technical norms, companies are required to be assessed on seven different criteria that include past performance, engineering and manufacturing capability, R&D

culture, infrastructure facilities, human resources structure and practices, quality control system, and maintenance and lifecycle support system.

Table 1: Proposed Group/Segments for Selection of SPs

Group I	*Group II*
Aircraft* Helicopters*	Metallic material and alloys
Aero Engines Submarines* Warships	Non-metallic material (including composites and polymers)
Guns (including artillery guns) Armoured vehicles including tanks*	Ammunition including smart ammunition*

* For these segments, SPs are recommended to be selected in the initial phase.

In a move to insulate the SPs from foreign control, the Task Force has suggested a maximum FDI of 49 per cent, with the CEO being an Indian citizen.

The Task Force has suggested the creation of an independent regulator and a specialised wing in MoD to deal exclusively with the chosen SPs. These two measures, if accepted by the government, will end a major trust gap that exists between MoD and the private sector.

A Critique of the Report

Given the sensitivity and complexity involved, the Aatre Task Force seems to have done a reasonable job in formulating detailed criteria for selection of SPs. However, it has not addressed two fundamental concerns, which would dilute the effectiveness of the whole exercise. First and foremost, the Task Force has not extended the principle of SP to the whole gamut of big contracts in which the private sector is supposed to play a major role. As initially suggested by the Dhirendra Singh Committee, the Task Force has also limited the participation of the SPs to the Buy and Make contracts involving transfer of technology. In other words, the SPs are not supposed to get preferential treatment for executing the crucial Buy and Make (India) and Make contracts. Given that capability creation and its nurture under the latter two categories is critical from the self-reliance point of view, it would have been prudent if the principle of SP would have been extended to them also.

Second, the SPs, in the present scheme of things, are not substitutes for the inefficient DPSUs and OFs. Rather, they are visualised as poor cousins of the state-owned entities. This is amply clear from the Task Force's giving liberty to MoD to buy items from DPSUs/OFs subject to their capacity constraints. In other words, only when DPSUs/OFs are not able to deliver in a stipulated timeframe (because of their overflowing orders), SPs would be considered. This is a highly inefficient way of protecting the state-owned entities, whose inefficiency has so far been the main reason for India's poor self-reliance.

Annexure C

Foreign Investment Proposals Approved in Defence Sector (As on July 2015)

Sl No	*Name of JV/Implementing Company*	*Items to be manufactured*
		DPSUs
1	Multirole Transport Aircraft Ltd	Co-development & Co-production of a Multirole Transport Aircraft of 15-20 Ton category jointly with Russian partners.
2	HAL-Edgewood Technologies Limited	Development and Manufacture of high technology miniature electronic modules and avionics systems for aerospace applications.
3	HALBIT Avionics Private Limited	Design, Development, Market and Support products such as Aircraft Simulators and Services and to subsequently enhance the scope of products to airborne avionics products. Development of State of the Art technology.
4	Multirole Transport Aircraft Ltd	Co-development & Co-production of a Multirole Transport Aircraft of 15-20 Ton category jointly with Russian partners.
		Private Sector
5	Alpha-ITL Electro Optics Private Limited	Manufacture of optical goods and equipment and optical instruments.
6	HBLElta Avionics Systems Private Limited	Radar, EW Systems, Electronics Communication systems.
7	BF Systems Limited	To provide complete support for Light Weight Howitzer and other small & medium caliber weapons programs, inclusive of engineering, design & development, manufacturing services and upgrading.

Sl No	Name of JV/Implementing Company	Items to be manufactured
8	Alpha Electronica Defence Systems Pvt. Ltd.	Production, assembling, testing, repair and support for EW equipment and systems for land/shipbased/airbased platforms.
9	ArmetArmored Vehicles (India) Ltd.,	Manufacture of bodies (including Cabs) designed to be mounted on motor vehicles chassis for special purpose motor lorries, armoured cars etc.
10	Samtel Thales Avionics Pvt. Ltd. New Delhi	Development, Manufacture & selling of helmet mounted sight display.
11	Astra Microwave Products Ltd, Hyderabad	Design, development, manufacture & supply of components & sub-systems for wireless communication for application in defence, space & cellular communication.
12	Mahindra Defense Systems Ltd, New Delhi	Manufacture & marketing of defence equipment in the land sector.
13	Taneja Aerospace & Aviation Limited	(i) Armour panel for helicopter, (ii) Body armour.
14	M/s Vyoneesh Technologies Pvt Ltd., New Delhi	Manufacturing, Designing, Selling, Undertaking Overhauling and Maintenance Activities for all kind of Engg. And Technology Related Equipment and Products including Aircrafts.
15	ICOMM Tele Ltd, Hyderabad	Engaged in engineering, procurement and construction services in the telecommunication, power transmission and distribution, water and sewerage sectors, manufactures telecommunications and power transmission towers, research, development and manufacture of active telecommunications infrastructure and equipment for a variety of sectors including defence related telecommunications equipment.
16	Lakshmi Machine Works Limited, Coimbatore	Manufacturing of entire range of Textile Spinning machinery. Proposed additional activities: manufacturing of parts, components and accessories for aircraft and spacecraft to be supplied to civil and defence sector.
17	Tata Aerostructure Limited, Mumbai	Design, manufacture, supply procurement and life cycle support of advanced aerospace and aero structures items for defence aircrafts, helicopters, and unmanned airborne vehicles including empennages and centre wing boxes (NIC Code-377.8).
18	Larsen & Toubro Ltd, Mumbai	Manufacturing, distributing, and marketing of products in the market segments of electronic warfare, military avionics, mobile systems (defence related) and radars (NIC code 359.4).
19	ABG Shipyard Ltd, Mumbai	Existing Activities: Shipbuilding, ship repair (NIC Code: 3899 & 3402)Proposed Activities: Defence products: NIC Code: 370,359,359.4, 365, 366, 367 & 370.8.

Sl No	*Name of JV/Inplementing Company*	*Items to be manufactured*
20	Jubilant Aeronautics Pvt Ltd, Delhi	Manufacture of different types of Unmanned Aerial Systems and accessories (NIC Code: 3770).
21	Maini Precision Products Pvt Ltd.	Existing activities: Engaged in the business of manufacture and export of high precision parts for automotive, material handling, general engineering purposes. Proposed additional activities: to manufacture parts and accessories of aircraft and spacecrafts (NIC Code: 377.8).
22	Park Controls & Communications Ltd, Bangalore	Existing Activities: Engaged in the business of defence Avionics solution provider. Proposed addition activities: activities to manufacture of onboard/data acquisitions systems, avionics, timing products, time code readers, ground based telemetry systems and other electronic aerospace and defence equipment.
23	Rossell Aviation Private Ltd.	Proposed Activities: To engage in civil &defence aviation filed with focus on product support services, repair and maintenance facility, providing training solutions in project.
24	Indian Rotorcraft Ltd.	To engage in the business of undertaking final assembly of both military and civil versions of AgustaWesland'sAW119Kx Helicopters.
25	Tara Aerospace Systems Ltd, Mumbai	Existing: Manufacture of parts for civilian aircrafts. Proposed: Design, development, engineering, manufacturing, integration, assembly, testing and inspection and fixed-wing aircrafts, including products such as aerospace and aero structures components, kits and accessories in the defence sector.
26	Larsen & Toubro Ltd, Mumbai	Defence Production.
27	Space Era Materials and Processes Pvt Ltd.	Engaged in the business of design, development, manufacture, assembly, repair and overhaul of the equipment of telecommunication and avionics used in aircrafts, radars and other electrical and electronics defence components, aggregates and equipment in India.
28	Track Systems India Private Limited	Manufacturing, assembling, marketing, trading, dealing in import and export of tracks and parts thereof and running gear components required for the defence sector.
29	Amertec Systems Pvt Ltd.	Manufacturing of advanced electronic systems, test systems, simulators and electronic systems for military applications.
30	Hical Technologies Pvt Ltd.	Manufacture of wiring, cable and harness for aeronautics and defence sectors (civil and military) and test benches.

Sl No	*Name of JV/Implementing Company*	*Items to be manufactured*
31	BF Elbit Advanced Systems Pvt. Ltd.	Manufacture of Artillery Guns/Howitzers, Mortars, Ammunition, manufacture of Tactically protected vehicles.
32	SasMos Het Technologies Limited	Existing: Assembly/Manufacturing of Cable Assembly, interconnection systems, Electrical & Electronic Panels for Aerospace & Defence applications.Proposed: Manufacturing of Electronic Warfare Sub-systems, Automatic Test Equipment, Avionics & Radar Sub-Systems, Unmanned Vehicle Sub-Systems, Command & Control Systems and Navigational Sub-systems and related parts and accessories for Airborne, Ground & Naval application in addition to existing activities.
33	Quest Global Manufacturing Private Ltd	Manufacturing for Indian Defence Sector including defence aerospace and participate in offset program.
34	Ideaforge Technology Pvt Ltd.	Existing Manufacturer of Unmanned Aerial Systems mainly supplied to defence sector.

Annexure D

Details and Status of Major Ongoing Projects (Cost above Rs. 100 crore) of DRDO

Sl.No.	*Project Name*	*Developing Agency*	*Date of Sanction*	*Original Estimated Cost (Rs in Crore)*	*Revised Cost (Rs. in Crore)*	*Original Likely Date of Completion*	*Revised Date of Completion*	*Expenditure till Date (Rs in Crore)*
1	Medium Range Surface-to-Air Missile (MRSAM)	RCI	Feb 2009	10075.68	No revision	Aug 2016	No revision	424.24
2	Light Combat Aircraft (LCA): Phase-II	ADA	Nov 2001	3301.78	6066.43	Dec 2008	Dec 2015*	5479.64
3	Airborne Warning and Control System (India) AWACS (I): Phase I	CABS	Fe 2013	5113.00	5113.00	Feb 2020	No revision	1.96
4	Kaveri Engine	GTRE	Mar 1989	382.81	2839.00	Dec 1996	Dec 2009*	2044.04
5	Long Range Surface-to-air Missiles (LRSAM)	DRDL	Dec 2005	2606.02	No revision	May 2012	Jun 2016	526.39
6	Light Combat Aircraft (LCA): Phase-III	ADA	Nov 2009	2431.55	No revision	Dec 2018	No revision	999.24
7	Airborne Early Warning and Control system (AEW&C)	CABS	Oct 2004	1800.00	2402.00	Apr 2011	Jun 2016	2017.17
8	Naval Light Combat Aircraft (LCA Navy Phase-II)	ADA	Dec 2009	1921.11	No revision	Dec 2018	No revision	426.85
9	Naval Light Combat Aircraft (LCA Navy Phase-I)	ADA	March 2003	948.90	2103.21	Mar 2010	Dec 2014*	1501.33
10	Medium Altitude Long Endurance (MALE) Unmanned Aerial Vehicle (UAV) and Development of Aeronautical Test Range (ART) at Chitradurga	ADE	Feb 2011	1540.74	No revision	Aug 2016	No revision	223.16
11	Air-to-Air Missile System 'Astra'	DRDL	Mar 2004	955.00	No revision	Feb 2013	Aug 2016	439.45
12	Nirbhay-Development & Flight Trials	DRDL	Dec 2010	56.93	102.28	May 2013	Dec 2016	23.28
13	Quick Reaction Surface-to-Air Missile (QR-SAM)	DRDL	Jul 2014	476.43	No revision	Jul 2017	No revision	4.43

(Contd.)

Sl.No.	Project Name	Developing Agency	Date of Sanction	Original Estimated Cost (Rs in Crore)	Revised Cost (Rs. in Crore)	Original Likely Date of Completion	Revised Date of Completion	Expenditure till Date (Rs in Crore)
14	National Open Air Range	DRDL	Aug 2014	468.00	No revision	Feb 2018	No revision	0.88
15	Active Electronically Scanned Array Radar	LRDE	Jan 2012	459.65	No revision	Jul 2016	No revision	39.08
16	Kautilya	RCI	Jul 2012	432.80	487.80	Jul 2017	No revision	123.64
17	Development of 1500 hp Engine	CVRDE	Dec 2013	398.02	No revision	Dec 2018	No revision	0.01
18	Solid Fuel Ducted Rocket Ramjet Technology for Air Launched Tactical Missiles (SFDR)	DRDL	Feb 2013	366.00	No revision	Feb 2018	No revision	116.50
19	Hypersonic Wind Tunnel (HWT)	DRDL						
20	EW systems for Capital Ships, Aircrafts & Helicopter of Indian Navy, 'Samudrika'	DRDL	Jul 2012	342.29	No revision	Jul 2017	No revision	33.91
21	New Generation Anti-Radiation Missiles (NGARM)	DRDL	Dec 2012	317.20	No revision	Dec 2017	No revision	30.04
22	Post Development Support of AEW&C System (PDSAS)	CABS	Sep 2013	314.32	No revision	Sep 2018	No revision	45.46
23	EW Suite for Fighter Aircraft (EWSFA)	DARE	Sep 2005	279.62	330.31	Mar 2013	Under closure	262.33
24	NBC Defence Technologies	DRDE	Mar 2010	284.96	181.65	Mar 2015	No revision	120.76
25	Dual Colour Missile Approach Warning System	DARE	Nov 2008	228.80	273.80	Jun 2013	Jun 2015**	199.75
26	AIP System on P-75 Submarines and Development of Deliverable LOX System	NMRL	Jun 2014	270.00	No revision	Jun 2017	No revision	17.57
27	D-Jag System Internal RWJ System for Jaguar DARIN III Upgrade Aircraft	DARE	Aug 2012	268.27	No revision	Jun 2015	Jun 2016	20.81
28	Low Vulnerable High Performance Propellant with Low Temperature Co-efficient and Improved Shelf Life of Ammunition	HEMRL	Sep 2014	267.02	No revision	Mar 2018	No revision	1.08
29	155 mm/52 Caliber Advanced Towed Artillery Gun System (ATAGS)	ARDE	Sep 2012	247.90	No revision	Sep 2015	Mar 2017	25.81
30	Land Based Prototype for AIP	NMRL	Aug 2010	216.60	No revision	Feb 2015	Mar 2016	121.00

(Contd.)

Sl.No.	*Project Name*	*Developing Agency*	*Date of Sanction*	*Original Estimated Cost (Rs in Crore)*	*Revised Cost (Rs. in Crore)*	*Original Likely Date of Completion*	*Revised Date of Completion*	*Expenditure till Date (Rs in Crore)*
31	40 GHz Upgradation of MMIC Facility	SSPL	Feb 2012	198.72	208.98	Aug 2015	Sep 2017	165.50
32	Advanced Light Weight Torpedo	NSTL	Feb 2008	194.53	No revision	Aug 2013	Dec 2017	73.80
33	Flying Test Bed	LRDE	Sep 2012	173.48	No revision	Sep 2017	No revision	97.21
34	D-29 System (Internal EW System for MiG-29 Aircraft Upgrade)	DARE	Mar 2010	168.85	No revision	Dec 2012	Dec 2015*	95.50
35	Submarine Periscope	IRDE	Mar 2014	163.77	No revision	Mar 2019	No revision	0.35
36	D-249 Grade Steels, Plates, Bulb Bars and Weld Consumables	DMRL	Dec 2012	159.30	No revision	Dec 2016	No revision	36.51
37	Consultancy for AB3 Steel and Establishment of Indigenous Production	DMRL	Jan 2013	148.50	No revision	Jan 2016	No revision	54.57
38	Sea Keeping and Maneuvering Basin (SMB)	NSTL	Sep 2007	84.00	168.58	Sep 2011	Jun 2015**	76.46
39	Development of Multi KV Fibre Laser	LASTEC	Mar 2015	289.55	No revision	Nov 2020	No revision	0.00
40	Instrumented Airborne Platform for Real-time Snow Cover, Avalanche and Glacier Monitoring	SASE	Sep 2011	125.94	No revision	Sep 2016	No revision	0.47
41	Augmentation of Environmental Test Facility for Warheads and Electronic System	TBRL	Sep 2013	121.17	No revision	Oct 2018	No revision	1.59
42	Advanced Light Towed Array Sonar (ALTAS)	NPOL	Apr 2012	114.42	No revision	Apr 2016	No revision	31.90
43	Technology Development for Engine Fuel Control System	GTRE	Oct 2014	177.72	No revision	Apr 2021	No revision	0.83
44	Project Pralay	RCI	Mar 2015	332.88	No revision	Mar 2018	No revision	0.34

Note: *: Under revision; **: under closure.

Index